COGNITION AND
EMOTIONAL DISTURBANCE

COGNITION AND EMOTIONAL DISTURBANCE

Edited by

Russell Grieger, Ph.D.
University of Virginia
Charlottesville, Virginia

Ingrid Zachary Grieger, Ed. D.
University of Virginia
Charlottesville, Virginia

With Contributors

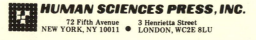

HUMAN SCIENCES PRESS, INC.
72 Fifth Avenue   3 Henrietta Street
NEW YORK, NY 10011 ● LONDON, WC2E 8LU

Library of Congress Cataloging in Publication Data

Main entry under title:

Cognition and emotional disturbance.

Includes bibliographies and index.
1. Mental illness—Etiology. 2. Cognition disorders. 3. Cognition. I. Grieger, Russell. II. Grieger, Ingrid. [DNLM: 1. Affective symptoms—Etiology. 2. Cognition. WM 171 G848c]
RC454.4.C6   616.89′071   L.C. 81-6461
ISBN 0-89885-022-3   AACR2

*To
Todd and Marcus,
whose voices help
it all make sense*

CONTENTS

CONTRIBUTORS

ELLIOT ABRAHMS, M.D. Department of Psychology, Hartford Hospital, Hartford, Connecticut

JOHN BOYD, PH.D. Associate Professor, University of Virginia, Charlottesville, Virginia. Clinical Psychologist in private practice in and around Charlottesville, Virginia

RAYMOND DIGIUSEPPE, PH.D. Director of Health Psychology, Hofstra Center for Health; Supervising Psychologist, Psychological Evaluation Center, Hofstra University, Hempstead, New York; Supervisor, Institute for Rational-Emotive Therapy, New York City

ALBERT ELLIS, PH.D. Executive Director, Institute for Rational-Emotive Therapy, New York City

9

INGRID ZACHARY GRIEGER, ED.D. Counseling Psychologist/Coordinator of Training, University of Virginia Counseling Center, Charlottesville, Virginia

RUSSELL GRIEGER, PH.D. Associate Professor, University of Virginia, Charlottesville, Virginia. Clinical Psychologist in private practice in and around Charlottesville, Virginia

WILLIAM J. KNAUS, ED.D. Director of Fort Lee Consultation Center, Fort Lee, New Jersey. Psychologist in private practice in New York City and Springfield, Massachusetts

JOHN RUSH, M.D. Associate Professor, Department of Psychiatry, University of Texas, Southwestern Medical School, Dallas, Texas

SUSAN WALEN, PH.D. Associate Professor of Psychology, Towson State College, Towson, Maryland

JAN WEISSENBURGER, M.A. Psychological Assistant, Department of Psychiatry, University of Texas, Southwestern Medical School, Dallas, Texas

JANET WOLFE, PH.D. Associate Executive Director and Director of Clinical Services, Institute for Rational-Emotive Therapy, New York City

PREFACE

The field of psychopathology is undergoing rapid change. New theories and treatments of anxiety, depression, schizophrenia, and other emotional disturbances keep emerging. More and more is being learned about the differential effects of drugs on people with various emotional and behavioral symptoms, suggesting in turn that further clues to the etiologies of these disorders will be found. In the third edition of its *Diagnostic and Statistical Manual of Mental Disorders* (DSM III), the American Psychiatric Association has amazingly dropped some of its traditional classifications, most notably neurosis, psychosis, and psychophysiological disorders. All of this, and much more, has led William Sahakian (1970, 1979) to correctly comment that "such rapid progress [in psychopathology] has had the effect of relegating the giants of the past (such as Freud) to the background."

Amidst this flux, perhaps no other phenomenon has had a greater impact on the field of psychopathology during the last two decades than the emergence of cognitive and cognitive-behavior psychotherapy, particularly rational-emotive therapy (RET)

(Grieger & Boyd, 1979; Mahoney, 1977). Basic to this movement is a large and growing body of literature on the cognitive basis of emotional and behavioral disorders. This theory is rich and varied, yet consistent in the view that peoples' psychological problems derive largely from conscious or partially conscious misconceptions and/or irrational ideas, beliefs, attitudes, or philosophies, not from the press of putative underlying personality structures in conflict. Put into the now-famous ABC theory of RET, the cognitive camp states that it is not the events we experience (at A) that determine how we react (at C), but rather our thoughts or ideas (at B) that do.

As Albert Ellis (1977) has himself stated, however, no theory of personality and psychopathology stands up well, regardless of how internally logical it is, without a good deal of empirical evidence to support its basic hypothesis. Fortunately, the main hypotheses that underlie cognitive theory in general and RET in particular are well supported by a plethora of such evidence. Not intending this to be a lengthy treatise on the personality theory of cognitive therapy, we list the basic hypotheses below, and refer the reader to Beck (1976), Ellis (1973, 1974, 1977), Ellis and Harper (1977), Meichenbaum (1977), and Raimy (1975), among others, for thorough reviews of this literature. For each hypothesis the experimental data is overwhelmingly supportive.[1]

1. Cognition, emotion, and behavior are not separate and independent entities but intimately and significantly effect each other. Cognition significantly effects emotion and behavior; emotion effects cognition and behavior; and behavior likewise effects cognition and emotion. When one is significantly changed, the other two also will change in some way as well.

2. People are chronic thinkers. The kinds of things they think, or tell themselves, as well as the manner in which they do so, significantly contributes to how they feel and behave. When people think and believe cheerful

---

[1]These are derived from Ellis (1977).

thoughts, they tend to feel happy, contented, enjoyful; when they think and believe cynical, sad, or upsetting thoughts, they will tend to feel depressed, morose, or down.

3. Thinking creates emotions. Thoughts, or cognitions, mediate between events or stimuli and emotional responses. In RET terms, A (the activating event) does not exclusively or even predominantly cause C (the emotional or behavioral consequence); rather, B (the thought or belief about A) most importantly contributes to or "causes" C.

4. Not only do people think about their experiences in words, phrases, and sentences, but they also do so via pictorial representations, including images, fantasies, and dreams. Such representations contain the same kind of cognitive mediations as do words and likewise significantly effect emotion and behavior. Some people are prone to think in pictorial representations and powerfully "cause" their emotion and behavior, while others do as less powerfully.

5. People not only think about the outside events they experience, but they also are aware of and think about their thinking. Furthermore, they perceive and think about their own emotions, behavior, and physiological processes. By this self-monitoring process, they significantly effect their subsequent reactions in both healthy (or self-helping) and unhealthy (or self-defeating) ways.

6. People have both innate and acquired tendencies to think rationally (thereby aiding their basic values and goals) and to think irrationally (thereby interferring with their basic values and goals). Irrational thoughts by definition are absolutistic and antiempirical, and they logically lead to what we commonly call disturbed emotional states—anxiety, anger, depression, guilt, and severe frustration. These irrational cognitions

correlate with almost all forms of emotional disturbance, and disturbed populations employ significantly more irrational thinking than do nondisturbed populations.

7.   Although hundreds of specific irrational thoughts exist, emotional disturbance by and large consists of three forms of irrational ideas: demandingness (of approval, achievement, comfort), awfulizing, and self-rating.

8.   Humans have a tendency to have low frustration tolerance; to say it differently, they consistently demand immediate gratification and abhor the slightest pain, hassle, or frustration. Emotional disturbance has a large component of low frustration tolerance—people very often decide they cannot stand hassles from their world and pain in their guts, and they regularly disturb themselves when they indubitably experience these events.

9.   When people feel upset or see themselves as emotionally disturbed, they tend to think about their upset or disturbance and make themselves feel further upset or disturbed about their troubles. In effect, they have a tendency to create emotional problems about their emotional problems.

10.   People not only make themselves disturbed by real events, but they also imagine, fantasize, expect, and anticipate events and make themselves upset about these "events" as well.

Having said this, we find it striking that no single text has overviewed the cognitive basis of psychopathology. It is the intention of this book to present this perspective on the major psychopathological conditions. Included is a first chapter by Albert Ellis describing the dynamics of psychoneurotic disorders, detailing both the faulty ideas that lead to anxiety in general and categorizing neurotic problems into ego anxiety and low frustration tolerance anxiety. Following this are chapters by Russell Grieger on the cognitive base of anger problems (Chapter Two), a chapter coauthored by Grieger and John Boyd on self-acceptance and guilt-based disturbances (Chapter Four), and one by John Rush and Jan Weissenburger outlining the cognitive underpinnings of depressive reactions (Chapter Three). Then, in Chapter Five, Eliot Abrahms overviews some of the significant contributions faulty cognition makes to many of the major mental disorders, including schizophrenia and manic-depressive reactions.

The remainder of the text addresses itself to some special categories of problems. In Chapter Six Janet Wolfe and Susan Walen offer an innovative approach to understanding sexual behavior in general and sexually dysfunctional behavior in particular. William Knaus follows with a discussion of the parameters of procrastination problems, and then Ingrid Grieger presents a cognitive perspective on issues crucial to the mental health of women. Finally, the book concludes with a chapter by Raymond DiGiuseppe detailing how children and their parents become emotionally disturbed.

Before concluding, we hasten to add that we do not consider this to be the final treatise on cognitive psychopathology. We ourselves eagerly await the new ideas and new data that the coming years will surely provide in understanding how people get and remain emotionally disturbed. What we present here is the "state of the art" today.

Russell Grieger
Ingrid Grieger
Charlottesville, Virginia
September 1979

References

Beck, A. T. *Cognitive therapy and the emotional disorders*. New York: International Universities Press, 1976.

Ellis, A. *Growth through reason*. Palo Alto, Calif.: Science and Behavior Books, 1971; Hollywood, Calif.: Wilshire Books, 1974.

Ellis, A. Research data that supports the basic theory of rational-emotive and other forms of cognitive-behavioral psychotherapy. In A. Ellis & R. Grieger (Eds.), *Handbook of rational-emotive therapy*. New York: Springer Publishing Co., 1977.

Ellis, A. Rational-emotive therapy. In R. Corsini (Ed.), *Current psychotherapies*. Itasco, Ill.: Peacock Publishers, 1973.

Ellis, A., & Harper, R. A. *A new guide to rational living*. Hollywood, Calif.: Wilshire Books, 1975.

Grieger, R., & Boyd, J. *Rational-emotive therapy: A skills-based approach*. New York: Van Nostrand Reinhold, 1979.

Mahoney, M. J. Reflections on the cognitive-learning trend in psychotherapy. *American Psychologist*, 1977, *32*, 5–13.

Meichenbaum, D. H. *Cognitive-behavior modification: An integrative approach*. New York: Plenum Press, 1977.

Raimy, V. *Misunderstandings of the self*. San Francisco, Calif.: Jossey-Bass Publishers, 1975.

Sahakian, W. *Psychopathology today: the current status of abnormal psychology*. Itasca, Ill.: Peacock Publishers, 1970, 1979.

Chapter 1

PSYCHONEUROSIS AND ANXIETY PROBLEMS

Albert Ellis

The relationship of psychoneurosis and anxiety problems to cognition in general and to what, in particular, people say to themselves as they experience difficult or "traumatic" experiences has been seen vaguely at least for many centuries. Buddha recognized that people make themselves miserable by concentrating too much on the fulfillment of their desires, including their goals and values; and he advocated that they become nonanxious or nonfrustrated by surrendering these values and making themselves desireless (achieving Nirvana) or at least less desirous. Epictetus (1890) and Marcus Aurelius (1890), a student of Epictetus, even more clearly saw that people's unrealistic cognitions made them anxious or miserable, and that these could distinctly be changed so that they then made themselves serene or happy. Other philosophers, such as Spinoza (1901) and Russell (1950), have also clearly seen that what we call "emotions" and "emotional disturbance" are largely created by cognitions, and that changing our beliefs and philosophies significantly modifies our disturbances (Ellis, 1977a).

In the realm of psychology and psychotherapy, several out-standing thinkers have arrived at similar conclusions, often with-out any real knowledge of their philosophic predecessors. Thus, pioneers like Adler (1927, 1968), Kelly (1955), Low (1952), Berne (1957), and Rotter (1954) have stressed the cognitive ele-ments in psychoneurosis and anxiety; and, even more specifically, for the last quarter of a century I have emphasized the significance of what people say to themselves, and how they can disturb and undisturb themselves by cognitive intracommunication (Ellis, 1957a, 1957b, 1962, 1971, 1973, 1979a; Ellis & Abrahms, 1978; Ellis & Grieger, 1977). In turn, a number of other prominent cognitive behavior therapists have gotten on the bandwagon and made the concept of cognition in psychoneurosis quite popular (Beck, 1976; Davison & Neal, 1974; Diekstra & Dassen (1976); Goldfried & Davison, 1976; Greenwald, 1977; Hauck, 1975; Knaus, 1974; Lembo, 1976; Mahoney, 1974, 1977; Maultsby, 1975; Meichenbaum, 1977; Morris & Kanitz, 1975; Raimy, 1975; Rimm & Masters, 1974; Tosi, 1974).

In this article, I shall review some of the main hypotheses and findings about cognition and emotional disturbance, and I shall particularly concentrate on several major forms of anxiety and how human thinking significantly helps to create feelings of overcon-cern, phobias, worthlessness, and various other forms of "ner-vousness." Since the field of human neurosis is almost incredibly broad and wide-ranging, I shall not attempt to cover it completely but shall concentrate on several of its major aspects, and on the cognitions and ideas that tend to go with these aspects.

Let me first define some terms in this respect, so that the various forms of anxiety that I shall concentrate on in this chapter will be clearly understood. These forms are as follows:

Ego anxiety. Ego anxiety is perhaps the most dramatic form of nervousness and one of the most pernicious because it involves people rating themselves, their essence, and feeling almost totally worthless or inadequate if they do not perform some task(s) well enough, or if they are not sufficiently approved or loved by others. When they have ego anxiety, they usually have emotional tension (or, better, hypertension) that results when they feel (1) that their self or personal worth is threatened; (2) that they *should* or *must* perform well and/or be approved by others; and (3) that it is *awful* or *catastrophic* when they don't perform well and/or are not approved by others as they supposedly *should* or *must* be (Ellis, 1978). Ego anxiety is frequently called performance anxiety, since it is experienced when people feel that they have not performed some task or project well enough and are pretty rotten individuals for having failed to do better on it.

Discomfort anxiety. Discomfort anxiety is a term that I have recently coined and that I define as emotional tension (or hypertension) and that results when people feel (1) that their comfort (or life) is threatened; (2) that they *should* or *must* get what they want (and *should not* or *must not* get what they don't want); and (3) that it is *awful* or *catastrophic* (rather than merely inconvenient or disadvantageous) when they don't get what they supposedly *must* (Ellis, 1978). Discomfort anxiety is usually less dramatic than ego anxiety, but it is probable that it is just as frequent or even more so, and that it is a secondary symptom (as I shall note below) of acute or longstanding ego anxiety.

Phobias. Phobias are feelings of anxiety or panic about specific things, situations, or people—such as phobias of riding on elevators, appearing in public places, talking in social groups, speaking in public, taking examinations, etc. Some phobias (e.g., fears of social situations) largely consist of ego anxiety: the fear that one will do poorly in these situations and will therefore find himself worthless. Many phobias (e.g., fear of riding in elevators) largely consist of discomfort anxiety: the fear that one will be highly inconvenienced or physically harmed in the elevator and therefore has to avoid it at all costs. But one can also have both anxieties in a given situation by: (1) feeling that elevators are too dangerous and too uncomfortable to ride in; and (2) feeling that if one rides in elevators one will act poorly (e.g., show panic), be disapproved by others, and therefore feel ashamed of oneself.

Obsessions. Obsessions frequently result when people are so terrified of something—such as social situations or elevators—that they keep dreading any actual or symbolic contact with this thing, and hence think of it continually, obsessively. Thus, knowing that one will have to speak in public a few weeks hence, one may think of almost nothing but that "horrible" experience until the scheduled performance; and then may obsess for weeks or months about how "terribly" they spoke in public after they have already done so.

Compulsions. Compulsions normally are performed in a rigid, invariant manner to defend against and ward off the anxiety that presumably would have to occur if people did not perform them. Thus, if a man is afraid of having dirty hands (and thereby offending others and proving to them and oneself that one is worthless), he may literally be compelled to wash his hands 20 or 30 times a day, and even then only partially ward off his anxiety.

Anxiety about anxiety. Once people make themselves anxious about almost anything, and experience extreme and uncomfortable states of panic about that thing, they know that they will be highly disadvantaged if they become anxious again. Therefore, they make themselves anxious about their anxiety, panicked about the possibility of recurring panic. Thus, if someone first makes him or herself anxious about riding in elevators, s/he knows that s/he will be highly uncomfortable if forced to ride or even if thinking about riding in a lift; hence s/he becomes more anxious than ever about the thought or the actuality of elevator rides—and very likely has both ego anxiety ("Isn't it shameful that I am afraid of riding in elevators!") and discomfort anxiety ("Isn't it horribly painful to experience anxiety about riding in elevators!") whenever anything connected with elevators comes to mind.

Anxiety about psychotherapy. Once people see that they are emotionally disturbed and once they go for psychotherapy, they frequently make themselves quite anxious about how they are doing or will do in therapy. Thus, one can put oneself down for not being a "good" client and responding well to therapy; and one can make oneself "anxious" about the hard work that therapy requires and have abysmally low frustration tolerance or discomfort anxiety about this required work.

BIOSOCIAL ELEMENTS IN COGNITION AND ANXIETY

If cognition plays an extremely important role in the creation and sustaining of neurosis in general and anxiety in particular, as this chapter will contend, the questions may be asked: Why is this so? What makes cognition so important in human affairs and in human disturbances?

The first answer to these questions is: Biology does. Humans are born with an unusually large and complex cerebral cortex; and they not only have the power to think, as do innumerable lower animals, but also to think about their thinking and think about thinking about their thinking. This power, moreover, is enormously enhanced by their invention and use of language: of verbal, mathematical, symbolic, and other forms of language. Again, while other animals have rudimentary language and can communicate with each other (and perhaps with themselves) to some extent, humans can do so to a much greater degree; and they almost invariably do. All human groups that we have any knowledge of appear to use language and cognition much more, and in many more complex ways, than do subhuman creatures.

Human biology, moreover, seems to predispose people to social living: to gregariousness, teaching, and to culture. Children are very suggestible or easily influenced animals; and so are adolescents and adults. They therefore are greatly influenced by their parents, schools, churches, books, TV shows, and other organizations and modes of mass communication. Since social learning largely takes place through language and verbal activities, the natural propensity of humans to think and to affect their emotions and behaviors by their thinking becomes enormously enhanced by cognitive means; and the influence of thinking on normal and pathological processes becomes even more profound. Even if reared by wolves on a desert island, people would probably think much more and differently than the wolves. But when reared in families, clans, and cultures, their cognitive processes take over even more and tend to run much of their other existence (Ellis, 1962, 1977a).

Human thinking, if it can be said to have a purpose, probably is mainly designed to help humans live longer and more successfully, to be alive and happy. But it also has its liabilities: to a considerable degree it manages to help humans live less long, as when it addicts them to cigaretts, overeating, alcohol, drugs, etc.; and it helps them live less happily, as when it addicts them to anxiety, depression, hostility, and feelings of worthlessness. Some of their disordered and disturbed thinking may well result from their social learning as Bandura (1977, 1978), Maslow (1962, 1970), Rogers (1961), and others have pointed out. But much of it—in fact, may also result from their biological tendency to think irrationally and to behave dysfunctionally (Ellis, 1976, 1979b). People are *so* prone to defeat their own chosen goals and values, and do this *so* widely, in just about every time and clime, that we may well hypothesize that they have a strong innate tendency to do so; and that even though this tendency may be partially overcome notably by teaching and by psychotherapy—as I have particularly claimed in many of my writings (Ellis, 1962, 1973, 1979a)—they still often and intensely fall back on disturbing themselves in powerful ways.

COGNITIVE ELEMENTS IN EGO ANXIETY

Ego anxiety, as I noted above and as I shall now indicate in more detail, has many pronounced cognitive elements, all of which lead to fears of worthlessness. The main and most important one is what I call *mus*turbation (Ellis, 1979a; Ellis & Abrahms, 1978; Ellis & Grieger, 1977; & Ellis & Harper, 1975). This arises because people do not merely wish, want, or prefer to perform important tasks adequately; they insist that they *must,* that they *have to* do so. They have what Karen Horney (1965) called the "tyranny of the shoulds."

Whenever people resort to absolutistic, *mus*turbatory thinking, it is virtually inevitable that they make themselves emotionally disturbed. For if they don't do as well as they think they *should* or *must,* they will certainly make themselves anxious or nervous about doing well, and also anxious about being worthwhile; and even when they *do* perform adequately, they will have no guarantee whatever that they will continue to do as well in the future; so, once again, they will make themselves distinctly anxious (Ellis, 1979a, 1979c).

More concretely, *musturbatory* thinking goes as follows. Let us say you rationally start off with the idea that "It would be highly preferable or desirable that I do well at important tasks" (that is, those I have chosen to see as important to my health and happiness); and "It would be undesirable and deplorable if I fail at such tasks and win the disapproval of significant people in my life." This is a rational or sensible or empirically confirmable belief because you can almost always show or prove that if you do poorly at these tasks and if others disapprove of you you will reap distinct disadvantages. For example, you will not get or keep a position you want; or will be paid poorly; or will not have others do various favors for you; or will reap other "disbenefits" by failing to do well. So, for all practical purposes, since you bring to almost any situation or experience your fairly strong desire to stay alive and to be happy, it *is* desirable for you to succeed and to be approved by others; and, by the same token, it *is* undesirable or unfortunate or regrettable if you fail and win others' disapproval.

If you were consistently rational, efficient, and sane, therefore, you would not like failing or being disapproved; and you would feel *appropriately* disappointed, sorry, sad, and frustrated when you did not do as well as you preferred to do and when others disliked you for failing. In RET, we distinctly and specifically differentiate your appropriate feelings in this respect from your *in*appropriate feelings of anxiety, depression, hostility, self-downing, and self-pity. We call the former set of feelings or emotions appropriate because they tend to help you, motivate you to go back to your original desires (for success and approval), and to achieve them; while inappropriate feelings tend to sabotage your goals, and deprive you of motivation (or give you misguided, desperate motivation), and thereby help you continue to fail in the future.

Let us assume in the examples in this chapter, however, that you have highly inappropriate anxiety (or nervousness or panic); and that this is largely (though not entirely) ego anxiety. In this case, you are not *merely* telling yourself the kinds of rational, sane beliefs listed above; but you are *also* telling yourself irrational, self-defeating beliefs; and it is these latter ideas that largely (though not exclusively) result in your anxious feelings. The main or paramount irrational belief that you are devoutly holding to, when you have ego anxiety, is: "I *must* succeed; I *have to* do well at this important task I have undertaken!" And this belief almost always has several important correlates, or supplementary irrational ideas:

1. "It is *terrible, awful* when I do not do what I *must* do: succeed and get approved or loved for my good efforts!"
2. "I *can't stand* failing and being rejected, and I *must not* be!"
3. "I have *no right* to fail in this dismal manner and to bring this amount of disapproval for failing!"
4. And, especially, "Because I failed, as I *must* not do and as I have *no right* to do, I am *a failure,* a pretty *rotten person,* who hardly *deserves* any goodness or any approval in the future!"

These irrational ideas all tend to be derivatives of or to stem from your original *must*urbatory command. For if you rigorously stayed with the rational belief, "I *prefer* to succeed at this task and be approved by significant others in my life, but I *don't* have to," you would then tend to conclude, "Because I don't have to succeed, I *can* stand failing and being rejected. It is highly inconvenient for me to fail and be rejected—but that's all it is, inconvenient, and not *awful.* As a fallible human, I always have the right to fail and merit disapproval, even though I don't like to do so. And although my performance is bad and unfortunate, it is only a part of me, an aspect of what I do, and never the whole of me. I am therefore not a bad person; and I fully deserve to succeed and be approved in the future, if I can manage this."

Ego anxiety, however, is anxiety about one's *self*, one's *being*, one's *essence*. It stems from *"needing"* (not just preferring) to do well and be approved by others; and from rating one's entire self, one's totality, as "bad" just because one has performed badly in some important areas. It results from self-rating, not just from rating (as one had better do!) one's acts, deeds, and performances. Although it is often called "performance anxiety," it is better called "ego anxiety" because it really is about one's self or ego; and it is most pernicious in that it involves the putdown, the damnation, of this entire self or ego.

Like almost all anxiety, ego anxiety is cognitive in that it is philosophical or ideological. It really begins with the basic assumptions, "I prefer to do well and be approved by others, and therefore I *must!*" This is an idea—a philosophy of life. Important emotional and behavioral consequences almost immediately, and in a sense automatically, flow from this basic assumption; and it is easy for us to focus upon these and to call ego anxiety an "emotional disturbance" or a "behavioral dysfunction." But it is also, essentially, an ideological disorder; and it is highly doubtful whether it would ever exist if humans were not philosophical, did not set up fundamental rules of behavior for themselves, and did not insist that they absolutely *must* follow these rules in a "good" or "perfect" manner.

COGNITIVE ELEMENTS IN DISCOMFORT ANXIETY

Rather than a fear of worthlessness, discomfort anxiety is a fear of (or overconcern about) pain, frustration, or discomfort. Like ego anxiety, it begins with the same kind of *shoulds* or *musts* and is also basically a product of *must*urbation. But instead of being a rating of oneself or ego as awful, it is a rating of others or of the world conditions under which one exists, as awful, and an evaluation that one cannot bear what one experiences. Thus, when you suffer from discomfort anxiety, you begin with the demand: "People and conditions *must* be the way I want them to be and *must not* exist in any manner that will cause me severe discomfort or death." The basic correlates or supplementary irrational ideas that accompany or follow this unrealistic demand then include:

1. "People and the world have *no right* to treat me in a manner so that I am seriously deprived of the things I want or am forced to live with things that I don't want!"

2. "Because conditions exist so as to bring about serious deprivations or to force me to live with things I don't want, the world is a thoroughly *rotten place* in which to live!"

3. "It is *awful* and *horrible* when conditions exist, as they *must* not, and seriously deprive me of the things that I want or cause me to experience things that I don't want!"

4. And, especially, "I *can't stand it* when conditions exist, as they must not, and seriously deprive me of the things that I want or cause me to experience things that I don't want!"

Ego anxiety and discomfort anxiety are in at least one fundamental way the same; in both there is a fear of something imagined, worthlessness in the case of ego anxiety and pain or frustration in discomfort anxiety. But, discomfort anxiety, or extreme low frustration tolerance, is in some ways almost the opposite of ego anxiety: In the latter condition one ends up by severely condemning oneself because one is not as glorious and great as one insists that one *must* be; while in the former condition one ends up by damning other people and the world because they do not treat one as gloriously and greatly as one insists that they *must*. Whereas ego anxiety, therefore, winds up with extreme self-downing and feelings of worthlessness, discomfort anxiety may wind up with feelings of depression, self-pity, and extreme anger or irritability, as well as anxiety, but with an underlying sense of grandiosity: one feels that the world indubitably stinks but that oneself is something of a marvelous person who does not deserve this kind of a stinking world (Ellis, 1978).

Ego anxiety, in other words, starts with feelings of grandiosity—or would-be grandiosity—and finishes up with self-immolation; and discomfort anxiety starts with similar feelings of grandiosity and may finish up with the same kind of feelings and/or with self-pity. You begin by assuming that because you have been given the boon of life and *should* be given it forever and assuming that because you can be happy and *must* always be happy, it is *horrible,* you *can't stand* it, and the world is a pretty *rotten place* whenever you are not accorded long life and great joy by others or by the universe. Childish grandiosity, which seems to be native to most children, thereby reigns forever!

Once you devoutly believe these fundamental irrational premises, you are prone to believe several irrational correlates of discomfort anxiety or low frustration tolerance. These irrational beliefs tend to be along the following lines:

1. "I *need* what I want and it is *awful* when I don't have it!"
2. "I *must* have the power to ward off dangerous and obnoxious conditions!"
3. "There *must* be a high degree of order or certainty in the universe."
4. "I *must* not be forced to face life's great difficulties and responsibilities."
5. "Many things are *too* hard and *must* not be *that* hard!"
6. "I can't stand my disturbed feelings and *must* not feel them!"
7. "Now that I am alive, I *must* not die!"

Cognitive Elements in Phobias

Phobias, as noted above, may stem from either feelings of ego anxiety or discomfort anxiety, or a combination of both. In phobias about presentations or situations where there is a good chance that people will fail or at least not come up to their own (often unrealistic) expectations, ego anxiety is largely involved. Thus, in phobias about attending social groups, speaking in public, or taking examinations, you usually start with the basic assumption: "I *must* not perform poorly in this situation; and if I do it is *terrible* and will prove that I *am* something of a worm!" And you then conclude: "I'd better not risk taking part in this performance and *must* avoid it at all costs!" These irrational ideas (irrational because they are pushed to the point of absolutistic *musts* instead of self-helping *preferences*) lead to avoidance of these phobic situations or even (sometimes) to avoidance of thinking about them.

Instead of this, or in addition to this, phobias are sparked by discomfort anxiety: "I *must* not be inconvenienced or harmed in any way when riding in an elevator; there is at least a slight chance that this kind of horrible inconvenience or harm will occur if I ride in elevators; that would be *terrible;* therefore I *must not,* under any condition, ride in elevators!" Again, in these instances, a preference has been irrationally escalated to an absolutistic demand or command: for although virtually all humans *prefer* to avoid harm or severe inconvenience when riding in elevators, most of them easily convince themselves that the chances of such accidents occurring are very slight; therefore they are willing to take the risk of using this means of transportation. But as soon as you insist, to yourself and/or others, "I absolutely *must* not be inconvenienced or harmed in elevators," and there is of course always *some* chance that you may be, you will bring on feelings of terror or horror about riding in them, and will become phobic about them. Virtually any *must* leads to feelings of anxiety—unless you are (foolishly) certain that there is *no chance* that your *must* will not be fulfilled. And even when you get what you think you *must* (e.g., a safe and enjoyable ride in an elevator) you will inevitably worry about your *next* ride if you still cling to, "I *must* not experience discomfort or harm in an elevator!"

COGNITIVE ELEMENTS IN OBSESSIONS

Obsessions almost always seem to result when one will not "drop" worrying about something and, instead, continues to insist that it would be horrible and terrible if this thing occurred or recurred. Obsessions may spring from irrational ideas that lead to both ego anxiety and discomfort anxiety. Thus, using the illustrations of phobias mentioned in the preceding paragraph, if you are afraid of social situations, and keep insisting to yourself, "I *have to* do well in such situations. Wouldn't it be *terrible* if I didn't! What a *rotten person* I would be if I failed socially!," and if you then have a social situation coming up in the near future, you will find it almost impossible not to keep thinking about it, obsessing about it. For the idea that it would be *terrible* to fail in such a situation and that you, as a total person, would be *completely no good* for failing is so dramatic, so overwhelming, that it tends to stay with you almost continually. Even when the situation has passed, and you have not done so poorly in it, you will still tend to obsess, for you still haven't done as well as you supposedly *must* have done. Feelings of terror and of self-castigation are so powerful that they easily preempt much or most of your waking thoughts; and also tend to get into your dreams. Knowing that you *may,* even with a high outside chance, be tortured to death tomorrow, you will obsess yourself, almost certainly, with the "horror" or being so tortured. Similarly, feeling that you *may* lose your "self" or "ego" by failing socially will tend to obsess you with thoughts about any event or performance that you may fail at to "lose" it.

A similar dynamism exists in the case of discomfort anxiety. If you are afraid, for example, of riding in an elevator because you are defining potential inconvenience or harm when you do so as *awful, terrible,* or *horrible,* you will thereby highly dramatize this possible inconvenience or harm, and will hardly be able to think about anything except the elevator you are about to ride in and the "horror" that will then ensue. Under these conditions, you will tend to obsess about injury, elevators, feelings of terror, people who see how terrified you are, and a host of other things that you may easily connect with riding in elevators; and only when you surrender your ideas about the "horror" of inconvenience or harm in elevators are you likely to become "unobsessed" about them.

COGNITIVE ELEMENTS IN ANXIETY ABOUT ANXIETY

Rational-emotive therapy is one of the main psychotherapies that duly emphasizes the element of anxiety about anxiety—or the secondary symptoms of anxiety that frequently follow the primary symptoms (Ellis, 1962, 1978, 1979a, 1979c, 1979d; Ellis & Abrahms, 1978; Ellis & Grieger, 1977; Ellis & Harper, 1975; Grieger & Boyd, 1979). This element has also been emphasized by a few other leading therapists, such as Low (1952) and Weekes (1969, 1972, 1977). It is exceptionally important to note this factor in anxiety and in neurosis since it usually is highly important and almost inevitably follows the continued or the intense existence of almost any feeling of anxiety.

A good example in this respect exists in the case of agoraphobia. When people are agoraphobic, they first tend to be extremely afraid of open or unfamiliar places, and therefore confine themselves to their homes or offices. They later often become afraid of many other things, such as trains, automobiles, elevators, etc. Their first level of anxiety usually is a combination of discomfort anxiety and of ego anxiety. In terms of the latter, they tell themselves something like, "I can't stand open spaces, because there is little structure there, and in an unfamiliar surrounding I might well make more mistakes than usual. If so, that would be awful and I would be something of a shit!" In terms of the latter, of discomfort anxiety, they tell themselves something like, "I can't stand open spaces, because there is little structure there, and in an unfamiliar surrounding I have to work harder to do well and to mind my p's and q's. It's *too* hard and it shouldn't be that hard! Therefore, I'd better take the easier way out and avoid all open spaces!"

Once they become terrified of open spaces—for either or both of these reasons—they frequently feel extremely uncomfortable (1) when actually in such spaces, or (2) even when thinking about being in them. They then frequently—I would say usually—acquire some degree of ego anxiety and of discomfort anxiety about their extreme feelings of discomfort or about their anxiety.

In terms of ego anxiety, they tell themselves something like, "It's awful to feel anxious about open spaces. Other people are not agoraphobics; and it's downright silly for me to be one. What an incompetent person I am for having such a foolish fear!" In terms of discomfort anxiety, they say to themselves something along these lines: "It's awful to feel anxious about open spaces. Anxiety is very painful; in fact, it's too painful to bear. How horrible for me to suffer such pain! I absolutely must stay away from open spaces, or even from thinking about open spaces, in order to stave off this horribly painful anxiety!" (Ellis, 1979d).

Things can get even more complicated than this in terms of one's secondary symptoms, or one's anxiety about anxiety. For just as one can think about one's thinking and also think about thinking about one's thinking, one can go to a tertiary level and conclude: "Not only am I anxious about open spaces, but I can see that I'm anxious about my anxiety. That means that I'm *really* very anxious—and much more so than are most people. What an idiot I therefore am! Moreover, if I have both anxiety and anxiety about anxiety—both of which are horrible to experience—I just *can't bear* this abominable kind of pain. Oh, woe is me if I continue to have these terrible feelings!"

Ego anxiety and discomfort anxiety, moreover, can easily reinforce and aggravate each other—especially in the case of agoraphobia. Thus, if you are an agoraphobic you can say to yourself, "I'm really no good if I act incompetently in open and unfamiliar places; and because I'm no good, people will see that I am and will tend to boycott me and not do anything good for me. This means that I will be extremely deprived; and I can't stand being deprived! My God, I must not be deprived, I must not be deprived! And the more anxious I am about open spaces, the more I will be boycotted and deprived; and the more I am deprived, the more anxious I will be. If people see I am incompetent, they are right, and I am pretty worthless; and if they see I can't stand the anxiety of being agoraphobic or can't stand the deprivation of their boycotting me, they will think I'm a terrible baby. And that's awful, if they think I'm a baby and put me down for that! Then they will boycott me all the more—and I can't stand their depriving me for that (or any other) reason!"

Round and round you can easily go: starting with ego anxiety, having discomfort anxiety about that; then creating more ego anxiety about your original anxiety and your discomfort anxiety; then creating more discomfort anxiety about your increased ego anxiety, etc., etc. The interaction of these two neurotic feelings seems endless—and quite often is!

Cognitive Elements in Anxiety about Psychotherapy

Just as people make themselves anxious about their own inadequacies, about the "unniceties" of others, and about the conditions and hassles of their lives, they also bring their anxiety-creating cognitions into the realm of psychotherapy. For many of them, particularly those who have high degrees of intelligence and education, soon see that they are anxious and try to do something about their neurotic feelings, either in the form of self-help procedures or by undergoing some form of individual or group therapy. And—what do you know!—they then tend to experience intense ego anxiety as well as discomfort anxiety about their therapeutic endeavors.

Take, for example, people with a simple fear of, for example, escalators. They know that they have this fear after having it a short while; they know that escalators are quite safe means of transportation; and they therefore conclude that they are "foolish" for maintaining their escalator phobias. They also know, in many instances, that if they (1) face their fear of escalators; (2) force themselves, however uncomfortably, to take many escalator rides; (3) read pamphlets and books on how to overcome fears; and (4) go for intensive psychotherapy, they will most probably overcome their phobia. But very frequently they do few or none of these things, and thereby "resist" curing themselves, for a number of reasons:

1. They tell themselves that it is utterly foolish to have such a "ridiculous" fear, and they are ashamed to fully admit that they have it. Consequently, even though they may avoid riding on escalators, they make rationalizations for doing so (e.g., "My foot is sore today and I may harm it," or "It's faster walking up the stairs than using the escalator," or "This is an unusually steep and fast escalator and is one of the few that really *is* dangerous."). They thereby never quite admit they truly have an escalator phobia, because of their ego anxiety.

2. Whenever they admit that they are afraid of escalators and vow to keep riding on them, they experience feelings of panic. They then tell themselves, "I can't stand this feeling of panic! It will make me do something really awful—such as actually get in a serious escalator accident! It's too hard to go on the escalators when I feel this way. I'll wait until I feel better about it and then take many rides." Their discomfort anxiety then prevents them from carrying out their resolution to practice *in vivo* desensitization on the escalators.

3. When they consider riding escalators, they often tell themselves, "I can do it; but I'm sure I'll feel panicked doing it. Other people will then see that I am panicked; and that will be shameful! I'd better look around for an escalator that practically no one ever uses, so that no one will see how shamefully panicked I am!" In this instance, their ego anxiety prevents them from curing themselves of their fear.

4. When they are reading pamphlets or books about overcoming fears of escalators (or of anything else), they frequently feel very uncomfortable (because they are then facing their phobia and admitting they have it and putting themselves down for having it), and they abandon the reading because of their discomfort. Here, their discomfort anxiety bolixes up their self-help efforts. They also may have difficulty in reading and under-

standing this material on overcoming fear and may tell themselves, "It's hard to read this difficult and boring material. In fact, it's *too* damned hard—much harder than it *should* be! I'll read it later." Again, their discomfort anxiety inteferes with their therapeutic efforts.

5. When they consider going for individual or group therapy, they tell themselves that seeing a therapist, and particularly letting others know that they see one, is shameful and that perhaps they'd better not go for that reason. Again: ego anxiety!

6. In considering therapy or actually undergoing it, they insist that they *have to* understand everything the therapist says and put his/her advice into almost perfect effect; and aren't they horrible people when they don't understand or don't perfectly actualize the therapeutic instructions. So they again refuse to go for treatment, or else they quit it prematurely. More ego anxiety!

7. They inwardly and/or outwardly rave about the *horrible* hardships of therapy such as: (1) they have to pay for it; (2) it requires steady appointments; (3) it involves homework assignments; (4) it calls for their doing hard things that they have never ever done before in their lives; (5) it takes too long; (6) it provides no guarantees of success; (7) it is often boring. They not only view these hardships as unfortunate and undesirable, but as hassles that *should* not, *must* not exist, and that are therefore totally abominable! More discomfort anxiety!

8. They frequently compare themselves to other clients who have undertaken therapy, such as their friends or other members of their therapy groups. They tell themselves that "I *should* do as well in therapy as these others are doing; and isn't it *awful* when I am not. That simply proves that I am a *hopelessly incompetent individual* who will *never* learn how to help myself and who will have to suffer this phobia forever!" Again, ego anxiety rears its ugly head!

9. Whenever they make temporary advances in therapy

and then fall back again, they tend to think, "There I go ahead! Falling back! What a rotten person am I!" And: "Obviously, this therapy is too hard for me. I'll never be able to keep it up! How impossible a task when I have to continue to work practically forever!" Here we have both ego anxiety and discomfort anxiety.

In many ways, then, and on several important levels, humans tend to create ego anxiety and discomfort anxiety: in regard to their original symptom; in the fabrication of secondary and tertiary symptoms; and about their attempts at helping themselves get over their symptoms. Again I hypothesize: in relatively mild, short-lived neurotic disorders, either ego anxiety or discomfort anxiety tends to exist; but in almost all severe and longstanding disorders, both these manifestations hold sway and usually continue to exist in an intense and prolonged manner. Whenever ego anxiety is profound, it leads to such heightened feelings of discomfort (such as panic, horror, and terror) that people conclude that these feelings absolutely *must* not, *should* not exist, that it is awful that they do, and that life is just too much of a hassle for them to experience almost any enjoyment whatever under these conditions. They then are in the throes of discomfort anxiety. And whenever extreme discomfort anxiety or feelings of low frustration tolerance exist, most humans sooner or later tend to put themselves down for having and indulging in such feelings. They tell themselves cognitions like, "What a baby I am! I should be able to face my panic and get over it and I obviously cannot. I'm just a rotter and a highly incompetent person!"

By the same token, feelings of discomfort anxiety may easily be followed by discomfort anxiety about discomfort anxiety. If you are horrified about the difficulty of speaking well in public, you can also easily horrify yourself about the difficulty of having these horrible feelings. And ego anxiety may easily be followed by ego anxiety. If you down yourself for being unable to cope with open spaces, you may down yourself for downing yourself! As noted above, ego anxiety and discomfort anxiety powerfully interact; and, whenever one powerfully exists, there is an excellent chance that the other does, too. Moreover, when you experience either ego or discomfort anxiety as a primary symptom, there is a good chance that you will experience either or both as a secondary (and perhaps also a tertiary) symptom. And since both ego and discomfort anxiety are largely created by irrational beliefs, we can truly say, with the poet, "O what fools we mortals be!" Except that, in RET terms, we *are* not foolish (about this or anything else); we merely *behave* foolishly much of the time!

RESEARCH FINDINGS ON COGNITION IN PSYCHONEUROSIS

It would seem a relatively simple task to check on the cognitions of individuals with emotional problems, and to see whether these significantly differ from, and in what ways they differ from, individuals having less of these problems. Indeed a great deal of research has been done in this area, especially in the realm of the irrational ideas that I hypothesized some 25 years ago as concomitants of neurotic behavior (Ellis, 1957b, 1958, 1962). My first papers on RET outlined from 10 to 12 major irrational ideas that presumably accompany, and in some significant ways contribute to or cause, emotional problems. A good many researchers expanded on these irrationalities and made them into paper and pencil tests (Argabite & Nidorf, 1968; Bassai, 1925; Fox & Davies, 1971; Jones, 1968; MacDonald & Games, 1972; Shorkey & Whiteman, 1977). These tests have subsequently been given to a wide variety of groups of disturbed and "normal" individuals; and they have also been correlated with the test results of some of the other standard personality and neurosis scales, such as the Minnesota Multiphasic Personality Inventory.

Most of the studies of tests of irrationality based on the main RET hypotheses have produced statistically significant results. Thus, O'Connell, Baker, Hanson, and Ermalinski (1974) found active participants in therapy groups to be significantly more rational than inactive participants. Kassinove, Crisci, and Tiegerman (1977) showed that older grade school students displayed less irrationality than younger ones. Nelson (1977) indicated that depression was related most strongly to high self-expectations, frustration reactivity, overconcern about possible misfortunes in the future, helplessness, and the total score on the R. G. Jones Irrational Beliefs Test (1968), derived from RET principles. Morelli and Friedman (1978) found that positive correlations existed between self-reported anxiety and irrationality. Shorkey and Reyes (1978) reported significant correlations between a rational behavior inventory and several self-actualization variables. Brandt (1976) discovered that basic irrationalities, as posited by me, are cross-cultural and exist in the British as well as the American populace. Nolan (1977) reported that selected irrational beliefs were responsible for the observed differences in the negative effects of anxiety, hostility, and depression of community college students.

Waugh (1976) found a significant correlation between rationality and emotional adjustment. Fox and Davies (1971) showed highly significant differences in irrationality scores between a group of normal Canadians and groups of mental hospital patients and of alcoholics. MacDonald and Games (1972) indicated that the Ellis irrational values scale was "significantly related to neuroticism, anxiety, external locus of control, and many of the California Psychological Inventory subscales." Barry (1974) found that prison inmates functioned more from irrational beliefs than a normal population sample. Eisenberg and Zingle (1975) showed that "individuals who experience marital difficulties demonstrate higher degrees of irrational thinking than individuals who do not experience such difficulties." Zingle (1965) reported that a test of irrationality based on RET discriminated school underachievers from normal achievers. Fox (1969) found that a rationality Life Orientation Test significantly differentiated between Erich Fromm's designations of individuals with biophilia and necrophilia.

Hoxter (1967) discovered that problem children in a school setting had more irrational beliefs than nonbehavior problem children in the same setting. Sanche (1968) reported that educationally retarded youngsters had significantly fewer irrational beliefs after a cooperative schoolwork training program than they did before taking this program. Sharma (1970) found that underachievers exposed to rational group counseling showed significantly greater reduction in irrational beliefs than did underachievers not exposed to this kind of counseling. Taft (1968) noted that a group that scored high on the Zingle (1965) Irrational Ideas Inventory exceeded a low irrational-belief group in anxiety. Vargo (1972) found mentally healthy people to be more rational than mentally disturbed people. Winship (1972) showed that a high irrational-belief group in every case exceeded a low irrational-belief group in anxiety proneness. Zingle (1965) found that a group of underachieving students counseled according to an RET orientation showed a significantly greater improvement than did an untreated group on his own Irrational Ideas Inventory.

Studies such as those just listed give fairly impressive evidence that in tests of irrationality, based on my originally posited basic irrational ideas, psychoneurotic and other emotionally disturbed groups of individuals are almost always found to differ significantly from control groups of "normal" or less disturbed individuals; and these and a good many other studies indicate that when disturbed groups are treated with RET or some variation of cognitive-behavior therapy they almost always show significant improvement on tests of rationality and other personality indicators (Ellis, 1977a, 1977c; DiGiuseppe, Miller & Trexler, 1977; & Murphy & Ellis, 1979).

In addition, literally scores of other studies have been done that indicate that people who are diagnosed as being emotionally disturbed—that is, either in the neurotic, borderline, or psychotic range of behavior—have various kinds of cognitive deficiencies or aberrancies. Thus, researchers have found that disturbed individuals are likely to have significant degrees of problem-solving difficulty (Platt, Spivack, Altman, & Altman, 1974); internally elicited cognitive activity (May, 1977); unplanned, impulsive action (Hill, Foote, Aldons, & MacDonald, 1970); closed-style perceptual orientation (Heilbrun, 1973); inconsistent attitude communication (Newman, 1977); dogmatic thinking (Kemp, 1961); less formal operational capacities (Kilburg & Siegel, 1973); deficit of mnemonic orientation (Larsen & Fromholt, 1976; dispersal behaviors (Horowitz, Sampson, Siegelman, Weiss, & Goodfriend, 1978); poor degree of construct differentiation (Hayden, Nasby, & Davids, 1977); disordered thinking (Harrow, 1977); a higher level of intrusive and stimulus-repetitive thoughts (Horowitz, Becker, & Malone, 1973); more authoritarian attitudes (Becker, Spielberger, & Parker, 1963); more overinclusive thinking (Craig, 1973); excessive response to strong aspects of meaning and deficient response to weak aspects of meaning of words (Chapman, Chapman, & Daut, 1976); deficiency in word association (DeWolfe, Kluczny, & McDonald, 1972); deficits in self-editing (Davis & Blaney, 1976); conceptual organization deficiencies and response interference problems (Depue & Fowles, 1974); greater misperceptions about people (Widom, 1976); and a clear abstraction deficit (Braff & Beck, 1974).

Pioneering hypotheses and studies of self-instruction, or of how children and adults talk to themselves and thereby control their own behavior, have been done by Vygotsky (1962), Luria (1961), and Arnold (1960); and applications of this idea to people's creation and control of their own emotional and psychosomatic disturbances have been done by many outstanding investigators, including Beck (1967, 1976), Graham, Lundy, Benjamin, and Kabler (1962), Schacter and Singer (1962), and Velten (1968). I review much of the literature showing the effect of cognitions on human emotions and on behavioral change in my article, "Rational-Emotive Therapy: Research Data That Supports the Clinical and Personality Hypotheses of RET and other Modes of Cognitive-Behavior Therapy" (Ellis, 1977a). Girodo (1977) also reviews the specific relationship between cognition and anxiety in his article, "Self-talk: Mechanisms in Anxiety and Stress Management."

This material, together with literally hundreds of other pertinent studies that could be quoted if space permitted, tends to show that human psychoneurosis, and anxiety in particular, is significantly related to cognition; and also (what is beyond the scope of the present article) that when people change their cognitions, attitudes, ideas, philosophies, or self-talk they also significantly change their disturbed emotions and behaviors. Of all the hypotheses about emotional disturbance and personality change that now exist, I would say that this one has, at the moment, immense empirical support.

REFERENCES

Adler, A. *Understanding human nature*. New York: Fawcett World, 1927, 1968.

Argabite, A. H., & Nidorf, L. J. Fifteen questions for rating reason. *Rational Living*, 1968, *3*(1), 9–11.

Arnold, M. *Emotion and personality* (2 vols.). New York: Columbia University Press, 1960.

Bandura, A. The self system in reciprocal determinism. *American Psychologist*, 1978, *33*, 344–358.

Bandura, A. *Social learning theory*. Palo Alto, Calif.: Stanford University Press, 1977.

Beck, A. T. *Depression*. New York: Hoeber, 1967.

Beck, A. T. *Cognitive therapy and the emotional disorders*. New York: International Universities Press, 1976.

Becker, J., Spielberger, C. D., & Parker, J. B. Value achievement and authoritarian attitudes in psychiatric patients. *Journal of Clinical Psychology*, 1963, *19*, 57–61.

Becker, S. S., Horowitz, M. J., & Campbell, L. Cognitive responses to stress: effects of changes in demand and sex. *Journal of Abnormal Psychology*, 1973, *87*, 519–522.

Berne, E. Ego states in psychotherapy. *American Journal of Psychotherapy*, 1957, *11*, 293–309.

Bessai, J. *A factorial assessment of irrational beliefs*. Unpublished M. A. thesis, Cleveland State University, 1975.

Braff, D. L., & Beck, A. T. Thinking disorder in depression, *Archives of General Psychiatry*, 1974, *31*, 456–459.

Brandt, F. M. J. *An inquiry into the underlying philosophy of rational emotive therapy*. A cross-cultural inquiry. Unpublished M. A. thesis, Central Michigan University, 1976.

Chapman, L. J., Chapman, J. B., & Daut, R. L. Schizophrenic inability to disattend from strong aspects of meaning. *Journal of Abnormal Psychology*, 1976, *85*, 35–40.

Craig, R. J. Interpersonal competition, overinclusive thinking, and schizophrenia. *Journal of Consulting and Clinical Psychology*, 1973, *40*, 9–14.

Davies, R. L. *Relationship of irrational ideas to emotional disturbance*. Unpublished M.Ed. thesis, University of Alberta, 1970.

Davis, K. M., & Blaney, P. R. Overinclusion and self-editing in schizophrenia. *Journal of Abnormal Psychology*, 1976, *85*, 51–60.

Davison, G. R., & Neale, J. M. *Abnormal psychology: an experimental clinical approach*. New York: Wiley, 1974.

Depue, R. A., & Fowles, D. C. Conceptual ability, response interference, and arousal in withdrawn and active schizophrenia. *Journal of Consulting and Clinical Psychology*, 1974, *47*, 509–518.

DeWolfe, A. S., & McDonald, R. K. Sex differences and institutionalization in the word association of schizophrenics. *Journal of Consulting and Clinical Psychology*, 1972, *39*, 215–221.

DiGiuseppi, R. A., Miller, N. S., & Trexler, L. A review of rational-emotive psychotherapy: Outcome studies. *The Counseling Psychologist*, 1977, *7*, 64–72.

Diekstra, R. F. W., & Dassen, W. F. M. *Rationele therapie*. Amsterdam: Swets and Zeitlinger, 1976.

Eisenberg, J. M., & Zingle, H. W. Marital adjustment and irrational ideas. *Journal of Marriage & Family Counseling*, 1975, *2*, 81–91.

Ellis, A. *How to live with a "neurotic."* New York: Crown Publishers, 1957, 1975. (a)

Ellis, A. Outcome of employing three techniques of psychotherapy. *Journal of Clinical Psychology*, 1957, *13*, 334–350. (b)

Ellis, A. Rational psychotherapy. *Journal of General Psychology*, 1958, *59*, 35–49.

Ellis, A. *Reason and emotion in psychotherapy*. New York: Lyle Stuart, Inc., 1962. Paperback ed. New York: Citadel Press, 1977.

Ellis, A. *Growth through reason*. Palo Alto, Calif.: Science and Behavior Books, 1971; Hollywood, Calif.: Wilshire Books, 1974.

Ellis, A. *Humanistic psychotherapy: the rational-emotive approach*. New York: Crown Publishers and McGraw-Hill Paperbacks, 1973.

Ellis, A. The biological basis of human irrationality. *Journal of Individual Psychology*, 1976, *32*, 145–168. Reprinted in A. Ellis & R. Grieger, *Handbook of rational-emotive therapy*. New York: Springer, 1977.

Ellis, A. Rational-emotive therapy: research data that supports the clinical and personality hypotheses of RET and other modes of cognitive-behavior therapy. *Counseling Psychologist*, 1977, *7*(1), 2–42. (a)

Ellis, A. *How to live with—and without—anger*. New York: Reader's Digest Press, 1977. (b)

Ellis, A. Elegant and inelegant RET. *Counseling Psychologist*, 1977, 7(1), 73–82.

Ellis, A. Discomfort anxiety: A new cognitive-behavioral construct. Invited address to the Association for Advancement of Behavior Therapy Annual Meeting, November 17, 1978. New York: BMA Audio Cassettes, 1978.

Ellis, A. *Theoretical and empirical foundations of rational-emotive therapy*. Monterey, Calif.: Brooks/Cole, 1979. (a)

Ellis, A. The biological basis of human irrationality: A reply to McBurnet and LaPointe. *Journal of Individual Psychology*, 1979, in press. (b)

Ellis, A. Rational-emotive therapy. In R. J. Corsini, *Current psychotherapies* (rev. ed.). Itasca, Ill.: Peacock, 1979. (c)

Ellis, A. A note on the treatment of agoraphobics with cognitive modification versus prolonged exposure *in vivo*. *Behaviour Therapy and Research*, 1979, in press. (d)

Ellis, A., & Abrahms, E. *Brief psychotherapy in medical and health practice*. New York: Springer, 1978.

Ellis, A., & Grieger, R. *Handbook of rational-emotive therapy*. New York: Springer, 1977.

Ellis, A., & Harper, R. A. *A new guide to rational living*. Engelwood Cliffs, N.J.: Prentice-Hall; Hollywood, Calif.: Wilshire Books, 1975.

Epictetus. *The works of Epictetus*. Boston: Little, Brown, & Co. 1890.

Fox, E. E. *A life orientation scale: Correlates of biophilia and necrophilia*. Unpublished doctoral dissertation, University of Alberta, 1969.

Fox, E. E., & Davies, R. Test your rationality. *Rational Living*, 1971, 5(2), 23–25.

Girodo, M. Self talk: mechanisms in anxiety and stress management. In C. Spielberger & I. G. Sarason (Eds.), *Stress and anxiety* (Vol. 4). Washington, D. C.: Hemisphere, 1977.

Goldfried, M. R., & Davison, G. C. *Clinical behavior therapy*. New York: Holt, Rinehart and Winston, 1976.

Graham, D., Lundy, R., Benjamin, L., & Kalber, F. Some specific attitudes in initial research interviews with patients having different "psychosomatic" diseases. *Psychsomatic Medicine*, 1962, *24*, 257–266.

Greenwald, H. *Direct decision therapy*. San Diego, Calif.: Edits, 1977.

Grieger, R., & Boyd, J. *Rational-emotive therapy: A skills-based approach*. New York: Van Nostrand Reinhold, 1979.

Harrow, M. Is disordered thinking unique to schizophrenics? *Archives of General Psychiatry*, 1977, *34*, 15–21.

Hauck, P. *Overcoming worry and fear*. Philadelphia: Westminster Press, 1975.

Hayden, B., Nasby, W., & Davids, A. Interpersonal conceptual structures, predictive accuracy and social adjustment of emotionally disturbed boys. *Journal of Abnormal Psychology*, 1977, *86*, 312–320.

Heilbrun, A. B. Adaptation to aversive maternal control and perception of simultaneously presented evaluative cues. *Journal of Consulting and Clinical Psychology*, 1973, *41*, 301–307.

Hill, R., Foote, N., Aldons, J., & MacDonald, R. *Family development in three generations*. Cambridge, Mass.: Shenkman, 1970.

Horney, K. *Collected writings*. New York: W. W. Norton, 1965.

Horowitz, L. M., Sampson, H., Siegelman, E. Y., Weiss, J., & Goodfriend, S. Cohesive and dispersal behaviors: two classes of concomitant change in psychotherapy. *Journal of Consulting and Clinical Psychology*, 1978, *46*, 556–564.

Horowitz, M. J., Becker, S. S., & Malone, P. Stress: different effects on patients and nonpatients. *Journal of Abnormal Psychology*, 1973, *82*, 547–551.

Hoxter, A. L. *Irrational beliefs and self-concept in two kinds of behavior*. Unpublished doctoral dissertation, University of Alberta, 1967.

Jones, R. *A factored measure of Ellis' irrational belief system with personality and maladjustment correlates*. Unpublished doctoral dissertation, Texas Technological College, 1968.

Kassinove, H., Crisci, R., & Tiegerman, S. Developmental trends in rational thinking: implications for rational-emotive school mental health programs. *Journal of Community Psychology*, 1977, *5*, 266–274.

Kelly, G. *The psychology of personal constructs*. New York: W. W. Norton, 1955.

Kemp, C. C. Influence of dogmatism on counseling. *Personnel and Guidance Journal*, 1961, *39*, 662–665.

Kilburg, R., R., & Siegel, A. W. Formal operations in reactive and process schizophrenia. *Journal of Consulting and Clinical Psychology*, 1973, *40*, 371–376.

Knaus, W. *Rational emotive education*. New York: Institute for Rational Living, 1974.

Larsen, S. F., & Fromholt, P. Mnemonic organization and free recall in schizophrenia. *Journal of Abnormal Psychology*, 1976, *85*, 61–65.

Lembo, J. *The counseling process: a rational behavioral approach*. New York: Libra, 1976.

Low, A. *Mental health through will training*. Boston: Christopher, 1952.

Luria, A. *The role of speech in the regulation of normal and abnormal behaviors*. New York: Liveright, 1961.

MacDonald, A., & Games, R. Ellis' irrational ideas: a validation study. *Rational Living*, 1972, *7*(2), 25–29.

Mahoney, M. *Cognition and behavior modification*. Cambridge, Mass.: Ballinger, 1974.

Mahoney, M. Personal science: a cognitive learning therapy. In A. Ellis & R. Grieger (Eds.), *Handbook of rational-emotive therapy*. New York: Springer, 1977.

Marcus Aurelius. *Mediations*. Boston: Little, Brown, 1890.

Maslow, A. H. *Toward a psychology of being*. Princeton, N.J.: Van Nostrand, 1962.

Maslow, A. H. *Motivation and personality* (2nd ed.). New York: Harper, 1970.

May, J. R. Psychophysiology of self-regulated phobic thoughts. *Behavior Therapy*, 1977, *8*, 150–153.

Maultsby, M.C., Jr. *Help yourself to happiness*. New York: Institute for Rational Living, 1975.

Morelli, G., & Friedman, B. Cognitive correlates of multidimensional trait anxiety. *Psychological Reports*, 1978, *42*, 611–614.

Morris, G. B. *Irrational beliefs, life orientation and temporal perspective of prison inmates*. Unpublished doctoral dissertation, University of Alberta, 1974.

Morris, K. T., & Kanitz, H. M. *Rational-emotive therapy*. Boston: Houghton Mifflin, 1975.

Murphy, R., & Ellis, A. *A comprehensive bibliography of books, articles and other materials on rational-emotive therapy and cognitive-behavior therapy*. New York: Institute for Rational Living, 1979.

Nelson, R. E. Irrational beliefs in depression. *Journal of Consulting and Clinical Psychology*, 1977, *45*, 1190–1191.

Newman, E. H. Resolution of inconsistent attitude communications in normal and schizophrenic subjects. *Journal of Abnormal Psychology*, 1977, *86*, 41–46.

Nolan, E. J. *Toward a theory of low frustration tolerance: a cognitive-emotive approach*. Ed.D. thesis, University of Virginia, 1977.

O'Connell, W. E., Baker, R. R., Hanson, P., & Ermalinski, R. Types of negative nonsense. *International Journal of Social Psychiatry*, 1974, *20*, 122–127.

Perls, F. *Gestalt therapy verbatim*. Lafayette, Calif.: Real People Press, 1969.

Platt, J. J., Spivack, G., Altman, N., & Altman, D. Adolescent problem-solving thinking. *Journal of Consulting and Clinical Psychology*, 1974, *42*, 787–793.

Raimy, V. *Misunderstandings of the self*. San Francisco, Calif.: Jossey-Bass, 1975.

Rimm, D., & Masters, J. C. *Behavior therapy*. New York: Academic Press, 1974.

Rogers, C. R. *On becoming a person*. Boston: Houghton Mifflin, 1961.

Rotter, J. B. *Social learning and clinical psychology*. New York: Prentice-Hall, 1954.

Russell, B. *The conquest of happiness*. New York: Pocket Books, 1950.

Sanche, R. P. *Self-concept and beliefs of educationally retarded youth*. M. Ed. thesis, University of Alberta, 1968.

Schachter, S., & Singer, J. E. Cognitive, social and physiological determinants of emotional state. *Psychological Review*, 1962, *69*, 379–399.

Sharma, K. L. *A rational group therapy approach to counselling anxious underachievers*. Unpublished doctoral dissertation, University of Alberta, 1970.

Shorkey, C. T., & Reyes, E. Relationship between self actualization and rational thinking. *Psychological Reports*, 1978, *42*, 842.

Shorkey, C. T., & Whiteman, V. L. Development of the rational behavior inventory. *Educational and Psychological Measurement*, 1977, *37*, 527–534.

Spinoza, B. Improvement of the understanding. New York: Dunne, 1901.

Taft, L. M. *A study to determine the relationship of anxiety to irrational ideas*. M.Ed. thesis, University of Alberta, 1968.

Tosi, D. J. *Youth: Toward personal growth. A rational-emotive approach*. Columbus, Ohio: Merrill, 1974.

Velten, E. A laboratory task for induction of mood states. *Behaviour Research and Therapy*, 1968, *6*, 473–482.

Vargo, J. W. *Two concepts of mental health*. Unpublished doctoral dissertation, University of Alberta, 1972.

Vygotsky, L. *Thought and language*. New York: Wiley, 1962.

Waugh, N. M. Rationality and emotional adjustment: a test of Ellis's theory of rational emotive psychotherapy. *Dissertation Abstracts International*, 1976, *36*, 6406.

Weekes, C. *Hope and help for your nerves*. New York: Hawthorn, 1969.

Weekes, C. *Peace from nervous suffering*. New York: Hawthorn, 1972.

Weekes, C. *Simple, effective treatment of agoraphobia*. New York: Hawthorn, 1977.

Widom, C. S. Interpersonal and personal construct systems in psychopaths. *Journal of Consulting and Clinical Psychology*, 1976, *44*, 614–623.

Winship, W. J. *The relationship of anxiety and cognitive style to irrational beliefs*. M.Ed. thesis, University of Alberta, 1972.

Zingle, H. W. *A rational approach to counselling underachievers*. Unpublished doctoral dissertation, University of Alberta, 1965.

Chapter 2

ANGER PROBLEMS

Russell Grieger

Agression and violence have drawn more attention from the behavioral science and philosophic communities than perhaps any other human phenomena. Experimental studies on the psychology of aggression are legion, as attested by recent texts by Bandura (1973), Ellis (1977b), Geen and O'Neal (1976), Johnson (1972), and Novaco (1975). From a social perspective, aggression has been discussed in relation to such variables as criminal justice (Chappell & Monahan, 1975), social alienation (Daniels, Gilula, & Ochberg, 1970), and violence on television (Feshback & Singer, 1971). Indeed, a recent edition of *Look* magazine (March 19, 1979) displayed a dramatic pictorial series showing English, German, Sicilian, Lebanese, and Irish children modeling the violence they directly and vicariously observed in their own countries. These pictures showed the children entertaining themselves with such games as "firing squad," "guillotine," and "soldier," among others.

Contrasted with aggression, anger is a rarely studied human reaction, except as it serves to instigate aggression or to reduce aggression through catharsis (Berkowitz, 1970; Feshback, 1961; Kahn, 1966). Novaco (1975) explains this by the fact that the dimensions of aggression can be easily observed and studied, whereas anger elements are more phenomenological in character. Regardless of the reason, anger problems populate clinical calendars, yet are probably the least studied of human emotions (Novaco, 1975).

Three perspectives on anger, and indeed all emotions, have been articulated (Lazarus, Averill, & Opton, 1970). The biological perspective assigns emotion to the more phylogenetically old portions of the brain: the reticular formation (Lindsley, 1950), the hypothalamus (Bard, 1950), and the limbic system (MacLean, 1960). Ignoring the fact that these structures play as vital a role in cognitive functioning as in emotion (Douglas, 1967; Pribram, 1960), this perspective views emotion as basically instinctual and related to earlier steps on the phylogenetic ladder. Accordingly, anger control depends on the development of both intellectual and social forces to contain the beast in humans.

The cultural perspective suggests that emotions are shaped by various societies in order to provide for the affective needs of their citizens (Hebb & Thompson, 1954), and in turn to maintain their own existence. It does so in many ways depending on economic, political, geographic, and historical factors, including influencing how people perceive or appraise emotional stimuli (Tursky & Sternbach, 1967) and how people can express emotions (LaBarre, 1947).

Following Magda Arnold (1960), Richard Lazarus (1966, 1968), and especially Albert Ellis (1962, 1971, 1973, 1977a), the cognitive perspective is based on the conviction that cognitive theorizing, appraising, and evaluating are primary human functions and that emotional reactions are directly determined by such cognitive activity. Furthermore, the cognitive determinants of emotion can be either dispositional (reflecting the basic values, attitudes, or philosophies of an individual) or situational (an individual's interpretation and evaluation of specific situational cues) in nature. Thus, in understanding a particular emotional reaction, anger in this case, an understanding of the nature of the underlying cognitions is essential.

This chapter largely follows the cognitive model of emotional arousal in general and the RET model of emotional disturbance in particular. After first outlining this model, it will discuss in more detail the cognitive mediators of anger and suggest a distinction between anger that is healthy and that is not.

COGNITIVE MEDIATION OF ANGER

As an affective phenomenon, anger can be seen as both an autonomic (Ax, 1953; Funkenstein, King, & Drolette, 1954, 1957; Schacter, 1957) and a central (Moyer, 1971, 1973) nervous system reaction to some real or imagined events, plus a cognitive labeling of that arousal as anger based on both physiological and behavioral cues (Konocni, 1975a, 1975b; Lazarus, 1967; Schachter & Singer, 1962). Thus, on a descriptive level, anger is a combination of physiological arousal and cognitive labeling.

Etiologically speaking, cognitive theorists generally follow the maxim of the Stoic philosopher, Epictetus, who stated: "Men are disturbed not by things, but by the view they take of them." Accordingly, they define anger (and all other emotional reactions as well) not so much by physiological or affective arousal as by the cognitions or appraisals that prompt the arousal. To determine if a person is angry, the cognitive theorist looks to the person's thoughts or ideas, not to his or her feelings.

The cognitive model presented here is an extension of the now famous ABC theory of RET (Ellis, 1962, 1971, 1973, 1975, 1977a, 1977b). Echoing Epictetus, RET states that perceived, imagined, remembered, or anticipated events (at point A) do not directly provoke anger (at point C). They only serve to prompt cognitive activity which in turn determines the anger. Each anger reaction is mediated by some cognitive event that logically leads to that reaction.

As previously stated, cognitions are significant to emotional arousal in at least two ways (see Figure 2–1). First, cognitions act as dispositional traits or strongly learned, enduring, personal values or life philosophies that people carry with them across situations (B_1). As such, they variously influence emotional arousal: (1) by providing a prejudicial set that leads people to search out and selectively attend to situational stimuli of a certain type; (2) by flavoring the evaluations or appraisals people make of particular experiences; (3) by directly keeping emotionally loaded past events "alive" and anticipated future happenings vivid; and (4) by indirectly creating events in the environment that prompt behavior from others consistent with the emotional reaction. In turn, consciously or unconsciously exercising the philosophy, and thus experiencing both the selectively perceived event and the emotional arousal, serves to further engrain it and make its activation more likely in the future.

Cognition plays a second significant role in emotional arousal by mediating aversive events (B_2). These situational attributions are the appraisals people make of the experienced event itself and of the likely outcome of various reactions to that event. They are in

Figure 2–1.   Cognitive Mediations of Anger

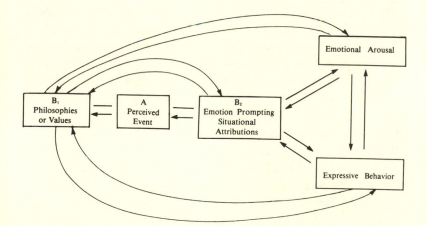

part determined by the characteristics of the event itself, but are also influenced by the person's life philosophies and past experiences in similar circumstances. The consequent emotional arousal and behavior reciprocally relate to these cognitive mediators by providing validating feedback to the appraisal and hence increase its likelihood in the future. The situational mediators also serve to validate and reinforce the associated life philosophies.

Both varieties of cognition can lead to emotional arousal singularly or more likely in concert with each other. In turn, emotional arousal and expressive behavior mutually influence each other. For example, anger arousal tends to prompt aggressive behavior (Rule & Nesdale, 1976). On the other hand, responding aggressively to negative events leads one to define one's emotional arousal as anger, which in turn increases anger (Konocni, 1975a, 1975b).

Having briefly outlined the model, I will now turn to a more detailed discussion of the cognitive mediators of anger. I will first discuss the irrational philosophies and situational attributions in anger, and then present processes whereby people get angry about being angry.

Irrational Philosophies in Anger

Consistent with rational-emotive theory (Ellis, 1962, 1971, 1975, 1976, 1977b), anger, like all other emotional reactions, in large measure results from (and is maintained by) a person holding ideas or philosophies that logically lead to anger. Accordingly, people who ardently endorse angry (or anger instigating) ideas are prone to anger and to act aggressively. Carrying these philosophies with them, they will tend to be oversensitive to elements of injustice or signs of hassle in situations; attribute hostile motivations to the actions of others; habitually evaluate situations in light of their angry philosophies; re-anger themselves by remembering (even obsessing about) past slights; and overreact to minor frustrations. In a very real sense, they are "programmed" time bombs ready to explode.

Albert Ellis (1973b, 1975) has proposed two separate, yet conceptually similar, forms of anger. In *autistic anger,* the individual childishly endorses the idea that because he or she does not personally like something or does not want something to happen, or because he or she finds someone's behavior undesirable or even obnoxious, it *should* not happen or that person *must* not behave that way. Then, when the event or act occurs, the person concludes that it is an *awful* thing that is too *unendurable* to bear. Finally, the person *condemns* either the world for allowing such a thing to happen or the offensive person for doing such a thing. The focus for these ideas is the "I": "Because *I* say so, it should not be."

In *impersonal anger,* the person invokes the magic of consensual validation. In this he or she concludes that, because everyone would agree that some event or action is bad, it *should* not have happened. Under this group umbrella, the person then goes on to conclude that it is *too awful to tolerate* and that he or she, like everyone, can legitimately rate the person as so thoroughly *rotten* as to deserve severe punishment. In this form of anger, then, the person is offended because of an allegiance to an implicit or explicit code of rules that pertain to some community, and he or she then acts as an avenging representative of that collective mass.

Both forms of anger have at least three common philosophical elements that directly lead to anger. The first is an assumption that an action or event that is deemed wrong *should not, must not* occur. In holding this view, the person acts as an arrogant, righteous rulemaker imposing laws over others and the universe that are absolute and incontrovertable, as per:

(1) others *must* behave the way I think best, in ways that I deem fair, moral, appropriate, ethical, considerate, or else . . .
(2) the world, and particularly the conditions under which I live, *must* be arranged the way I think best, in ways that are just, compassionate, and hassle free, or else . . . (Ellis, 1977a).

A second philosophical element common to both forms of anger is the person perceiving the action or event as negative (e.g., unfortunate, disadvantageous, inconvenient, deplorable) and then concluding that it is so *awful* to be virtually *unbearable*. When, for instance, a person is treated rudely at the theater and only concludes that it is a pain in the neck or an inconvenience to be subjected to such treatment, he or she will at worst be only irritated or annoyed. But, when he or she concludes that it is such a terrible thing that the offender had no right to do it, he or she will almost certainly become outraged and probably act in some revengeful way.

The third common philosophical element in both types of anger proposed by Ellis focuses on the person who performs the outlawed act itself. It consists of concluding that the offending person's acts are not only bad or rotten, but that the offending person is *rotten* and should therefore be severely punished for *being* that way, as per: "Because you have done this terrible thing you should not have done, you are a *total shit* and I can justifiably condemn you to a lifetime of misery"; or, "Because we all agree that you should not have done such a horrid thing, we can condemn you and we can conclude that severe retribution must take place."

The assumption throughout all this is that people prone to anger take the philosophic position that they can Jehovistically impose absolute demands on others for certain behaviors, and that it is legitimate for them to condemn the other if he or she violates the standards. Yet, while this is true for most if not all angry people, two other themes, already discovered to be central to a number of other emotional disturbances, underlie most all angry reactions (Grieger, 1977; Grieger & Boyd, 1979). These stimulate the irrational ideas proposed by Ellis and fuel the anger. One theme has to do with self-worth and the other with frustration tolerance.

SELF-WORTH ANGER.   Often lurking behind anger is a perceived threat to one's sense of being worthwhile. Indeed, while not directly related to anger, experimental evidence suggests that subjects who report themselves high in self-esteem respond with less aggression to provocations than subjects who report the opposite (Green & Murray, 1973; Rosenbaum & de Charms, 1960;

Rosenbaum & Stanners, 1961; Veldman & Worchel, 1961; Worchel, 1960). Toch (1969), for instance, suggested that low self-esteem was a significant determinant of both anger arousal and aggressive behavior in the interactions between the police and criminals he studied.

In cognitive therapy terms, people prone to self-worth anger believe that their self-worth depends on what others think of them and on how well they do in gaining the acknowledgment, acceptance, and love of others. In addition to austic and /or impersonal anger themes, they ardently adhere to the idea that: "I *must do well* and *win approval,* particularly from those I deem significant, *or else I rate as a rotten person."* Individuals who hold this idea quite often interpret the negative actions of others as discounting them, as somehow threatening or taking away their self-worth. With the precious commodity of self-worth at stake, this person sees an unjust or insulting act as a horrible affront that absolutely should not happen and sees the perpetrator as a terrible person for doing that. Thus, when confronted with the slings and arrows of fortune, the person reflexively concludes: "His actions communicate that he finds me insignificant. If that is true, it does make me insignificant. He shouldn't do that to me, the SOB!"

A double-level problem thus operates in self-worth anger. On the more conscious, accessible level the typical "shoulding" and "condemning" takes place. At a less conscious, less accessible level looms the individual's predisposed tendency to generalize from the negative actions of others to his or her self-worth. Instead of simply accepting the validity of the insult and turning inward to condemn the self, this person turns on and condemns the other person in the picture. The important point is that the turning on the other person or event is a self-protective action designed to prevent the person from facing his or her fears of worthlessness. An analogy that I think captures the concept of self-worth anger has to do with two waitresses who serve a rude, critical customer. The waitress experiencing autistic or impersonal anger only carries food on the tray and strongly objects to the customer subjecting her to such behavior. The waitress experiencing self-worth anger carries her self-worth, as well as the customer's food, on the tray, and she strongly objects to the customer taking away her self-respect. She is personally hurt.

Let me illustrate what I am talking about through two clinical examples. In each instance, a significant feature of the client's anger was a perceived threat to self-worth.

CASE 1.   Carol was a member of a RET group who wanted to overcome her anger problems. Not a wilting lily, she quickly took advantage of the group situation. She readily acknowledged the fact that she "shoulded" other people and condemned them as rotten for behaving in the particular ways they did that she did not like. She also acknowledged the irrationality of these stances and with our help correctly thought them through. But, she did not improve.

Then in one group session Carol discussed how angry she had become at a woman who rented a room at her house. It seemed that this woman used Carol's iron and left her kitchen untidy, despite the fact that Carol repeatedly told her not to do either. After she and the group again went over the same ground as before, the following interchange took place between Carol and me.

> Therapist: We don't seem to be getting anywhere here. Let me ask you a question, Carol. Do you find this woman's behavior positive, negative, or neutral?
>
> Carol: Well, negative of course.
>
> Therapist: Then, finish this sentence for me. "I don't like her using my iron, particularly since I've told her not to, because . . ."
>
> Carol: (pause) Because it discounts me.
>
> Therapist: What do you mean when you say it discounts you?
>
> Carol: She invalidates me.
>
> Therapist: That sounds a little mystical to me. Do you mean that she somehow devalues your worth by ignoring your wishes?
>
> Carol: Yes. That's exactly right.
>
> Therapist: Well, aren't you confusing her negative value

of you, assuming that that is true, with your own value of yourself as a person? Aren't you putting your self-worth on the line depending on whether she obeys you or not?

Carol: In a way, I guess I am.

Therapist: With that being at stake, I can see why you are so angry at her and why you would demand that she toe the line. It's a logical reaction from an illogical premise. But, isn't the real problem the fact that you don't really accept yourself?

Carol: Yes. I guess that is the problem.

CASE 2. Bill was a relatively new teacher on the faculty of a private school for emotionally disturbed and learning disabled youngsters to which I consulted. Following an in-service workshop on anger, Bill approached me to talk about his intense anger at the students. He expressed a concern that he might soon lose control and physically lash out when the following interchange took place.

Bill: I've certainly lost my ideals around here. When I started work, I would ride home each night wondering how I could be more effective the next day. Now I fantasize getting even with them.

Consultant: Well, what exactly do they do that you find so irritating?

Bill: Everything from the typical things like talking in class and fighting to not remembering my name. I've really worried about some of them and put extra effort into working with them, but they don't listen. They just don't appreciate me!

Consultant: Bill, it sounds like you might have an anger problem pretty much like we were talking about just a little while ago—a self-worth anger problem.

Bill: How so?

Consultant: Well, you just said they don't appreciate you. Go with that for a minute. What if they don't? What if they don't? What does that mean to you?

Bill: Look, I've put my life into this. If they don't appreciate what I'm doing, what's the use. My life is purposeless.

Consultant: Wow! That's quite a conclusion to draw—that your life's purposeless if some 12-year-olds don't appreciate you. Doesn't that tell you what's at stake for you in their behavior!

Bill: OK, you're right. I'm thinking that they take away my meaning by their acts. They steal away my insides, my worth. Just like we talked earlier.

Consultant: Right! That's what you think. And, what do you then do with that toward them in your head?

Bill: It's: "Goddamn them! They're not going to get away with putting me down like that, the little bastards." And then I feel like lashing out.

Thus, a self-worth issue very often lies at the bottom of many angry problems. Like with Carol and Bill, self-worth anger results, first, from a person believing that the negative treatment of others or the adverse conditions of the world threaten his or her self-worth or value, and, second, from vehemently *demanding* that different treatment result in order to present this loss of self. Given this, an interesting question is why a person who believes that he or she must have approval and acknowledgment to be worthwhile reacts with anger instead of anxiety and depression. In my clinical experience, people with self-worth anger are also prone to anxiety and depression as well so that their negative emotional states are often more frequent and more complex. Beyond this, I frequently find that self-worth angry people have what Cohen (1966) calls "defensive high self-esteem." That is, they have often been successful in getting people to approve of them so that they frequently feel good about themselves. They are, thus, often able to focus on the offensive agent and the insult in a blameworthy way. But, their sense of well-being is fragile and dependent on the continued good grace of others so that prolonged or frequent assaults can easily shatter their facade. The result then is either an entrenchment of the anger and/or depression coupled with lowered self-esteem.

LOW-FRUSTRATION-TOLERANCE-ANGER. Besides perceived threats to self-worth, a low tolerance for frustration or hassle can also prompt the "shoulding," "awfulizing," and other person rating that Ellis (1973b, 1975) has shown to fuel anger reactions. He (1976) contends that low frustration tolerance (LFT), or overreacting to frustration, is a predictable consequence of a person holding one or more of the following ideas in the face of difficult, hassling, or frustrating circumstances: (1) the world *has* to be arranged so that I get pretty much what I want, when I want it, without too much hassle; (2) it is *awful, horrible,* and *terrible* when I am thwarted or presented with such difficult circumstances; and (3) I *can't stand it* when things go wrong. By holding these ideas, the person creates an unrealistic exaggeration of the badness of aversive events and connotes a gross underestimation of his or her ability to tolerate or deal with the event, thus making an emotional and/or behavioral overreaction likely.

To test these contentions, Nolan, Boyd, and Grieger (1979) had subjects who scored in the upper and lower quartiles on the frustration-reactive subscale of Jones' (1968) Irrational Beliefs Test try to solve three problems that, unbeknownst to them, were insolvable. Following this task, subjects who scored in the upper quartile reported significantly higher negative affect, as measured by the Multiple Affect Adjective Checklist (Zuckerman & Lubin, 1965), than did subjects who scored in the lower quantile. The results of this investigation lend strong support to the contention that the mediating cognitive appraisals of frustrating situations have a profoundly instrumental effect upon people's emotional reactions to those frustrating circumstances.

For the purpose of this discussion, it is important to note that the subjects in this study who highly endorsed the beliefs in the frustration-reactive subscale reported significantly more anger (P < .025) than did subjects who only minimally endorsed this belief. To understand this, it is helpful, as with self-worth anger, to think of frustration-related anger as a double-level problem. On the first or more surface level, the LFT-angry person engages in the shoulding toward, awfulizing about, and condemning of the frustrating person or set of circumstances. On the second, perhaps less conscious level, the person strongly *demands* that things be easy, smooth, and hassle free, and then evaluates the frustration as awful, as per: "This hassle is *too much to bear;* it is such a hassle that it *shouldn't* exist, particularly for me; and you (or the world) are *rotten* for subjecting me to such a thing." All in all, low frustration tolerance anger is a scream of outrage against any interruption of the smooth flow of events.

Against let me illustrate LFT anger with a clinical example. Michael was a client I previously showed to have a profound case of self-worth anger (Grieger, 1977). What precipitated his decision to seek psychological help was his increasing anger that resulted in his physically abusing his 12-year-old son. After confronting and making significant inroads into his self-worth issues, he then turned to the element of low frustration tolerance, or, to say it another way, to his belief that he should not have to contend with the hassles that his children, his wife, his house, and his job inevitably presented. Note the following interchange.

Michael:	This damn thing just keeps coming at me. If I'm not angry at one thing its another.
Therapist:	What happened this week, Michael?
Michael:	Nothing in particular. I just seem to get madder as the day wears on. It starts sometime in the afternoon and really gets to me at night.
Therapist:	What's going on at work in the afternoon?
Michael:	Nothing, really. Students just keep coming by my office and wanting to talk to me. And I have this stupid report to write for the Dean, and . . .
Therapist:	So, you keep getting interrupted from doing

what is important for you to do at work, and
you also seem to see the report as an inane,
bureaucratic thing. And, what goes through
your head at these times? ,

Michael: (pauses) That I have to do this and its a pain in
the ass.

Therapist: Is that all?

Michael: No. I also think that I shouldn't be bothered by
all this nonsense. The Dean's report is basically just busy work, and the student interruptions
are pointless.

Therapist: And they *shouldn't* hassle me like this.

Michael: Right! They shouldn't! It's all a bunch of shit.

Therapist: And what about home?

Michael: That just continues it. Its one thing after
another. The gutters need painting, the lawn
needs mowing, and . . .

Therapist: . . . and what? "I . . ."

Michael: . . . shouldn't have to put up with it either! It's
such a pain in the ass.

Therapist: Those things are indeed a pain in the ass. But,
Michael, I hear you really holding two philosophies, one that feeds into or actually mirrors
the other. The one is that I shouldn't have to
deal with these hassles. Right?

Michael: Right.

Therapist: But, I also hear you holding another idea,
which I suspect includes the first. It is that life
should always be easy and simple for you. It
simply should not be difficult! How does that
sound to you?

Michael: Pretty accurate.

Situational Attributions in Anger

What has been discussed so far are the enduring irrational
philosophies people endorse and carry with them accross situa-

tions that prompt them to become angry. Individuals who hold these philosophies may be seen as angry people because they have adopted ideas that (1) are scientifically invalid, and which (2) logically and predictably lead to frequent anger reactions.

In addition to irrational philosophies, another set of cognitive variables also play an important role in mediating anger. These are situationally based and reflect current appraisals of a situation. Appraisal here refers to the cognitive interpretations and evaluations of situations that may not be but probably are influenced by one's more enduring philosophies. These include attributions about an aggressor's intent, the perceived arbitrariness of another's actions, one's own perceived power and control in the situation, expectation of outcome, and the badness of one's anger.

AGGRESSOR'S INTENT.   One of the more consistent findings in the literature has been that the magnitude of anger arousal and aggression relates to the perceived intent of an attacker (Epstein & Taylor, 1967; Greenwell & Dengerink, 1973; Taylor, 1967). That is, if a person determines that another intended to be aggressive or frustrating, then he or she is very likely to respond with anger and aggression. On the other hand, if the person decides that the aggressor's behavior was accidental, then the probability of anger and counterattack is significantly lessened.

This proposition has been ingeniously explored by Nickel (1974). He first had confederates give subjects high-intensity shocks for incorrectly guessing a color. Just prior to changing places with the confederate, the experimenter explained to half the subjects that the buttons had accidentally been reversed so that while the subjects had received high-intensity shocks the confederate had intended to give low-level shocks. Those subjects who were led to believe that the confederate's intent was opposite to what they had received gave significantly lower shocks to the confederate than those not given this information. Thus, subjects responded more to their perception of the opponent's intent than to the intensity of shock or the received aggression. It therefore appears that the attribution of hostile intent is a major mediator of anger and aggression: you will be much less likely to respond with anger and aggression if you perceive the obnoxious behavior of another as being accidential than if you see it as preplanned.

PERCEIVED ARBITRARINESS VS. MITIGATING CIRCUMSTANCES. Several investigators have found that attributing arbitrary, nonjustifiable, or selfish motivations to an aggressor will more likely lead to anger and counteraggression than when the aggressor's behavior is seen otherwise. Mallick and McCandless (1966), for instance, had a confederate child interfere with the performance of one half of their subjects on a task for which they could earn money. All subjects were then given the opportunity to play, to chat with the experimenters about irrelevant topics, or to be given a reasonable explanation for the confederate's frustrating behavior. Consistent with predictions, the experimenters found that when the subjects were given an opportunity to retaliate, those frustrated were more likely to interfere in kind than those who were not frustrated, unless they had been given a reasonable explanation for the confederate's behavior. It therefore seems that when a frustrator's behavior is labeled as inappropriate and arbitrary, children are more likely to behave aggressively.

It also appears that the specific motivations attributed to an aggressor are important in anger arousal. Using paper-and-pencil measures of anger and hostility, Frodi (1976) assessed the effects of different types of attributed mitigating circumstances on the anger of junior high students. After being highly criticized by an experimenter, students were told that he was either sick (sympathy condition), a high-achieving expert (achiever condition), or habitually obnoxious (habit condition). The sympathy and habit conditions produced the least anger while the achiever condition produced the greatest anger. In order to obtain a measure of perceived intentionality, a second group of students was given a typed description of the experiment and asked to judge whether, given the mitigating circumstances, the experimenter acted intentionally or not. The sympathy condition was seen as least intentional and the achievement condition most intentional. The results confirmed an earlier study by Frodi (1973) that found high school students were relatively less hostile when the investigator's behavior was attributed as being beyond his control.

To determine whether perceived mitigating circumstances result in response inhibition to already aroused anger or an actual failure to arouse anger, Zillman and Cantor (1976) measured the effects of mitigating circumstances on levels of physiological arousal and retaliatory behavior. The mitigating circumstance (E worrying about an exam) was told to subjects either prior to an aggressive act, following it, or not at all. On the physiological measures (heart rate), prior knowldege resulted in little change in arousal level in response to aggression, and knowledge following aggression resulted in a significant drop in arousal which had risen to high levels in response to aggression. In the no-knowledge condition, arousal levels remained high following aggression. On the retaliatory measure (an evaluation of the aggressor that would purportedly influence his job), subjects with prior knowledge showed comparatively little retaliatory behavior, while subjects with postaggression mitigating knowledge and subjects with no knowledge showed significant levels of retaliation. With regard to retaliation by subjects who had mitigating knowledge after the aggressive act, the authors suggest that intensely aroused anger may produce a disposition to retaliate that lasts beyond the physical excitatory residues. Once this commitment is made, the mitigating information is ignored on a conscious level.

PERCEPTION OF PERSONAL POWER AND CONTROL.   It seems that a person's perception that he or she can control or cope with a situation containing provacation serves to diminish the negative response to that situation. Davison (1967) made the observation that relaxation procedures not only teach a person to identify and undo anxiety, but also teach the person the comforting idea that he or she can control and regulate the anxiety. In a broader context, Lefcourt (1973), after reviewing the literature, concluded that the perception of control ameliorates negative situational reactions across species. He stated: "Pain-producing stimuli prove less painful and disruptive to individuals who can predict and control these stimuli, and these findings are obtained with different types of data . . ." (p. 420).

With regard to anger arousal, Rimm, DeGroot, Bourd, Reiman, and Dillow (1971) taught subjects how to effectively reduce their anger through muscle relaxation. Novaco (1975), following Meichenbaum and Cameron (1973), successfully taught subjects to dissect angry provocations into stages and to use self-instructional techniques to regulate the anger. More important to this discussion, Novaco (1975) asserts that learning nonangry and nonantagonistic responses to provocations reduces the probability of future anger in provocative circumstances. He reasons that "as one learns to handle provocations with nonantagonistic behavior, he develops a new sense of competence and discovers that he can take charge without being angry" (p. 10).

An interesting variation on this theme is offered by Brehm (1966). He suggested that anger and hostility can be reduced by convincing a person that he or she has the option or freedom to aggress. His reasoning is based on the assumption that whenever a person has a freedom (e.g., to become angry) and that freedom is denied, he or she is motivated to restore it. In testing this out, Nezlek and Brehm (1975) found that leading a victim to perceive that he or she had the opportunity to counteraggress against an instigator resulted in a significant decrease in counterhostility in comparison to those who did not have this perception. Thus, a perception of personal power, or choice, in a situation mediated angry and hostile responses.

EXPECTATION OF OUTCOME. The term "expectation" refers to the prediction a person makes about current or future events and is based on appraisals of past situations. According to Rotter (1954, 1972), the potential for a behavior in a particular situation is a function of the person's expectations for reward or punishment in that situation and the value of those consequences for that person. Accordingly, action is likely when there is a high expectation for reward plus a high value for that reward. Contrarily, a low expectation for reward, a low value for the rewards that seem available, or a high expectation for punishment would make an action highly improbable.

Expectation of outcome or consequence can be predicted to influence anger in at least three ways. First, high expectations for rewarding or desirable consequences that do not occur can make an outcome aversive, resulting in anger and even in aggression (Novaco, 1978). What happens in this case is that the person takes the positive outcome for granted and hence overreacts to the frustration.

Second, a perception or belief that anger and aggression will be rewarded, or alternatively that failing to respond with anger or aggression will be punished, will raise the probability of an angry and/or aggressive response. The now famous study by Stanley Milgram (1963) in which a subject "mercilessly" shocked confederates in response to pressure from the experimenter dramatically demonstrates this.

And, third, high expectations that anger or aggressive behavior will result in negative consequences of some kind will predictably reduce the probability of anger and aggression. Burnstein and Worschel (1962) and Mosher (1965), for instance, show that expectations for social disapproval, particularly among those with high approval needs, will inhibit anger and aggression in the presence of environmental cues indicating the existence of such negative consequences. Mosher (1963) has further suggested that an extremely powerful inhibitor of anger and aggression is the expectations of personally suffering guilt as a result of experiencing anger or acting aggressively. Studies by Buss (1966a, b), Baron (1971), James and Mosher (1962), and Knott, Lasater, and Shuman (1974) seem to bear this out. And finally, experimental evidence has shown that expectation of physical retaliation (but only if it is powerful or massive) will result in an inhibition of anger and aggression (Shortell, Epstein, & Taylor, 1970; Dengerink & Levendusky, 1972).

SELF-EVALUATION OF ANGER.   A final situationally specific cognitive mediator of anger and aggression to be mentioned is the person's negative evaluation of his or her own anger arousal. Thus, when a person becomes aware of being angry and sees it as bad (i.e., unwarranted by the circumstances), the likelihood that he or she will nullify the anger and antagonism is increased. Indeed, Borden (1975) showed this to be true, as did Berkowitz, Lepinski, and Angulo (1969). By manipulating awareness of anger level, Berkowitz et al. (1969) found that subjects very aware of their high level of anger had a significantly lowered incidence of aggression to a confederate instigator. They speculated that awareness of extreme anger causes people to conclude that their reactions are not justified.

Cognitive Elements in Anger About Anger

It is an axiom of RET that people rarely display only primary symptoms of emotional disturbance; they also typically present secondary symptoms about their primary symptoms (Ellis, 1962, 1978, 1979a, 1979c, 1979d; Ellis & Abrahms, 1978; Ellis & Grieger, 1977; Ellis & Harper, 1975; Grieger & Boyd, 1979). That is, they first make themselves emotionally upset or disturbed, and then they frequently make themselves emotionally upset about being emotionally upset. Secondary symptoms usually exacerbate primary problems and serve to interfere with solving the original problem.

The ABC theory of RET provides a nice framework with which to conceptualize this. Following the theory, people first experience some aversive event at point A, and they then disturb themselves at point C by thinking (and believing) some irrational, disturbance-producing idea at point B. Not content to stop there, they then observe their own disturbed reaction at C, in effect making it a new A or (A_2); and they then create a new disturbance (a C_2) by again thinking (and believing) irrational, disturbance-producing ideas (at B_2) about their disturbed state. In effect they create a double-level problem, or an emotional problem about an emotional problem (Grieger & Boyd, 1979).

Ellis has shown this to be a particularly powerful phenomenon in anxiety problems (see Ellis's chapter, "Psychoneurosis and Anxiety Problems," this volume). In addition, human beings, after becoming angry, are very likely to observe their anger and to further disturb themselves about it. Some note their anger and make themselves anxious by holding what Ellis has labeled ego anxiety thoughts ("Isn't it terrible to be so angry! I shouldn't be feeling this way!"). Others create guilt for themselves by putting themselves down ("Its an awful thing to feel this way. I'm a real heel.").

Those who make themselves angry about being angry are likely to hold ideas or philosophies that characterize low frustration tolerance (Ellis, 1976; Nolan, Boyd, & Grieger, 1979). Thus, one first makes oneself angry via some situational attribution or some irrational philosophy that logically leads to the anger. Then, noting and experiencing the anger as displeasurable or aversive, the person evaluates the emotional upset as *too much* of a hassle that he or she *shouldn't have to* bear it. He or she consequently experiences anger about having to bear the burden of experiencing the anger itself.

HEALTHY AND UNHEALTHY ANGER*

What has so far been presented is a cognitive mediation model of anger arousal and maintenance. An implication of all this is that it is very easy for human beings to become angry; and, given the myriad frustrations that everyday life indubitably presents, it is very likely that every person will periodically experience anger. Ignoring the issue of whether or not people must as a consequence of their existence feel angry, a question remains as how to differentiate between healthy and unhealthy, or rational and irrational, anger. How do we conceptualize those anger reactions which are appropriate and those that are not?

*This section is modeled after a paper by Albert Ellis presented at the 1973 Annual Meeting of the American Psychological Association titled "Healthy and Unhealthy Aggression."

To answer this, it is helpful to first consider the basic values that humans hold. Most people seem to hold a fairly limited number of basic values, including: (1) staying alive; (2) living happily or with an acceptable amount of pleasure and a minimum of pain; (3) living comfortably in a social group or community in which one is basically accepted; and (4) relating intimately and lovingly with one or a selected few individuals (Ellis, 1973b). People do indeed adopt many subvalues or subgoals, such as listening to music, playing golf, and the like, but these can be easily catalogued under one or more of the basic four listed above.

Assuming that humans do generally adopt these basic values, and that it is legitimate for them to do so, it follows that " . . . any thoughts, emotions, or actions [that] aid or promote these goals are rational, sensible, or healthy; while, by the same token, any behavior [that] blocks or sabatoges goals are irrational, insane, or unhealthy" (Ellis, 1973b, p. 2). Therefore, healthy anger can be seen as anger that aids and abets the human values (or goals) of remaining alive, being happy, successfully relating to a small social group, and relating intimately and pleasurably to one or a few select individuals. Unhealthy anger, then, is anger that thwarts, blocks, or undermines these basic goals. Neither the definition of healthy or unhealthy anger is offered in an absolute form, but rather in terms of probabilities.

Going beyond this, a cognitive therapist further defines healthy and unhealthy anger by the thoughts or ideas that lie behind and prompt the anger, rather than by the quality of the affective experience itself or by some behavioral correlate like aggression. Healthy anger (or, better, irritation or annoyance) is defined as a person holding thoughts that predictably (although not inevitably) lead to the realization of one's basic goals, with the opposite being true for unhealthy anger. So, using the ABC's of rational-emotive therapy, if I am insulted by you at point A, and feel angry at point C, I am thinking both rational and irrational thoughts at point B: (1) "I don't like the rotten thing you did, and I wish you would refrain from doing it in the future; (2) You *shouldn't* have done that *terrible* thing to me, and you're a *rotten person* for doing it!"

The first set of these thoughts is healthy or rational because they logically derive from my basic values. Being insulted, I can still survive, but to some degree it has interfered with my happiness and may possibly have interfered with my successfully relating with others. I can therefore legitimately conclude that I don't like to be insulted, that it was a bad thing to do, and that it was obnoxious. And I will probably behave in some self-assured, determined, and assertive ways to get my message across that will least likely do me in.

My second set of thoughts is unhealthy or irrational because they do not derive from my basic human values, they have no empirical or objective basis, and they probably will lead me to behaviors that further undermine my goals (Ellis, 1973b; Ellis & Abrahms, 1978; Goodman & Maultsby, 1974). There is absolutely no evidence that you shouldn't behave badly, that behaving badly is more than bad or unconvenient, nor that you are totally rotten for behaving badly (Ellis, 1977a). And, holding these beliefs, I will probably become oppositional, combative, insulting, argumentative, and even perhaps violent. In the process, I will further undercut my happiness and interfere with my interpersonal relationships.

The implications for treatment of differentiating healthy anger (or irritation) from unhealthy anger in this way are obvious. It argues against a squelching or denying of anger, for this makes people ignore the irrational ideas behind the anger. It also argues against a program designed to teach people to "creatively" express their anger, for this teaches people that anger is both unavoidable and acceptable. Finally, it argues against the free expression of anger, for evidence shows that such expression, by providing the person an opportunity to rehearse the anger-producing philosophies, tends to further engrain the philosophies and abet the anger (Bandura & Walters, 1963; Feshback, 1971).

Rather, such a differentiation suggests treatment strategies that help unhealthy angry people radically change their irrational philosophies (Ellis, 1973b). It argues for therapies, like RET and other cognitive-behavioral treatment programs, that first help people acknowledge their unhealthy anger, and then encourages them to: (1) assume full responsibility for their anger; (2) look for and find their anger-instigating philosophies; (3) dispute these philosophies via cognitive, emotive, and behavior means; and (4) act on and practice ideas that are contrary to the unhealthy ones (Ellis, 1976b).

SUMMARY

I have outlined in this chapter a RET-based, cognitive mediation model of anger development and maintenance. Within this model, anger is seen as being aroused when an individual holds irrational ideas or philosophies and/or when a person makes situationally specific assumptions that logically lead to anger. By the same token, a person can be said to have an anger problem when he or she strongly endorses these irrational philosophies or habitually and frequently makes these assumptions across situations. The irrational ideas articulated by Ellis (1977b) to be behind anger are buttressed either by self-worth and/or low frustration tolerance issues, and situational assumptions include attributions regarding the intent of an aggressor, the perceived arbitrariness of another's actions, the sense of personal power one has in a situation, outcome expectations for getting angry, and the perceived badness of being angry. Finally, following Ellis (1973b), healthy anger (i.e., irritation, annoyance) is differentiated from unhealthy anger by the different cognitions that lie behind them, one set being rational and goal-facilitating and the other being irrational and goal-blocking.

REFERENCES

Arnold, M.B. *Emotion and personality*. New York: Columbia University Press, 1960.

Ax, A.F. The physiological differentiation between fear and anger in humans. *Psychosomatic Medicine*, 1953, *15*, 433–442.

Bandura, A. *Aggression: a social learning analysis.* New York: Prentice-Hall, 1973.

Bandura, A., & Walters, R.H. *Social learning and personality development.* New York: Holt, Rinehart & Winston, 1963.

Bard, P. Central nervous mechanisms for the expression of anger in animals. In M.L. Reymert (Ed.), *Feelings and emotions: The Mooseheart symposium.* New York: McGraw-Hill, 1950.

Baron, R.A. Magnitude of victim's pain eves and level of prior anger arousal as determinants of adult aggressive behavior. *Journal of Personality and Social Psychology,* 1971, *17,* 236–243.

Berkowitz, L. Experimental investigations of hostility catharsis. *Journal of Consulting and Clinical Psychology,* 1970, *35,* 1–7.

Berkowitz, L., Lepinski, J., & Angulo, E. Awareness of our anger level and subsequent aggression. *Journal of Personality and Social Psychology,* 1969, *11,* 293–300.

Borden, R.J. Witnessed aggression: influence of and observer's sex and values on aggressive responding. *Journal of Personality and Social Psychology,* 1975, *31,* 567–573.

Brehm, T. *A theory of psychological acceptance.* New York: Academic Press, 1966.

Burnstein, E., & Worchel, P. Arbitrariness of frustration and its consequence for aggression in a social situation. *Journal of Personality,* 1962, *30,* 528–541.

Buss, A.H. The effect of harm on subsequent aggression. *Journal of Experimental Research in Personality,* 1966a, *1,* 249–255.

Buss, A.H. Instrumentality of aggression, feedback and frustration as determinants of physical aggression. *Journal of Personality and Social Psychology,* 1966b, *3,* 153–162.

Chappell, D., & Monahan, J. Violence and criminal justice. Lexington, Mass.: D.C. Heath, Lexington Books, 1975.

Cohen, A.R. Some implications of self-esteem for social influence. In I.L. Janis & C.I. Houland (Eds.), *Personality and persuasibility.* New Haven: Yale University Press, 1966.

Daniels, D.N., Gilula, M.F., & Ochberg, F.M. *Violence and the struggle for existence.* Boston: Little, Brown & Co., 1970.

Davison, G.C. Anxiety under total curarization: implications for the role of muscular relaxation in the desensitization of neurotic fears. *Journal of Mental and Nervous Diseases,* 1967, *143,* 443–448.

Dengerink, H.A., & Levendusky, P.G. Effects of massive retalization and balance of power on aggression. *Journal of Experimental Research in Personality,* 1972, *6,* 230–236.

Douglas, R.J. The hippocampus and behavior. *Psychological Bulletin,* 1967, *67,* 416–442.

Ellis, A. *Reason and emotion in psychotherapy*. New York: Lyle Stuart, Inc., 1962.

Ellis, A. *Growth through reason*. Palo Alto, Calif.: Science and Behavior Books, 1971; Hollywood, Calif.: Wilshire Books, 1974.

Ellis, A. *Humanistic psychology: The rational-emotive approach*. New York: Julian Press, 1973. (a)

Ellis, A. Healthy and unhealthy aggression. Paper presented at the first annual Convention of the American Psychological Association, Montreal, Canada, August, 1973. (b)

Ellis, A. *How to live with a neurotic*. New York: Crown Publishers, 1975.

Ellis, A. The biological basis of human irrationality. *Journal of Individual Psychology*, 1976, *32*, 145–168.

Ellis, A. Techniques of handling anger in marriage. *Journal of Marriage and Family Counseling*, 1976, *2*, 305–315. (b).

Ellis, A. The basic clinical theory or rational-emotive therapy. In A. Ellis & R. Grieger (Eds.), *Handbook of rational-emotive therapy*. New York: Springer Publishing Co., 1977, pp. 3–34. (a)

Ellis, A. *How to live with and without anger*. New York: Reader's Digest Press, 1977. (b)

Ellis, A. Discomfort anxiety: A new cognitive-behavioral construct. Invited address to the Association for Advancement of Behavior Therapy Annual Meeting, November 17, 1978. New York: BMA Audio Cassettes, 1978.

Ellis, A. A theoretical and empirical foundation of rational-emotive therapy. Monterey, Calif.: Brooks/Cole, 1979. (a)

Ellis, A. Rational-emotive therapy. In R.J. Corsini (Ed.), *Current psychotherapies* (rev. ed.). Itasca, Ill.: Peacock, 1979. (b)

Ellis, A. A note on the treatment of agoraphobics with cognitive modification versus prolonged exposure *in vivo*. *Behavior Therapy and Research*, 1979, in press. (c)

Ellis, A., & Abrahms, E. *Brief psychotherapy in medical and health practice*. New York: Springer Publishing Co., 1978.

Ellis, A., & Grieger, R. *Handbook of theory and practice*. New York: Springer Publishing Co., 1977.

Ellis, A., & Harper, R.A. *A new guide to rational living*. Englewood Cliffs, N.J.: Prentice-Hall, Inc., 1975.

Epstein, S., & Taylor, S.P. Instigation to aggression as a function of degree of defeat and perceived aggression intent of the opponent. *Journal of Personality*, 1967, *35*, 265–289.

Feshback, S. Dynamics and morality of violence and aggression. *American Psychologist*, 1971, *26*, 281–292.

Feshback, S. The stimulating vs. cathartic effects of a vicarious aggressive activity. *Journal of abnormal and social psychology*, 1961, *63*, 381–385.

Feshback, S., & Singer, R.D. *Television and aggression*. New York: Jossey-Bass, 1971.

Frodi, A. Alternatives to aggressive behavior for the reduction of hostility. *Guteborg Psychological Reports*, 1973, *3*, 11.

Frodi, A. Effects of varying explanations given for provocation on subsequent hostility. *Psychological Reports*, 1976, *38*, 659–669.

Funkenstein, D.H., King, S.H., & Drolette, M. The direction of anger during a laboratory stress-inducing situation. *Psychosomatic Medicine*, 1954, *76*, 404–413.

Funkenstein, D.H. King, S.H., & Drolette, M. *Mastery of stress*. Cambridge, Mass.: Harvard University Press, 1957.

Geen, R.G., & O'Neal, E.C. *Perspectives on aggression*. New York: Academic Press, Inc., 1976.

Goodman, D., & Maultsby, M.C. *Emotional well-being through rational behavior training*. Springfield, Ill.: Thomas Press, 1974.

Green, R., & Murray, E. Instigation to aggression as a function of self-disclosure and threat to self-esteem. *Journal of Consulting and Clinical Psychology*, 1973, *40*, 440–443.

Greenwell, I., & Dengerink, H. The role of perceived vs. actual attack in human physical aggression. *Journal of Personality and Social Psychology*, 1973, *26*, 66–71.

Grieger, R.M. An existential component of anger. *Rational Living*, 1977, *12*, 3–8.

Grieger, R., & Boyd, J. *Rational-emotive therapy: A skills-based approach*. New York: Van Nostrand Reinhold, 1979.

Hebb, D.O., & Thompson, W.R. The social significance of animal studies. In G. Lindzey (Ed.), *Handbook of social psychology. Volume 1, Theory and method*. Cambridge, Mass.: Addison-Wesley, 1954.

James, P., & Mosher, D. Thematic aggression, hostility-guilty, and aggressive behavior. *Journal of Projective Techniques*, 1967, *3*, 61–67.

Johnson, R. *Aggression in man and animals*. Philadelphia: W.B. Saunders, 1972.

Jones, R.G. A factored measure of Ellis's irrational belief system, with personality and maladjustment correlates. Unpublished doctoral dissertation, Texas Technological College, 1968.

Kahn, M. The physiology of catharsis. *Journal of personality and social psychology*, 1966, *3*, 278–286.

Knott, P.D., Lasater, L., & Shuman, R. Aggression-guilt and conditionability for aggressiveness. *Journal of Personality*, 1974, *3*, 332–344.

Konocni, V.T. Annoyance, type, and duration of post-annoyance activity, and aggression: "The cathartic effect." *Journal of Experimental Psychology*, 1975, *104*, 76–102. (a)

Konocni, V.T. The mediation of aggressive behavior: Arousal level vs. anger and cognitive labeling. *Journal of Personality and Social Psychology*, 1975, *32*, 706–712. (b)

La Barre, W. The cultural basis of emotions and gestures. *Journal of Personality*, 1947, *16*, 49–68.

Lazarus, R.S. *Psychological stress and the coping process*. New York: McGraw-Hill, 1966.

Lazarus, R.S. Cognitive and personality factors underlying threat and coping. In M.H. Appley & R. Trumbell (Eds.), *Psychology of stress*. New York: Appleton-Century-Crofts, 1967.

Lazarus, R.S. Emotions and adaptation: conceptual and empirical relations. In W.J. Arnold (Ed.), *Nebraska symposium on motivation*. Lincoln, Nebraska: University of Nebraska Press, 1968.

Lazarus, R.S., Averill, J.R., & Opton, E.M. Towards a cognitive theory of emotion. In M. Arnold (Ed.), *Feelings and emotions*. New York: Academic Press, Inc., 1970.

Lefcourt, H. The functions and illusions of control and freedom. *American Psychologist*, 1973, *28*, 417–425.

Lindsley, D.B. Emotions and the electroencephalogram. In M.R. Raymert (Ed.), *Feelings and emotions: The Mooseheart symposium*. New York: McGraw-Hill, 1950.

Look, March 19, 1979, pp. 18–24.

MacLean, P.D. Psychosomatics. In H.W. Magoun (Ed.), *Handbook of physiology. Action 1: Neurophysiology* (Vol. 3.). Washington, D.C.: American Physiological Society, 1960.

Mallick, S.K., & McCandless, B.R. A study of catharsis of aggression. *Journal of Personality and Social Psychology*, 1966, *4*, 591–596.

Meichenbaum, D., & Cameron, R. Stress inoculation: A skills-training approach to anxiety management. Unpublished manuscript, University of Waterloo, Ontario, Canada, 1973.

Milgram, S. Behavioral study of obedience. *Journal of Abnormal and Social Psychology*, 1963, *67*, 371–378.

Mosher, D.K. Interaction of fear and guilt in inhibiting unacceptable behavior. *Journal of Consulting Psychology*, 1965, *29*, 161–167.

Moyer, K.E. The physiology of aggression and the implications for aggressive control. In T.L. Singer (Ed.), *The control of aggression and violence*. New York: Academic Press, 1971.

Moyer, K.E. The physiological inhibition of aggressive behavior. In T.F. Knutson (Ed.) *The Control of Aggression*. Chicago: Aldine Press, Inc., 1973.

Nezlek, T., and Brehm, W. Hostility as a function of the opportunity to counter-aggress. *Journal of Personality*, 1975, *43*, 421–433.

Nickel, T.W. The attribution of intention as a critical factor in the relation between frustration and aggression. *Journal of Personality,* 1974, *42,* 482–492.

Nolan, E.J., Boyd, J.D., & Grieger, R.M. Influences of irrational beliefs and expectancy of success on frustration tolerance. Unpublished manuscript, 1979.

Novaco, R.W. *Anger control: The development and evaluation of an experimental treatment.* Lexington, Mass.: D.C. Heath, Lexington Books, 1975.

Novaco, R.W. Anger and coping with stress. In J.P. Foreyt & D.P. Rathjew (Eds.), *Cognitive behavior therapy.* New York: Plenum Press, 1978, pp. 135–173.

Pribram, K.H. Emotion: Steps toward a neuropsychological theory. In D.C. Glass (Ed.), *Neurophysiology and emotion.* New York: Rockefeller University Press, 1967.

Rimm, D.C., DeGroot, J.C., Bourd, P., Reiman, J., & Dillow, P.V. Systematic desensitization of an anger response. *Behavior Research and Therapy,* 1971, *9,* 273–280.

Rosenbaum, M.E., & de Charms, R. Direct and vicarious reduction of hostility. *Journal of Abnormal and Social Psychology,* 1960, *60,* 105–111.

Rosenbaum, M.E., & Stanners, R.F. Self-esteem, manifest hostility, and expression of hostility. *Journal of Abnormal and Social Psychology,* 1961, *63,* 646–649.

Rotter, J.B. *Social learning and clinical psychology.* Englewood Cliffs, N.J.: Prentice-Hall, 1954.

Rotter, J.B. An introduction to social learning theory. In J. Rotter, J.E. Chance, & E.J. Phares (Eds.) *Applications of a social learning theory of personality.* New York: Holt, Rhinehart, and Winston, 1972.

Rule, B., & Nesdale, A. Emotional arousal and aggressive behavior. *Psychological Bulletin,* 1976, *83,* 851–863.

Schachter, S., & Singer, T.E. Cognitive, social, and physiological determinants of emotional state. *Psychological Review,* 1962, *69,* 379–399.

Schacter, J. Pain, fear, and anger in hypertensives and normotensives: A psychophysiological study. *Psychosomatic Medicine,* 1957, *29,* 17–29.

Scheier, M. Self-awareness, self-consciousness, and angry aggression. *Journal of Personality,* 1976, *44,* 627–644.

Shortell, J.R., Epstein, S., & Taylor, S.P. Instigation to aggression as a function of degree of defeat and the capacity for massive retaliation. *Journal of Personality,* 1970, *38,* 313–328.

Taylor, S.P. Aggressive behavior and physiological arousal as a function of provocation and the tendency to inhibit aggression. *Journal of Personality,* 1967, *35,* 297–310.

Toch, H. *Violent Men.* Chicago,: Adline Publishing Co., 1969.

Tursky, B., & Sternbach, R.S. Further physiological correlates of ethnic differences in response to shock. *Psychophysiology,* 1967, *4,* 67–74.

Veldman, D., & Worchel, P. Defensiveness and self-acceptance in the management of hostility. *Journal of Abnormal and Social Psychology,* 1961, *63,* 319–325.

Worchel, P. Status restoration and the reduction of hostility. *Journal of Abnormal and Social Psychology,* 1960, *63,* 443–445.

Zillman, D., & Cantor, J.R. Effects of timing of information about mitigating circumstances on emotional responses to provocation and retaliatory behavior. *Journal of Experimental Social Psychology,* 1976, *12,* 38–55.

Zuckerman, M., & Lubin, B. *Manual for the Multiple Affect Adjective Check List.* San Diego, Calif.: Educational and Industrial Testing Service, 1965.

Chapter 3

DEPRESSION AND SUICIDE

John Rush
Jan Weissenburger

Behavioral and cognitive-behavioral psychologists have recently begun to study depression (Ferster, 1973; Lazarus, 1968). Lewinsohn (1974), for instance, links a low rate of response-contingent positive reinforcement to depression. According to this formulation, any number of factors may lead to a low rate of positive reinforcement. Even if response-contingent positive reinforcers are available, the depression-prone individual may lack the social skills to elicit these reinforcers, may actually thwart themselves by turning them off, or may perceive fewer response-contingent events as positively reinforcing than actually exist.

Partially supporting this, there is evidence that depressed individuals have social/interpersonal skill deficits (Lewinsohn, Biglan, & Zeiss, 1976; Lewinsohn, Weinstein, & Shaw, 1969). Several studies indicate that depressives have a negative perception of interpersonal relationships. Lunghi (1977), finding that depressives tend to report more negative interpersonal relations than nondepressed persons, suggested that a generally negative way of perceiving interpersonal situations may elicit a more negative response from others and actual negative relations may develop that in turn reinforce this negative view. Indeed, depressed persons often induce negative responses and feelings in others. For example, after phone conversations with depressed persons, interviewers reported having more feelings of depression, anxiety, hostility, and rejection (Coyne, 1976; Steiner, 1974). And persons enacting a depressed role were rejected more during phone conversations than persons playing a nondepressed role (Hammen & Peters, 1978).

Lewinsohn has developed a therapy program based on this theory. This treatment involves initial monitoring and subsequent behavioral changes to increase the level of response-contingent reinforcement (Lewinsohn, 1975; Lewinsohn, Biglan, & Zeiss, 1976). Treatment is time-limited (three months) and has the dual goals of (1) increased participation in positive events and (2) enhanced social skills.

A more thoroughly cognitive position is offered by RET (Ellis, 1962; Ellis & Grieger, 1977). RET is based on the idea that emotional disturbance arises when individuals hold and act on certain maladaptive assumptions or philosophies that lead to disturbed emotional reactions and maladaptive behavioral patterns. In the case of depression, these generally consist of: (1) awfulizing—things that are unfortunate or frustrating are chronically evaluated as catastrophic and unbearable; (2) self-downing—habitually downing or condemning oneself as bad for real or imagined mistakes or deficiencies (Grieger & Boyd, 1979; Hauck, 1973). RET focuses on helping people eliminate these self-defeating beliefs and developing ones that lead to more satisfying response styles.

Another cognitive theory of depression is based on the notion of learned helplessness (Seligman, 1974). This theory was derived from an experimental paradigm in which dogs previously subjected to inescapable shock became passive and "helpless" when subsequently placed in a situation in which escape from the shock was possible. Seligman proposed that this learned helplessness paradigm is a prototype for the development of neurotic depression: an individual's belief in his or her helplessness leads to depressive symptoms. This belief is derived from a prior history of situations in which the patient believed he or she lacked personal control.

Although initially focused on a behavioral explanation, a recent revision of this model stresses a cognitive mediation model of depression. In this the depressed person habitually makes a certain set of attributions that essentially leads to depression (Abramson, Seligman, & Teasdale, 1978). The depressive's attributional style consists in a tendency to make internal attributions for failure ("I did it.") but external attributions for success, to make stable attributions for failure ("I can't do better") but unstable attributions for success, and to make global attributions for failure ("I'm bad") but specific attributions for success.

All these viewpoints fall within the cognitive framework and provide a logical basis for clinical intervention. The focus of this chapter, however, will be on Aaron Beck's cognitive theory of depression, a theory that has been widely researched. It too has led to a well-developed intervention model which also has strong empirical support. We will first explain this model and then present empirical evidence attesting to its validity.

BECK'S COGNITIVE MODEL OF DEPRESSION

Beck's cognitive theory (Beck, 1967, 1974) views depression as activation of three major cognitive patterns (the cognitive triad) that induce the individual to respond emotionally and behaviorally in a negative manner. The first component of the triad focuses on a negative view of *self*. These patients see themselves as deficient, inadequate, or unworthy and tend to attribute their unpleasant experiences to some personal physical, mental, or moral defect. In their opinion, they are undesirable and worthless because of their presumed defects; and they tend to underestimate or criticize themselves because of them. Further, they regard themselves as lacking in attributes they consider essential for attainment of happiness or at least contentment.

The second component of the triad is the patient's distorted interpretations of *experience*. He or she tends to see the world as making exorbitant demands and/or presenting insuperable obstacles to reaching life goals. The patient consistently misconstrues interactions with the environment as evidence for defeat and deprivation. These misinterpretations are apparent by observing that the patient negatively construes situations even when less negative, more plausible, alternative interpretations are available.

The third component of the triad consists of viewing the *future* in a negative way. The depressed patient anticipates that current difficulties or suffering will continue indefinitely. Whenever he or she contemplates undertaking a specific task, he or she expects to fail. Thus, he or she is unable to see the future as more promising than the current view of reality.

According to this theory, the other signs and symptoms of the depressive syndrome are consequences of the activation of these negative cognitive patterns. The affective symptoms (feeling sad, lonely, bored) can be analyzed in terms of these negative concepts. If a patient incorrectly thinks he or she is being rejected, he or she will react with the same negative affect that occurs with actual rejection. Similarly, if a patient erroneously believes he or she is a social outcast, he or she will feel lonely. The motivational changes in depression (paralysis of the will, escape and avoidance wishes, suicidal ideas, and increased dependency) are also related to negative cognitions. Since he or she anticipates a negative outcome, he or she is reluctant to commit him or herself to a goal or undertaking. Convinced of failure, the depressed person cannot mobilize the desire and effort to undertake a task. Negative expectations also result in avoidance and escape wishes. Suicidal wishes are an extreme expression of the desire to escape from what appears to be insoluble problems or unbearable situations. Since he or she see him or herself as a worthless burden, the depressed patient believes that everyone will be better off when he or she is dead. Increased dependence may also be attributed to negative concepts. The patient sees him or herself as inept and undesirable; he or she tends to overestimate the difficulty of normal tasks in life and unrealistically expects things to turn out badly. Under these circumstances, many patients seek help and reassurance from others they consider competent. Similarly, indecisiveness is derived from the patient's belief that any decision he or she makes will be wrong.

The physical correlates of depression can also be related to the cognitive patterns. An example is profound motor inhibition. When a patient believes he or she is doomed to failure in all efforts, he or she feels apathetic and low in energy. The conviction of futility seems to be related further to "psychomotor inhibition." Patients in an experiment receiving feedback that their performances on tasks were inferior were less motivated to volunteer again than those informed that their performance was superior (Loeb, Feshback, Beck, & Wolf, 1964). When a patient can be encouraged to initiate an activity, however, psychomotor retardation and the sense of fatigue are reduced.

Beck (1963) also posited a number of specific logical errors depressed persons make to misinterpret events. Arbitrary inference refers to the process of drawing a conclusion in the absence of evidence to support the conclusion or when the evidence is contrary to the conclusion. Selective abstraction consists of focusing on a detail taken out of context, ignoring other more salient features of the situation, and conceptualizing the whole experience on the basis of this element. The third specific cognitive distortion refers to a pattern of drawing a general conclusion on the basis of a single incident and is labeled overgeneralization. Magnification and minization are other errors which are reflected in evaluations that are so gross as to constitute distortion. Personalization, the final distortion listed by Beck, refers to the patient's proclivity to relate external events to self when there is no basis for making such a connection.

A developmental hypothesis to explain the formation of a predisposition to depression is offered by the cognitive model. According to this hypothesis, the child develops many attitudes about self and surroundings, some of which may be realistic and facilitate healthy adjustment, while others deviate from reality and make the individual vulnerable to psychological disorders. An individual's concepts about self, the world, and the future are based upon specific beliefs or assumptions derived from personal experience, identificaion with significant others, and perceptions of the attitudes of others. Once a particular belief is formed it may form the basis for additional assumptions and cognitions which support these beliefs. Beliefs are reinforced by ongoing experience such that cognitions compatible with the beliefs are developed into enduring structures or schemas.

Because schemas constitute the basis for screening out, differentiating, and coding stimuli, they produce a predictable pattern of interpretations of specific sets of situations in an individual. Through a matrix of schemas, then, the individual categorizes and evaluates experiences, molding the data into cognitions (defined as any mental activity with verbal content). The schemas activated in specific situations directly determine the affective responses to them. If the content is relevant to being deserted, thwarted, undesirable, or negligent in one's duties, the schemas will produce, respectively, feelings of loneliness, frustration, humiliation, or guilt. Though schemas may be latent at a given time, they can be activated by specific circumstances that are analogous to experiences initially responsible for embedding the schemas. Persons sensitive to particular situations because of previous similar experiences tend to negatively construe these situations due to the activation of previously formed schemas. However, these persons are still able to maintain interest in and realistically appraise other nontraumatic aspects of life. In theory, these individuals function according to adaptive, realistic schemata and thus, process many events in accord with these adaptive beliefs. When situations are analogous to former traumas, however, maladaptive schemas are activated and negatively biased ideas about life develop.

A depressed person's thoughts are characterized by negative themes and schemas. As the depression deepens, thinking is increasingly dominated by these negative ideas, although there may be no logical connection between actual situations and negative interpretations. This impairment in thinking is due to negatively biased schemas which assume a dominant role in the thought processes of the depressed person, interfering with the operation of cognitive structures involved in reality testing and reasoning. The usual orderly matching of stimulus and appropriate schema is upset by the intrusion of the overactive, idiosyncratic schemas which displace the more appropriate ones. As idiosyncratic schemas become more active, they are evoked by a wider range of stimuli which are less logically related to them. The patient's conceptualization of reality situations is distorted to fit the schema. The systematic errors which lead to distortion of reality in depressed patients (arbitrary interpretation, selective abstraction, etc.) are a consequence of hypervalent schemas.

Beck employs a feedback model to more completely explain depressive phenomena. An unpleasant life situation triggers schemas related to loss, negative expectancies, and self-blame. These schemas stimulate related affective responses. These affects further energize the schemas to which they are connected. In phenomenological terms, the depressive's negative ideation leads to sadness; then sadness becomes a sign that life is painful and hopeless. Thus, negative interpretations of sadness further reinforce negative attitudes. Hence, a cycle is produced (Beck, 1971).

EMPIRICAL SUPPORT FOR THE COGNITIVE TRIAD

As already described, the cognitive triad (negative view of self, of experience, and of the future) leads to affective, behavioral, motivational, and other symptoms of depression. These cognitions are accompanied by specific logical errors (e.g., arbitrary inference). A number of studies have been conducted which provide partial evidence for these hypotheses.

Weintraub, Segal, and Beck (1974) devised a test consisting of incomplete stories involving a principal character with whom the subject was asked to identify. Subjects were asked to complete the stories by selecting one of four sentences. The sentences were grouped according to the following themes derived from the triad: expectation of discomfort, expectation of failure, negative interpersonal relations, and low self-concept. The story-completion test was administered to 30 normal male undergraduates on five occasions over a 2-month interval, preceded on each occasion by a measure of depressed mood (Lubin's Depression Adjective Checklist, 1965).

The authors found a time-specific relationship between cognition and mood: subjects who were thinking more negatively, as measured by responses to a story-completion test, reported feeling more "depressed." In addition, the four components of cognitive content were highly intercorrelated: each component correlated with the total cognitive content score and each was positively associated with depressed mood. The results indicate that the cognitive triad is a unified, cohesive entity, with a stable relationship to sad mood. Further, it was possible to demonstrate that the cognitive content was a relatively enduring characteristic, while "depressed" moods were more transient. Weintraub et al. (1974) argue on this basis that the negative attitudinal set, rather than depressed affect, may be the primary factor in depression.

Hammen and Krantz (1976) developed another story completion task that assessed the tendency for depressed subjects to show cognitive distortions. Subjects were asked to read a paragraph describing a person in a problematic situation, to picture themselves in the situation, and to select one of four possible responses for each story. Each group of responses contained depressed-distorted, depressed nondistorted, nondepressed distorted, and nondepressed nondistorted responses. Each depressed-distorted response contained one or more of the logical errors (overgeneralization, arbitrary inference, selective abstraction, magnification, or minimization) hypothesized by Beck. These responses also reflected negative interpretations of experience, especially in the interpersonal sphere, low self-concept, and negative expectations for the future. An example follows:

> Janice is a senior at a large university. She dislikes the lack of faculty-student contact so she usually makes an effort to talk to her teachers outside the classroom. So after she received an average

score on a midterm, she went to the professor, Dr. Smith, to talk over the test. Dr. Smith pointed out the correct answers and the reasons for them on the questions she missed. He also gave her some helpful tips on studying. After about 45 minutes, Dr. Smith said he was quite busy and hoped she would excuse him. He then walked her to the door and said it was nice talking to her. Put yourself in Janice's place, trying to imagine as vividly as you can what she probably thought and felt.

Are you satisfied with your meeting with Dr. Smith?

a.   Yes, because he was quite pleased with my visit and will probably give me a good grade in the course. (nondepressed-distorted)

b.   Although it's upsetting for me to realize it, I probably needed tips on studying. (depressed-nondistorted)

c.   Yes, he answered all my questions and I made a good contact. (nondepressed-nondistorted)

d.   No, he probably thinks I'm dumb, which is why he gave me tips on study habits. (depressed-distorted)

The Hammen and Krantz task was originally administered to depressed and nondepressed women as assessed by the Beck Depression Inventory. Depressed women selected significantly more depressed-distorted responses and significantly fewer nondepressed-nondistorted responses than did the nondepressed women.

In subsequent studies Krantz and Hammen (1978) administered the questionnaire to groups of male and female undergraduates, to students instructed to role-play a depressed or nondepressed part, to persons seeking therapy for depression in an outpatient setting, and to depressed inpatients. Results in all groups indicated a consistent relationship between level of depression as measured by depression inventories and choice of depressed-distorted responses. In addition, test-retest results indicated that individuals with the highest depressed-distorted response scores had the highest depression levels at retest. There were no significant effects of subject sex, sex of the story character, or nature of the story theme (whether achievement-competence or social-interpersonal).

Watkins and Rush (1978) devised a more projective measure

of cognitions, the Cognitive Response Test (CRT). In the CRT, items are presented in an openended sentence completion format and are scored by assigning responses to the following categories: rational (R), irrational-depressed (ID), irrational-other (IO), and not scorable. Comparing responses of depressed psychiatric out-patients, nondepressed psychiatric outpatients, nondepressed medical outpatients, and nondepressed controls, to the CRT, it was found that the depressed group gave significantly fewer rational responses and significantly more irrational-depressed responses than the other subject groups, who did not differ from each other on the response categories. The irrational-other and not scorable categories did not discriminate between groups.

Moyal (1977) used a "stimulus appraisal" test in which subjects imagined themselves in a variety of problem situations and predicted their likely responses to these situations. The depression scores of the children studied were negatively related to the choice of adaptive responses, but positively correlated with the selection of helpless or self-blaming responses. Responses to a second questionnaire revealed a strong negative correlation between depression and self-esteem. This study in children is consistent with those in adults.

Hollon and Kendall (in press) have developed a 30-item Automatic Thoughts Questionnaire (ATQ) consisting of items describing negative thoughts associated with depression. The questionnaire was devised by asking undergraduate students to imagine depressing situations and write down their associated thoughts. Of these responses, 100 of the most common were selected and given to another sample of undergraduate subjects. These subjects were additionally administered two measures of level of depression, the Minnesota Multiphasic Personality Inventory-Depression Scale and the Beck Depression Inventory. Thirty of the one hundred items were selected as discriminating depressed from nondepressed individuals and comprised the resultant ATQ. The questionnaire was validated on independent samples of under-graduates and found to significantly discriminate depressed from nondepressed groups. Results of a factor analysis of the questionnaire items are particuarly relevant to the cognitive theory of depression. The second of a four-factor solution consisted of items relating to negative self-concept and negative expectations, which correspond well with Beck's concepts of negative view of self and the future.

The preceding studies provide evidence for the existence of the cognitive triad in depression. They indicate that the three components of the triad are interrelated, that a time-specific relationship exists between mood and cognitive distortions, and that the degree of cognitive distortion discriminates between depressed and nondepressed persons. Additional empirical evidence for each component of the cognitive triad is described below.

Negative View of the Self

CORRELATION STUDIES. Beck (1967) noted a significant correlation between the severity of depression and a measure of self-concept. Depressed patients rated themselves high on socially undesirable traits and low on desirable traits. Beck (1974) again found significant correlations between Depression Inventory scores and negative self-concept. Changes (or differences) in the level of depression between admission and discharge correlated highly with changes in the measure of self-concept.

Similarly, Pachman and Foy (1978) reported a significant negative correlation between depression and self-esteem as measuared by the self-esteem index in inpatient male alcoholics (Barksdale, 1974). These results concur with the earlier experiments, indicating that there is a significant positive relationship between negative self-concept or self-esteem and depression.

EXPERIMENTAL STUDIES. Loeb, Beck, and Diggory (1971) exposed depressed outpatients and nondepressed controls to a card-sorting task, asking them (prior to undertaking the task) to estimate the probability they would succeed. Although the depressed patients indicated they would try as hard as, and indeed subsequently performed as well as, the nondepressed group, they were significantly more pessimistic in estimating their chances of success and rated their actual performances as poorer than did the nondepressed controls.

Several studies have demonstrated that depressed patients are particularly sensitive to failure. After inferior performance in a word-completion test, high-depressed patients showed a greater drop in mood level and in their level of expectation of future success at the same task than did nondepressed patients (Loeb, Feshback, Beck, & Wolf, 1964). Loeb, Beck, Diggory, and Tuthill (1967) found that depressed subjects reacted to failure on a card-sorting task with significantly greater pessimism and lower levels of aspiration than nondepressed patients. Hammen and Krantz (1976) obtained comparable results when they gave depressed and nondepressed subjects a test supposedly designed to assess therapeutic potential and then reported to them bogus scores. They found that depressed subjects who had received "failure" scores had the least positive predictions of future success of all groups. The authors concluded that depressed subjects were more sensitive to the experience of failure.

Giles (1978) has found that hospitalized depressed women rate themselves as less likely to achieve a goal, as anticipating a lower likelihood of future success, as performing worse than others, and as expecting failure when the outcome is unknown when compared to nondepressed psychiatric and nonpsychiatric hospitalized groups of women. These results were consistent across two types of tasks: an impersonal card-sorting task and an interpersonal-oriented means-end problem-solving procedure. However, a significant effect of feedback, whether success or failure, was not found. That is, following failure feedback, all groups lowered their expectations for future success, with no significant difference between groups. These results support Beck's negative cognitive triad theory in depression and suggest that the cognitive distortions are present when the person is engaging in either an impersonal- or an interpersonal-oriented situation. The failure to find a differential effect of feedback suggests all subjects realistically responded to their feedback but that depressed subjects maintained their negative bias.

Self-criticism and self-blame are strongly associated with low self-concept. Beck's observations suggested that depressed people tend to blame themselves and their inadequacies for negative outcomes. Experimental support for this hypothesis was offered by Rizley (1978) who instructed depressed and nondepressed subjects to perform a task in which they were to predict the order of numbers presented. The numbers were actually in a random order, and the experimenter controlled which subjects "succeeded" and which "failed." Subjects were asked to judge the degree to which luck, effort, ability, or task difficulty contributed to the outcome. In assessing the reasons for failure, depressed subjects ascribed more causal importance to internal factors (effort and ability) whereas nondepressed subjects rated these factors as less important determinants of failure. In a second experiment, Rizley asked depressed subjects to instruct another person in a task. Compared to nondepressed subjects, the depressed persons tended to invoke their own efforts or abilities to explain the performances of the instructees.

Recent studies by Diener and Dweck (1978) also suggested that helpless children attribute failure to a lack of ability, whereas nonhelpless children tend to concentrate on problem-solving strategies rather than assigning attribution for failure. In a similar vein, Klein, Fencil-Morse, and Seligman (1976) found that depressed subjects were more likely than nondepressed subjects to attribute failure to their own abilities in an anagram problem. Thus, these experimental paradigms tend to support the relationship between a negative view of self and depression.

Negative View of Experiences

According to the cognitive model, the depressed person consistently construes experiences in a negative way. Studies supporting this are of four kinds, as follows.

DREAMS.   Early studies analyzing thematic content of dreams of depressed patients revealed a disproportionate number in which the dreamer was deprived, frustrated, deserted, or injured. These findings were replicated in a sleep laboratory by Beck and Ward (1976) with remitted depressed patients, and by Beck and Ward (1961) in a well-controlled study utilizing both inpatients and outpatients. The latter study concluded that background factors had no effect on the dream content.

PROJECTIVE TESTS.   The Focused Fantasy Test consists of a set of four picture cards. Each card has four frames that portray a continuous sequence of events. The action in the sequence enters around a pair of identical twins. In the last frame, one of the twins is subjected to an unpleasant experience, and the other twin avoids the unpleasant experience or has a pleasant experience. After being presented with the pictures, the patient is asked to tell a story about the sequence. After listening to the story, the examiner determines with which twin the patient identifies. The test score is based on the number of identifications with the hurt or injured figure. In the Focused Fantasy Test, depressed patients identified more often with outcomes in which the protagonist was hurt compared to nondepressed patients (Beck, 1961). These typical themes also appeared in the depressed patient's early memories (Beck, 1967, p. 181).

MEMORY TESTS.   Lishman (1972) found the tendency to recall more positive than negative material was less marked in overtly depressed patients than in hypomanics and patients recovered from depression. He attributed this result to the higher negative tone of material which depressed patients recalled. A later study (Lloyd & Lishman, 1975) reported a highly significant relationship between degree of depression and speed of recall of pleasant and unpleasant experiences. A high level of depression was associated with a lower ratio between the speed of recall of pleasant and unpleasant memories. This indicates that the usual bias toward more easy recall of pleasant events diminishes as depression increases. The authors argue that the results are not likely due to premorbid personality characteristics or to an excess of unpleasant previous life experiences, since subjects retested when less depressed showed a slight tendency as a group to recall pleasant memories more quickly. The results therefore suggest a tendency for selective recall of negative experiences during the depressive episode.

EXPERIMENTAL STUDIES.   A number of experimental studies support the notion that depressed persons view experience in an unrealistically negative manner. Wener and Rehm (1975) found that depressed subjects frequently underestimated the percentage of "correct" feedback they received in a laboratory task. A number of other studies on informational feedback have examined how depressed persons recall and by inference experience positive reinforcement. Nelson and Craighead (1977) used a predetermined reinforcement schedule with subjects performing a task. They predicted that depressed subjects would recall less positive reinforcement and more punishment than nondepressed subjects, and that this effect would be greatest in high-positive and low-negative reinforcement conditions, since this schedule would be least consistent with their expectations. These predictions were confirmed. Nelson and Craighead also found that depressed subjects self-reinforced significantly less frequently than nondepressed subjects.

Using a similar technique in an experiment with psychiatric outpatients, DeMonbreun and Craighead (1977) found that depressed patients underestimated the amount of reinforcement received when recalling previous performance. Their recall of reinforcement was more inaccurate in the high-positive reinforcement condition than in the low-reinforcement condition (at which time they were fairly accurate). Nondepressed psychiatric patients overestimated positive reinforcement, whereas nondepressed, nonpsychiatric subjects were almost accurate in their recall.

The negative view of experience received further support from a study of the effects of positive reinforcement on depressed mood (Hammen & Glass, 1975). Contrary to what would be predicted by an operant model, depression was not alleviated when participation in pleasurable activities was increased for a two-week period. When subjects rated their enjoyment of activities, depressed subjects who increased activities rated their activities as *less* pleasurable than nondepressed subjects or depressed subjects, who self-monitored mood and activity but maintained their normal routines. In a recent correlational analysis, the tendency to underestimate positive reinforcement was positively correlated with depressed mood (Buchwald, 1977). These findings are congruent with the supposition that depressed patients view and experience the world as devoid of satisfactions.

Negative View of the Future

The storytelling tests reviewed earlier indicate that depression is associated with a negative view of the future. In the Weintraub et al. (1974) study, depressed mood was associated with the endorsement of items such as "I expect the trip will be a flop," "I doubted everything would be as good as I hoped," "I expect my plans will fail." The depressed women in the study by Hammen and Krantz (1976) chose such responses as "I feel like I'll never meet anyone who's interested in me."

Beck (1974) found a positive relationship between the severity of depression, a negative view of the future, and constricted sense of future time (measured by a Generalized Expectancy Scale (Vatz, Winig, & Beck, 1969). Furthermore, changes in both pessimistic attitudes toward the future and sense of future time constriction were significantly correlated with changes in level of depression. Likewise, Melges and Bowlby (1969) observed that a hopeless view of the future predominates in severely depressed patients. Further, Minkoff, Bergman, Beck, and Beck (1973) found that scores on the Generalized Expectancy Scale (later called the Hopelessness Scale) showed a highly significant positive correlation with Beck Depression Inventory scores, as did Beck, Kovacs, and Weissman (1976) and Abramson, Garber, Edwards, and Seligman (1978).

Consequences of Negative Cognitive Set

Beck (1967) contended that the depressed patient's negative, distorted views were responsible for the major symptoms of de-

pression: sadness, lack of motivation, suicidal wishes, and dependent and avoidant behavior. Both correlational and experimental
data support this hypothesis.

MOOD CHANGES.   A naturalistic, correlational study by Weintraub
et al. (1974) yielded some evidence that negative cognitions pre-
cede depressed mood. Further, experimental evidence suggests
that thinking produces sad affect. Velten (1968) examined the
ability of self-referent statements to induce mood changes that
progressed from a neutral to depressive mood. After first reading
neutral and then depressive mood self-referent statements, normal
subjects were significantly more depressed on a number of self-
report and behavioral measures. Opposite effects were produced
by reading statements that progressed from mood neutral to elation. These effects were confirmed by Strickland, Hale, and
Anderson (1975) and by Hale and Strickland (1976). In addition,
the effects have been extended to a situation in which thinking
(rather than reading) happy or sad thoughts was found to have an
effect on mood (Teasdale & Bancroft, 1977). In this study self-
report measures of mood were found to covary with corrugator
EMG which was implicated as a possible objective index of mood
state.
        Coleman (1975) modified the Velten procedure so that sub-
jects read statements of self-evaluation, either positive or negative, which avoided mention of mood. Again, these statements
produced significant differences in levels of elation and depression. Further, characteristically elated patients became "depressed" after this procedure and characteristically "depressed"
subjects became elated. Working within the learned helplessness
model, Wortman, Panciera, Shusterman, and Hibacher (1976)
demonstrated that subjects led to attribute failure at a laboratory
task to personal incompetence were significantly more depressed
than subjects led to believe their failure was externally caused.
Thus, an experimentally induced negative cognitive set appears to
result in depressed moods.

BEHAVIORAL CHANGES. Miller and Seligman (1975) compared depressed subjects to nondepressed subjects exposed to inescapable, aversive noise. Presumably, the inescapable noise pretreatment induced the cognition that responses would have no effect on reinforcement. Both groups showed performance deficits in subsequent anagram tasks compared to nondepressed subjects pretreated with escapable noise or no noise. A study by Klein, Fencil-Morris, and Seligman (1976) manipulated attribution by informing subjects either that most peers had succeeded at the task or that most had failed. Depressed subjects informed that most peers had succeeded showed the greatest performance deficits of all groups in a second task. Stockton (1975) reported significant differences in ability to express feelings, blocked expressions of hostility, dependency, and rigidity between outpatients with depressive neurosis and nondepressed controls, based on both observational and self-report data. Whether negative cognitions result in these differences was not determined.

SUICIDAL IDEATION. Another demonstrated consequence of negative thinking, particularly hopelessness, is suicidal preoccupation in the depressed patient. Ganzler (1967), studying life crisis and suicide in psychiatric outpatients, found that, in contrast with other psychiatric groups, only the suicidal group gave negative ratings of the future. Bjerg (1967) reported that 81% of suicide notes studied reflected a "desire . . . which could not, cannot or will not be fulfilled"; a prominent theme in these notes was the expectation of continued deprivation and suffering. Factor analytic studies of the Beck Depression Inventory have also related pessimism to suicidal wishes (Pichot & Lemperiere, 1964; Cropley & Weckowicz, 1966). Further, using a soliloquy technique to reevoke subjective experiences preceding suicide attempts, Melges and Weisz (1971) found that suicidal ideation was related to a hopeless, helpless, and narrow view of the personal future.

Several studies have indicated that hopelessness, defined as a cognitive factor involving negative expectations, may represent the link between depression and suicide. Minkoff, Bergman, Beck, and Beck (1973) interviewed 68 suicide attempters, and administered to them the Beck Depression Inventory, the Hopelessness Scale (Beck et al., 1974), a Suicidal Intent Scale (Beck, Herman, & Schuyler, 1973), a self-report measure to assess the circumstances surrounding the attempt, and the patient's intentions during the attempt. They found a highly significant positive relationship between hopelessness and suicidal intent. In fact, hopelessness appeared to be a better predictor of suicide attempt than the depression itself.

This study was replicated by Beck, Kovacs, and Weissman (1975) with 384 suicide attempters. Both clinical and psychometric ratings confirmed that hopelessness is more highly correlated with suicidal intent than is depression, and accounts for the variance in the relationship between depression and suicide. This relationship appeared to hold for schizophrenics as well as depressives. At another research center, Wetzel (1976) also replicated the findings of Minkoff et al. in a sample of 48 suicide attempters, and extended the inquiry to a group of 56 patients who had planned, but not carried out, suicide attempts. Findings for the patients thinking of suicide also showed hopelessness to be the mediating variable between depression and suicidal intent.

Reversing Effects of Negative Cognitive Set

There is empirical evidence that negative cognitions and their negative effects can be reversed. Loeb, Beck and Diggory (1971) showed that while depressed patients were particularly sensitive to failure, they also were encouraged by success. Depressed patients who had previously succeeded at a card-sorting task were more optimistic, showed higher levels of aspiration, and performed better on a second task than depressed patients who had failed. Klein and Seligman (1976) "inoculated" depressed subjects by having them succeed at a problem-solving exercise. Subsequently presented with an escape task, these subjects did not show performance deficits, while depressed subjects who did not receive prior "therapy" did show the expected deficits.

In another study, Beck (1974) presented depressed inpatients with a hierarchy of verbal tasks. The tasks ranged from reading a paragraph aloud to improvising a short speech on a chosen subject and attempting to convince the experimenter of their point of view. Patients began with the simplest task and progressed to the most difficult item on the hierarchy. After successfully completing the assignment, they showed significant improvement in global ratings of optimism and self-concept. In another study of depressed and nondepressed college students, McNitt and Thornton (1978) found that the depressed group showed a greater change in expectancy of success after exposure to a high reinforcement schedule (75% of all responses reinforced) than the nondepressed control group. These results lend support to the notion that depressed persons are particularly influenced not only by failure, but also by success experiences. This phenomenon was hypothesized by McNitt and Thornton to be an instance of overgeneralization. That is, the depressed subjects expected more future success because of the experience of a high rate of past success which was generalized to include future expectations of success. Lebow (1975) found that highly depressed college students exposed to a success experience were more likely to show increases in self-satisfaction than nondepressed controls. However, some evidence suggests that the actual experience of success rather than simply thinking of and recalling past success may be a necessary component in the process of altering negative cognitions and their effects. Teasdale (1978) reported that recalling past success in one task had no effect on improving performance deficits induced in a second task via a learned helplessness paradigm in depressed subjects.

Thus, the postulated negative cognitive set can be modified by specifically constructed experiences, and some experimental evidence suggests that changes in the negative set may provide at least temporary prophylaxis against subsequent events which usually result in depression.

In review, there appears to be evidence to support the existence of the cognitive triad in depression. The negative distortions about self, world, and future appear to be interrelated as shown by story completion studies. Experimental and correlational studies lend support to each of the three components of the triad. The triad leads to changes in mood and behavior. Negative view of the future correlates with suicidal ideation and intent. Finally, the effects of this cognitive set on mood, behavior, and thinking can be modified by specific experiences.

EMPIRICAL SUPPORT FOR COGNITIVE ERRORS

Several systematic studies have attempted to determine whether depressed patients have a thinking disorder and whether the formal characteristics of the postulated disorder are consistent with Beck's clinical observations. Salzman, Goldstein, and their group (Goldstein & Salzman, 1967; Salzman, Goldstein, Atkins, & Babigian, 1966.) showed that depressives as well as schizophrenics manifested impairment in abstract conceptualization when a proverbs test was administered. Similarly, systematic studies by O'Reilly and Harrison (1960) and Brattemo (1962) have produced evidence for a thinking disorder in depression.

Braff and Beck (1974) measured abstraction ability in 67 depressed, schizophrenic, and normal subjects. Compared with normals, depressed and schizophrenic subjects showed a clear abstraction deficit. Schizophrenics showed more autistic responses than the depressives. Further, an important overall relationship was observed between degree of depression and degree of abstraction deficit. Moreover, whereas the concrete thinking improved with time for the depressives, it remained relatively stable for the schizophrenics.

Beck observed that depressed patients make absolute and negative judgments in their self-evaluations and attitudes toward their future. Evidence to confirm these observations come from studies by Neuringer (1961, 1964, 1967, 1968) and Rey, Silber,

Savarel, and Post (1978). Neuringer found that rigid and dichoto-mous thinking (the tendency to think in bipolar opposites) was characteristic of suicidal persons, many of whom were depressed. Rey et al. (1978) recently reported a more comprehensive test of the specific aberrations in language form and content among depressives. In moderately to severely depressed patients, subtle disturbances in the formal aspects of language appeared to be as prominent as disturbances of content and affect typically associated with depression. These included rigidity of thought, polarization or thinking in extremes, arbitrary interpretation of events, magnification or minimization, and alterations in time perspective. These findings essentially confirmed Beck's "typology of thinking" (Beck, 1963).

Finally, it should be noted that the story completion test administered by Hammen and Krantz (1976) was developed to include specific examples of Beck's (1963) categorizations of idiosyncratic thinking in depression: for example, arbitrary inference, overgeneralization, minimization of the positive, etc. The options selected by depressed patients showed a significant proportion of these types of distortions. Whether these logical errors are specific to depression remains unclear. Controlled studies comparing nonpsychotic disorders with depression are indicated to determine the specificity of these formal thought characteristics.

EMPIRICAL SUPPORT FOR SCHEMAS

Depressogenic Schemas

Cognitive schemas consist of a complex of assumptions or beliefs through which the individual construes the world. These beliefs or assumptions are unspoken, abstract rules by which the patient judges experience and behavior and makes predictions. For example, recurrent cognitions of failure might reveal demands for perfection. When this idea is not met, the individual concludes that he or she has failed and is, therefore, "a failure." The underlying assumption might be "Unless I am doing a perfect job all the time, I am a failure". The cognitive paradigm of depression assumes that depression is precipitated when a stressful situation interacts with particular cognitive structures, since many individuals would *not* become depressed had they been in the same situation as the person who *does* become depressed.

In order to test for the existence and importance of these underlying assumptions in predisposing to or operating in depression, a Dysfunctional Attitude Scale (DAS) Weissman, 1977) was designed to measure the extent in which a person holds these beliefs. For a statement of belief or attitude seven response categories are presented ranging from totally agree to totally disagree. The higher the total DAS score, the greater the number of dysfunctional beliefs endorsed. Some sample items are listed below:

> [1]I can find happiness without being loved by another person.
> People will probably think less of me if I make a mistake.
> People who have the marks of success (good looks, fame, wealth) are bound to be happier than people who do not.
> I must be a useful, productive, creative person or life has no purpose.
> [1]If I demand perfection in myself, I will make myself very unhappy.

In a preliminary investigation on 35 depressed patients (Weissman & Beck, 1977), the high correlation ($r = 0.58$, $p < .001$) between the DAS and the Beck Depression Inventory (BDI) indicated in significant relationship between the salience of an individual's dysfunctional attitudes and the intensity of depression. In a subsequent investigation utilizing 25 graduate students (Weissman & Beck, 1978), the DAS was found to correlate .65 with the BDI, .62 with the Hammen and Krantz story-completion measures of cognitive distortions, and .76 with the depression

---

[1]For these items an agreement response indicates an adaptive reaction to the belief in question. For the other items, an agreement response indicates a maladaptive reaction.

scale of the Profile of Mood States (POMS) (McNair, Lorr, & Droppleman, 1971). In addition, reliability measures revealed a high degree of internal consistency for the DAS (.93 alpha coefficient), as well as a test-retest reliability coefficient of .71. Further cross correlational analyses of the BDI and DAS at test and retest administrations resulted in a lower correlation coefficient at the second administration which appeared to have been primarily due to alterations in BDI scores. This implies that cognitive distortions, such as those tapped by the DAS may be more stable than affect or mood. In addition, the relatively high correlation between the DAS scores at administration time one and the BDI scores at the second administration suggests a causal relationship between dysfunctional cognitions and depressed mood.

Origin of Dysfunctional Schemas

To explore the origin of the depressogenic attitudes, past histories have been studied to determine whether depressed patients have been exposed to any particular types of developmental stresses that might account for their sense of deprivation and hopelessness. It was anticipated that the death of a parent in childhood, because of the intensity and finality of the loss, might be expected to sensitize the child to regard future life deprivations and problems as irreversible and insoluble.

In a group of 100 severely depressed adult patients, 27% had lost one or both parents through death before the age of 16, whereas in a control group of nondepressed psychiatric patients, only 12% had been orphaned before age 16 (Beck, 1967). These data are consistent with the idea that as a result of traumatic life experiences, depressed patients may develop certain cognitive-affective patterns which, when activated, produce inappropriate or disproportionate reactions of deprivation and despair.

In a recent study, Stockton (1975) found that depressed outpatients reported more self-deprecating childhood experiences (mean 6.9) than nondepressed controls (mean 3.5). Whether depressed persons actually experienced a greater frequency of such events or whether they simply recalled negative as opposed to positive past experiences, cannot be ascertained by such a study. Further studies on the developmental etiologies of such schemas are needed.

COGNITIVE THERAPY OF DEPRESSION: OUTCOME STUDIES

The foregoing has presented empirical data to support the cognitive model of depression. This model has been the basis for developing and testing new hypotheses. It has also been a basis for developing a specific treatment for depression called cognitive therapy. Studies of the efficacy of cognitive therapy have implications for the model itself. If techniques to correct cognitions offer no specific advantage over no treatment or nonspecific treatment controls, we might conclude that negative cognitions, although present in association with a depressed mood, may simply be a secondary effect of the mood itself, an epiphenomenon, rather than as causal to the disorder. Secondly, if dysfunctional attitudes contribute to a predisposition to depression and if these attitudes are corrected with cognitive therapy, then patients treated with cognitive therapy may be afforded some prophylaxis against relapse compared to no treatment and to other treatments.

The rationale for the cognitive therapy of depression is derived from this cognitive formulation: if the source of the depression is a hypervalent set of negative concepts, then the correction of these schemas may be expected to alleviate the depressive symptomatology. In cognitive therapy, the therapist and patient work together to identify distorted cognitions derived from his or her dysfunctional beliefs. These distorted negative cognitions and dysfunctional beliefs are subjected to logical analysis and empirical testing. Moreover, through the assignment of behavioral tasks, the patient learns to master probems and life situations which he or she previously considered insuperable and consequently learns to realign his or her thinking with reality.

Space limitations do not allow for a detailed account of the efficacy of the application of the techniques of cognitive therapy to depression. The interested reader may turn to Beck and Shaw (1977) and to Shaw and Beck (1977) to review this literature. Suffice it to say that psychotherapy outcome studies of both depressed students (Gioe, 1975; Shipley & Fazio, 1973; Taylor & Marshall, 1977) and psychiatric outpatients (Morris, 1975; Rush, Khatami, & Beck, 1978; Rush & Watkins, 1979; Schmickley, 1976; Shaw, 1977) generally indicate that cognitive therapy is more effective than waiting-list controls and various other active treatments. One study (Rush, Beck, Kovacs, & Hollon, 1977) suggests that cognitive therapy is more effective than antidepressant medication for treatment with the depressive syndrome. Secondly, the potential prophylactive value of cognitive therapy is implied by the follow-up data available (Kovacs, Rush, Hollon, & Beck, 1979). These findings are consistent with the notion that cognitions and schemas play a major role in the induction or maintenance of depression. Further studies are needed to identify the predictors of response to this treatment, to assess the applicability of this treatment to other types of depression, and to determine whether cognitive changes uniquely result from cognitive therapy.

Summary

The cognitive model of depression has provided a number of testable hypotheses about the psychological functioning of depression and has been a basis for the development of an affective short-term therapy. The data thus far gathered is strongly supportive of this model and the evidence is quite positive with regard to the affectivness of the treatment paradigm. We can therefore safely conclude that the therapy has validity such that negative cognitions are both part of and causal to depressive phenomenon. Furthermore, changing these negative cognitions leads to changes in or alleviation of the depression.

REFERENCES

Abramson, L. Y., Garber, J., Edwards, N. B., & Seligman, M. E. P. Expectancy changes in depression and schizophrenia. *Journal of Abnormal Psychology*, 1978, *87*, 102–109.

Abramson, L. Y., Seligman, M. E. P., & Teasdale, J. D. Learned helplessness in humans: critique and reformulation. *Journal of Abnormal Psychology*, 1978, *87*, 49–74.

Barksdale. W. The self-esteem index. Unpublished manuscript, 1974.

Beck, A. T. A systematic investigation of depression. *Comprehensive Psychiatry*, 1961, *2*, 163–170.

Beck, A. T. Thinking and depression: 1. Idiosyncratic content and cognitive distortions. *Archives of General Psychiatry*, 1963, *9*, 324–333.

Beck, A. T. Cognition, affect and psychopathology. *Archives of General Psychiatry*, 1971, *24*, 495–500.

Beck, A. T. *Depression: Clinical, experimental, and theoretical aspects*. New York: Harper and Row, 1967. (Republished as *Depression: Causes and treatment*, Philadelphia: University of Pennsylvania Press, 1972.)

Beck. A. T. The development of depression: A cognitive model. In R. Friedman & M. Katz (Eds.), *Psychology of depression: Contemporary theory and research*. Washington, D.C.: Winston-Wiley, 1974.

Beck, A. T., & Beamesderfer, A. Assessment of depression: The Depression Inventory In P. Pichot (Ed.), *Psychological measurements in psychopharmacology, Modern Problems of Pharmacopsychiatry, 7*. Basel, Switzerland: Karger, 1974.

Beck, A. T., Herman, I., & Schuyler, D. Development of suicidal intent scales. In A. T. Beck, H. L. P. Resnick, & D. LeHieri (Eds.), *Measurement of suicidal behaviors*. New York: Charles Press, 1973.

Beck, A. T., Kovacs, M., & Weissman, A. Hopelessness and suicidal behavior: An overview. *Journal of the American Medical Association*, 1975, *234*, 1146–1149.

Beck, A. T., Rush, A. J., & Shaw, B., *Cognitive Therapy of Depression—A Treatment Manual*, mimeograph, University of Pennsylvania, 1977.

Beck, A. T., Rush, A. J., Shaw, B. F., & Emery, G. *Cognitive Therapy of Depression: A Treatment Manual*. New York: The Guilford Press, in press.

Beck, A. T., & Shaw, B. F. Cognitive approaches to depression. In A. Ellis & R. Grieger (Eds.), *Handbook of rational-emotive theory and practice*. New York: Springer Publishing Co., 1977.

Beck. A. T., & Ward, C. H. Dreams of depressed patients. *Archives of General Psychiatry*, 1961, *5*, 66–71.

Beck, A. T., Weissman, A., Lester, D., & Trexler, L. The measurement of pessimism: The Hopelessness Scale. *Journal of Consulting and Clinical Psychology*, 1974, *42*, 861–965.

Bjerg, K. The suicidal life space. In E. S. Shneidman (Ed.), *Essays in Self-Destruction*. New York: Science House, 1967.

Blaney, P. Contemporary Theories of Depression: Critique & Comparison. *Journal of Abnormal Psychology*, 1977, *86*, 203–223.

Braff, D. L., & Beck, A. T. Thinking disorder in depression. *Archives of General Psychiatry*, 1974, *31*, 456–459.

Brattemo, C. E. Interpretations of proverbs in schizophrenic patients: Further studies. *Acta Psychologica* (Amsterdam), 1962, *20*, 254–263.

Buchwald, A. M. Depressive mood and estimates of reinforcement frequency. *Journal of Abnormal Psychology*, 1977, *86*, 443–446.

Coleman, R. E. Manipulation of self-esteem as a determinant of mood of elated and depressed women. *Journal of Abnormal Psychology*, 1975, *84*, 695–700.

Covi, L., Lipman, R., Derogatis, L., Smith, J., & Pattison, I. Drugs and group psychotherapy in neurotic depression. *American Journal of Psychiatry*, 1974, *131*, 191–198.

Coyne, J. C. Depression and the response of others. *Dissertation Abstracts International*, 1976, 36, (11-B), 5785.

Cropley, A. J., & Weckowicz, T. E. The dimensionality of clinical depression. *Australian Journal of Psychology*, 1966, *18*, 18–25.

DeMonbreun, B. G., & Craighead, W. E. Distortion of perception and recall of positive and neutral feedback in depression. *Cognitive Therapy and Research*, 1977, *1*(4), 311–329.

DePue, R. A., & Monroe, S. M. Learned helplessness in the perspective of the depressive disorders: conceptual and definitional issues. *Journal of Abnormal Psychology*, 1978, *87*, 3–20.

Diener, C. I., & Dweck, C. S. An analysis of learned helplessness: continuous changes in performance, strategy, and achievement cognitions following failure. *Journal of Personality and Social Psychology*, 1978, *36*, 451–462.

Dilling, C. A., & Rabin, A. I. Temporal experience in depressed states and schizophrenia. *Journal of Consulting Psychology*, 1967, *31*, 604–608.

Ellis, A. *Reason and Emotion in Psychotherapy*. Secaucus, N.J.: Lyle Stuart, Inc., 1962.

Ellis, A., & Grieger, R. *Handbook of rational-emotive therapy*. New York: Springer Publishing Co., 1977.

Ferster, C. B. A functional analysis of depression. *American Psychologist*, 1973, *28*, 857–870.

Ganzler, S. Some interpersonal and social dimensions of suicidal behavior. *Dissertation Abstract*, 1967, *288*, 1192–1193.

Giles, D., Cognitive and perceptual abnormalities in depression. Unpublished manuscript, 1978.

Gioe, V. J. Cognitive and positive group experience as a treatment for depression. Unpublished doctoral dissertation, Temple University, 1975. *Dissertation Abstracts International*, 1975, *36*, 3039B–3040B, University Microfilms No. 75–28, 219.

Goldstein, R. H., & Salzman, L. F. Cognitive functioning in acute and remitted psychiatric patients. *Psychological Reports*, 1967, *21*, 24–26.

Grieger, R., & Boyd, J. *Rational-emotive therapy: A skills-based approach.* New York: Van Nostrand Reinholdt, 1979.

Hale, W. D., & Strickland, B. R. Induction of mood states and their effect on cognition and social behaviors. *Journal of Consulting and Clinical Psychology*, 1976, *44*, 155.

Hammen, C. L., & Glass, D. R. Depression, activity, and evaluation of reinforcement. *Journal of Abnormal Psychology*, 1975, *84*, 718–721.

Hammen, C. L., & Krantz, S. Effect of success and failure on depressive cognitions. *Journal of Abnormal Psychology*, 1976, *85*, 577–586.

Hammen, C. L., & Peters, S. D. Interpersonal consequences of depression: responses to men and women enacting a depressed role. *Journal of Abnormal Psychology*, 1978, *87*, 322–332.

Hauck, P. A. *Overcoming depression.* Philadelphia: Westminster Press, 1973.

Hollon, S. D., Beck, A. T., Kovacs, M., & Rush, A. J. Cognitive therapy of depression: an outcome study with six-month follow-up. Paper presented at the Society for Psychotherapy Research, 1977.

Hollon, S. D., & Kendall, P. C. Cognitive self-statements in depression: development of an automatic thoughts questionnaire. manuscript submitted for publication, 1978.

Kelly, G. A. *The Psychology of Personal Constructs* (Vol. 1.). New York: W. W. Norton & Co., 1955.

Klein, D. C., Fencil-Morse, E., & Seligman, M. E. P. Learned helplessness, depression and the attribution of failure. *Journal of Personality and Social Psychology*, 1976, *33*, 508–16.

Klein, D. C., & Seligman, M. E. P. Reversal of performance deficits and perceptual deficits in learned helplessness and depression. *Journal of Abnormal Psychology*, 1976, *85*, 11–26.

Kovacs, M., Rush, A. J., Beck, A. T., & Hollon, S. P. A one year follow-up of depressed outpatients treated with cognitive therapy or pharmacotherapy.

Unpublished manuscript, University of Pennsylvania, School of Medicine, 1979.

Krantz, S., & Hammen, C. The assessment of cognitive bias in depression. Manuscript submitted for publication, 1978.

Lazarus, A. A. Learning theory and the treatment of depression. *Behavior Research and Therapy*, 1968, *6*, 83–89.

Lebow, J. D. The effects of success and failure upon depresse, non-depressed and post-depressed subjects. *Dissertation Abstracts International*, 1975, *35*, (10-B), 5118.

Lewinsohn, P. M. A behavioral approach to depression. In R. Friedman & M. M. Katz, (Eds.), *Psychology of depression: Contemporary theory and research*. New York: Winston/Wiley, 1974.

Lewinsohn, P. M. The behavioral study and treatment of depression. In M. Hersen, R. M. Eisler, & P. M. Miller, (Eds.). *Progress in behavior modification* (Vol. 1). New York: Academic Press, 1975.

Lewinsohn, P. M., Biglan, A., & Zeiss, A. M. Behavioral treatment of depression. In P. O. Davidson, *The behavioral management of anxiety, depression and pain*. New York: Brunner/Mazel, 1976.

Lewinsohn, P. M., & Graf, M. Pleasant activities & depression. *Journal of Consulting and Clinical Psychology*, 1973, *41*, 261–268.

Lewinsohn, P. M., & Libet, J. Pleasant events, activity schedules and depression. *Journal of Abnormal Psychology*, 1972, *79*, 291–295.

Lewinsohn, P. M., Weinstein, M. & Shaw, D. Depression: a clinical-research approach. In R. O. Rubin & C. M. Frank (Eds.), *Advances in behavior therapy, 1968*. New York: Academic Press, 1969.

Lishman, W. A. Selective factors in memory. Part 2: Affective disorder. *Psychological Medicine*, 1972, *2*, 248–253.

Lloyd, G. G., & Lishman, W. A. Effect of depression on the speed of recall of pleasant and unpleasant experiences. *Psychological Medicine*, 1975, *5*, 173–180.

Loeb, A., Beck, A. T., & Diggory, J. Differential effects of success and failure on depressed and nondepressed patients, *Journal of Nervous and Mental Disease*, 1971, *152*, 106–114.

Loeb, A., Beck, A. T., Diggory, J. D., & Tuthill, R. Expectancy, level of aspiration, performance, and self-evaluation in depression. *Proceedings of the 75th Annual Convention of the American Psychological Association*, 1967, *2*, 193–194.

Loeb, A., Feshback, S., Beck, A. T., & Wolf, A. Some effects of reward upon the social perception and motivation of psychiatric patients varying in depression. *Journal of Abnormal and Social Psychology*, 1964, *68*, 609–616.

Lubin, B. Adjective check lists for measurement of depression. Archives of General Psychiatry, 1965, 12, 57–62.

Lunghi, M. E. The stability of mood and social perception measures in a sample of depressive in-patients. British Journal of Psychiatry, 1977, 130, 598–604.

McNair, D. M., Lorr, M., & Droppleman, L. F. Manual for the profile of mood states. San Diego, Calif.: Educational and Industrial Testing Service, 1971.

McNitt, P. C., & Thornton, D. W. Depression and perceived reinforcement: A reconsideration. Journal of Abnormal Psychology, 1978, 87, 137–140.

Melges, F. T., & Bowlby, J. Types of hopelessness in psychopathological process. Archives of General Psychiatry, 1969, 20, 690–699.

Melges, F. T., & Weisz, A. E. The personal future and suicidal ideation. Journal of Nervous and Mental Disease, 1971, 153, 244–250.

Miller, W. R., & Seligman, M. E. P. Learned helplessness, depression and the perception of reinforcement. Behavior Research and Therapy, 1976, 14, 7–17.

Miller, W. R., & Seligman, M. E. P. Depression and learned helplessness in man. Journal of Abnormal Psychology, 1975, 84, 228–38.

Minkoff, K., Bergman, E., Beck, A. T., & Beck, R. Hopelessness, depression, and attempted suicide. American Journal of Psychiatry, 1973, 130, 455–459.

Morris, N. E. A group of self-instruction method for the treatment of depressed outpatients. Unpublished doctoral dissertation, University of Toronto, 1975.

Moyal, B. A study of depression-related variables in children. Journal of Consulting and Clinical Psychology, 1977, 45(5), 951–952.

Nelson, R. E., & Craighead, W. E. Selective recall of positive and negative feedback, self-controlled behaviors, and depression. Journal of Abnormal Psychology, 1977, 86, 379–388.

Neuringer, C. Dichotomous evaluations in suicidal individuals. Journal of Consulting Psychology, 1961, 25, 445–449.

Neuringer, C. Dichotomous evaluations in suicidal individuals. Journal of Consulting Psychology, 1961, 25, 445–449.

Neuringer, C. The cognitive organization of meaning in suicidal individuals. Journal of General Psychology, 1967, 76, 91–100.

Neuringer, C. Divergencies between attitudes toward life and death among suicidal, psychosomatic and normal hospital patients. Journal of Consulting and Clinical Psychology, 1968, 32, 59–63.

O'Reilly, P. O., & Harrison, K. The Gorham Proverbs Test. Disease of the Nervous System, 1960, 32, 59–83.

Pachman, J. S., & Foy, D. W. A correlational investigation of anxiety, self-esteem and depression: new findings with behavioral measures of assertiveness. *Journal of Behavior Therapy and Experimental Psychiatry*, 1978, *9*, 97–101.

Pichot, P., & Lemperiere, T. Analyse factorielle d'un questionnaire d'autoévaluation des symptomes depressifs. *Revue de Psychologie Appliquée*, 1964, *14*, 15–29.

Rehm, L. P. A self-control model of depression. *Behavior Therapy*, 1977, *8*, 787–804.

Rey, A. E., Silber, E., Savard, R. J., & Post, R. M. Thinking and language in depression. Paper presented at meeting of the American Psychiatric Association, Toronto, May, 1978.

Rizley, R. C. Depression and distortion in the attribution of causality. *Journal of Abnormal Psychology*, 1978, *87*(1), 32–48.

Rush, A. J., Beck, A. T., Kovacs, M., & Hollon, S. Comparative efficacy of cognitive therapy and imipramine in the treatment of depressed outpatients. *Cognitive Therapy and Research*, 1977, *1*, 17–37.

Rush, A. J., Khatami, M., & Beck, A. T. Cognitive and behavioral therapy in chronic depression. *Behavior Therapy*, 1975, *6*, 398–404.

Rush, A. J., & Watkins, J. T. Group versus individual cognitive therapy: a pilot study. *Cognitive Therapy and Research*, 1979, in press.

Salzman, L. F., Goldstein, R. H., Atkins, R., & Babigian, H. Conceptual thinking in psychiatric patients. *Archives of General Psychiatry*, 1966, *14*, 55–59.

Schmickley, V. G. The effects of cognitive-behavior modification upon depressed outpatients. Unpublished doctoral dissertation, Michigan State University, 1976. *Dissertation Abstracts International*, 1976, *37*, 987B–988B. University Microfilms No. 76–18, 675.

Seligman, M. E. P. *Helplessness: on depression, development and death*. San Francisco: W. H. Freeman, 1975.

Shaw, B. F. Comparison of cognitive therapy and behavior therapy in the treatment of depression. *Journal of Consulting and Clinical Psychology*, 1977, *45*, 543–551.

Shaw, B. F., & Beck, A. T. The treatment of depression with cognitive therapy. In A. Ellis & R. Grieger (Eds.), *Handbook of rational-emotive theory and practice*. New York: Springer Publishing Co., 1977.

Shipley, C. R., & Fazio, A. F. Pilot study of a treatment for psychological depression. *Journal of Abnormal Psychology*, 1973, *82*, 372–376.

Steiner, R. E. A cognitive-developmental analysis of depression: interpersonal problem solving and event interpretation among depressed and nondepressed women. *Dissertation Abstracts International*, 1975, *35*,(8-B), 4197.

Stockton, C. T. The depressive style of life. *Dissertation Abstracts International*, 1975, *36*, (3-B), 1420–1421.

Strickland, B., Hale, W., & Anderson, L. Effect of induced mood states on activity and self-reported affect. *Journal of Consulting and Clinical Psychology,* 1975, *43,* 587.

Stuart, J. L. Intercorrelations of depressive tendencies, time perspective, and cognitive style variables. Unpublished doctoral dissertation, Vanderbilt University, 1962. *Dissertation Abstracts International,* 1962, *23,* 696. University Microfilms No. 62–3419.

Taylor, F. G., & Marshall, W. L. Experimental analysis of a cognitive-behavioral therapy for depression. *Cognitive Therapy and Research,* 1977, *1,* 59–72.

Teasdale, J. D. Effects of real and recalled success on learned helplessness and depression. *Journal of Abnormal Psychology,* 1978, *87,* 155–164.

Teasdale, J. D., & Bancroft, J. Manipulation of thought content as a determinant of mood and corrugator electromygraphic activity in depressed patients. *Journal of Abnormal Psychology,* 1977, *86,* 235– 241.

Vatz, K. A., Winig, H. R., & Beck, A. T. Pessimism and a sense of future time construction as cognitive distortions in depression. Mimeograph. University of Pennsylvania, 1969.

Velten, E. A laboratory task for induction of mood states. *Behavior Research and Therapy,* 1968, *6,* 473–482.

Watkins, J. T., & Rush, A. J. Cognitive Response Test. Presented at the Twelfth Annual Association for the Advancement of Behavior Therapy Convention, Chicago, November 18, 1978.

Weintraub, M., Segal, R., & Beck, A. T. An investigation of cognition and affect in the depressive experiences of normal men. *Journal of Consulting and Clinical Psychology,* 1974, *42,* 911.

Weissman, A. W. The Dysfunctional Attitude Scale: A scale designed to measure the relationship between cognitive distortions and emotional disorders. Unpublished doctoral dissertation, University of Pennsylvania, 1977.

Weissman, W. W., & Beck, A. T. A preliminary investigation of the relationship between dysfunctional attitudes and depression. Unpublished manuscript, University of Pennsylvania, 1977.

Weissman, A. N., & Beck, A. T. Development and validation of the Dysfunctional Attitude Scale: a preliminary investigation. Paper presented at the Annual Meeting of the American Educational Research Association, Toronto, 1978.

Wener, A. E., & Rehm, L. P. Depressive affect: A test of behavioral hypotheses. *Journal of Abnormal Psychology,* 1975, *84,* 221–227.

Wetzel, R. D. Hopelessness, depression, and suicide intent. *Archives of General Psychiatry,* 1976, *33,* 1069–1073.

Wortman, C. B., Panciera, L., Shusterman, L., & Hibacher, J. Attributions of casuality and reactions to uncontrollable outcomes. *Journal of Experimental Social Psychology,* 1976, *12,* 301–316.

Zuckerman, M., & Lubin, B. *Manual for the Multiple Affect Adjective Check List.* San Diego, Calif.: Educational and Industrial Testing Service, 1965.

Chapter 4

SELF-ACCEPTANCE PROBLEMS

John Boyd
Russell Grieger

Self-esteem is a concept which mental health professionals endorse as central to understanding personality and psychopathology. It is among those rare concepts that almost all therapeutic approaches seem intent on enhancing or improving (Adler, 1974; Berne, 1964; Branden, 1971, Freud, 1963; Jung, 1954; Perls, 1969; Rogers, 1961).

Cognitive systems in general, and RET in particular, take a rather radical position with regard to self-esteem. Simply stated, a major premise of RET is that pursuing or promoting self-esteem is an indubitably destructive endeavor and that therapeutic effect had best be made to get people to give up their self-esteem (Ellis, 1973, 1974, 1975, 1976). The authors support this position and will endeavor to define what self-esteem is and why it is destructive. We will then describe an alternative concept, self-acceptance, and show why being self-accepting, rather than self-esteeming, is more theoretically valid and pragmatically tenable. Following this, we will discuss emotional disturbances in which self-esteem issues are both central and secondary.

SELF-ESTEEM

The first personality theorist to focus on self-esteem as a central theoretical concept was Alfred Adler (1927). He posited that humans have an innate inferiority resulting from their infantile experience of complete helplessness, and that the remainder of their lives are motivated to a great extent by strivings to overcome their basic sense of inadequacy. From this point of view, much human behavior is motivated by a drive to compensate for low self-esteem.

Other early theorists attending to self-esteem, such as James (1890), Mead (1934), Horney (1950), and Fromm (1947), did not give the concept as primary a position as did Adler, and usually self-esteem was treated as one of several divisions of the total self, or the product of other fundamental personality processes. These theorists also tended to view self-esteem as a function of one's *learned attribution of worth*. One of the strongest contemporary explanations for the acquired nature of self-esteem comes from Rogers (1951, 1961). He has stressed that during the formative years children internalize the attitudes which they perceive significant others to have toward them. From these perceptions and internalizations they form self-attitudes which are carried for the remainder of their lives. "Self-regard" was Rogers's term for the personal worth which individuals create from their perceptions of others' reactions toward them.

This brief review is by no means exhaustive. There are numerous personality theories which include self-esteem as a major construct and each one has a somewhat different explanation for the antecedents of one's self-attribution of worth. Yet, there are similarities and common dimensions among these theories, and Coopersmith's (1967) analysis of them has yielded four interrelated and overlapping factors which contribute to the development of self-esteem: (1) treatment from significant others, (2) history of successes, (3) values and aspirations, and (4) style of defending self-esteem.

The first antecedent factor has already been mentioned in

regard to the position of Rogers and other phenomenologists. Rogers stresses that the facilitative relationship conditions of empathy, unconditional acceptance, and honesty, expressed through the behavior of significant others, encourages recipients to value themselves. Our self-esteem is built upon the attitude that others value us, and this attitude is most likely to arise when we receive facilitative relationship conditions.

History of success is the second antecedent of self-esteem, that is, the extent of which we have accomplished what we set out to do and have received social recognition for these accomplishments. By achieving valued goals we develop an "I can do it" belief, a sense of power and competence; and respectful treatment from other people is usually a by-product as well. But underlying success experiences are values and aspirations—the criteria by which we determine if a success has been achieved. One person's attainment of a sought-after goal may be viewed as a success by that individual, but be meaningless to someone else who does not aspire to or value the goal. Consequently, the development and constellation of one's values and aspirations is a prime determinant in self-esteem.

The fourth antecedent factor is one's manner of responding to negative personal events, such as failing at an important task, receiving negative appraisals from significant others, and having personal limitations. Sullivan (1953) has set forth the widely accepted notion that people continually guard against a loss of self-esteem, and they experience anxiety when they anticipate devaluation or are demeaned by others or themselves. Individuals differ in their ability to successfully deal with threatening circumstances and in their styles of responding. Many resort to distortions of reality as a defensive measure and thereby relinquish a degree of sanity. They lack the crucial mental health skill of "[defining] an event filled with negative implications and consequences in such a way that it does not detract from [one's] sense of worthiness, ability, or power" (Coopersmith, 1967, p. 37).

These four antecedents of self-esteem offer an eclectic foothold on the question of from where self-esteem comes. But in RET these antecedents are viewed as experiences which give rise to several *faulty* and *self-defeating* propositions, including the following major three (Ellis, 1974, 1976).

First, people equal their traits, particularly their character traits. Thus, if they have significantly bad traits, then they rate as bad people and justifiably have low self-esteem; if they have good traits, however, they rate as good people and can rightfully claim positive self-esteem.

This proposition represents faulty reasoning because it is predominantly an overgeneralization, suggesting that any individual trait or cluster of traits can legitimately generalize to the whole person. But, how can one or several aspects of a person equal all of him or her? It is like saying that a whole basket of fruit is rotten because one apple is spoiled. Do not people have almost unlimited traits that change from day to day? How can any person know all his or her traits in order to make a judgment? Where is the table of weights to differentially value certain traits over others? By what formula do we do the weighing—addition, geometry, multiplication? The questions such a proposition raises are many and the answers suggest that the proposition itself is senseless.

Second, people must succeed in life, must win the love of those whom they find significant, and must survive comfortably and happily. To do so gives them personal worth, or high self-esteem; to fail to do so makes them unworthy, or of low-esteem.

This proposition is blatantly false for a number of reasons. For one, it sets up absolute standards for self-worth, all of which are magical and tautological (Ellis, 1974, 1976). There are simply no universal, scientific standards for success. Furthermore, if people have low self-worth because of failures in their various enterprises, love affairs, and efforts for contentment, then by definition we must define all people as worthless, for all have surely failed in one or more of these at some point in their lives. No one is so totally outstanding or infallible to succeed all the time. Finally, there are numerous practical disadvantages of holding such a view, not the least of which are anxiety over failure and loss of creativity and spontaneity.

Third, people must have self-worth, or prove to themselves

that they have self-worth, in order to accept and respect themselves. Furthermore, they must be convinced that they are worthwhile in order to be happy and enjoy their lives.

In addition to all the fallacies of the first two propositions, this one is blatantly tautological. For it argues that self-worth is a criteria for happiness where no evidence exists that this is the case. In fact, as we shall soon discuss, those who are most happy, fulfilled, and free from psychological symptoms are those who basically stop worrying about whether or not they are worthwhile.

These, then, are the faulty propositions upon which self-esteeming is based. But, what about the consequence of the esteeming process? What happens when an individual rates himself or herself as unworthy and ends up with low self-esteem (LSE)?

A review of the self-esteem literature, a monumental task because of the plethora of articles and books on the subject, will produce many personality and psychopathological characteristics which have been clinically and/or empirically associated with LSE. For example, research has shown that individuals with high self-esteem (HSE) versus those with LSE exhibit a greater degree of interpersonal influence, are less likely to identify with their negative attributes, are less easily persuaded by threatening communications, and improve more after a success (Schneider & Turkat, 1975).

Coopersmith's (1967) overview of his and others' self-esteem studies extends the foregoing profile even further. Evidence suggests that, when compared with LSE people, those with HSE tend to:

1. Have lower anxiety and less psychosomatic symptoms, and in general are better at dealing with threatening situations;
2. Are more emotionally active and responsive, and are more likely to have deep interpersonal relationships;
3. Are more competent and effective, and have more positive expectations for success and less anticipation of failure and helplessness;

4. Set higher goals for themselves, and are prone to reach them;
5. Are more independent and creative;
6. Are more likely to be socially accepted, and have poise and social skills.

In view of the characteristics described, it is clear that LSE is a psychological liability. It should be stressed, however, that LSE certainly does not guarantee an inadequate personality, for there are those who struggle with a feeling of low worth yet maintain stable and productive lives. And there are probably many LSEers who have only a few of the problematic characteristics which have been described. Furthermore, LSE seems to exist in degree (Coopersmith, 1967), and a moderate level of LSE may not be as destructive to one's functioning as a chronic level. But substantive empirical and clinical evidence does indicate that LSE is a dimension within psychopathology which is widespread, deleterious to psychological health, and worthy of therapeutic treatment.

Holding ourselves in HSE is the other side of the coin. Is not this, however, unquestionably a desirable goal, one to strive for? The answer is No! When people hold themselves in high esteem, they are engaging in the same irrational process of evaluating their total worth based on some personal characteristic or on the affection offered by another. Thus to maintain HSE, people *must* continue to display their characteristic of worth and to maintain the affection from others—a highly anxious state of affairs; and, if they fail in this task, they lose their tenuous hold on self-esteem.

Those people who are blessed with many of the characteristics we associate with personal worth sometimes create a particularly troublesome problem for themselves. They become egotistical and narcissistic. Genuinely though neurotically believing they have more value than others, they act upon this belief in selfish and self-centered ways. When their criteria for aggrandizement slips away, as is eventually the case, their grandeur vanishes and they fall quickly to the depths of LSE. Suicides consequent to commercial failings are everpresent in contemporary society.

Self-Acceptance

The concept of self-acceptance is central to the theory of RET and a primary goal of a good many RET endeavors. Contrasted with self-esteem, self-acceptance starts from the premise that human beings are too multifaceted to be rated or evaluated as a total entity. With such human complexity, and with no means or tools to do such a rating anyway, self-acceptance means giving up the philosophical set of person rating and simply attending to one's traits skills, or performances, either individually or in small clusters.

Given that self-acceptance is more philosophically sound and psychologically helpful than self-esteem, there are several basic propositions which follow (Ellis, 1976). These are objective and valid statements about human nature which replace self-rating and a sense of self based on evaluative thinking.

1. Despite the almost infinite individual manifestations, people generally have two major goals or purposes in life: (a) to remain alive and (b) to live with a maximum of happiness and a minimum of pain.
2. People have an ongoing aliveness that continues for a certain period of time and then comes to an end.
3. People have a multitude of traits that make them separate and different from others, giving them uniqueness. Although some of these traits change, a good many have consistency over time, giving people an "identity" or "self" all their own.
4. People have awareness of their ongoingness and their traits. They can, within limits, therefore plan for their future, change some of their traits, discover what they enjoy, and work to realize their enjoyment.
5. People have awareness of themselves. They can choose to value themselves based on how well they do in meeting their goals; they can choose to value themselves on the grounds that it simply feels better and makes more practical sense to do so; or they can choose to unconditionally accept themselves, simply because

they are alive and because they realize that *self*-rating is both impossible and pernicious.

To summarize these propositions, RET strongly advises people to stop their self-rating process, never jumping from self-acceptance and trait-rating to self-esteeming and self-rating. Why? Because self-acceptance follows the rules of scientific evidence; because a self-acceptance stance does not hinder people from attaining their basic goals and, in fact, serves to facilitate them; and because self-acceptance certainly does not lead to the emotional problems that self-esteeming sooner or later does.

In the final analysis, RET proposes two alternatives to self-rating (Ellis, 1976; Ellis & Harper, 1975). The less elegant alternative is for people to arbitrarily define themselves as good or esteemable simply because they exist, thus making themselves feel worthwhile. The more elegant alternative is for people to recognize their extreme complexity, to acknowledge that any attempt at rating is scientifically doomed, and to recognize that they have no intrinsic worth, but rather aliveness. People can and certainly "should" rate their traits, for this will facilitate their meeting their goals; but in addition they can fully accept themselves no matter what helpful or harmful traits they discover.

Self-Rating and Emotional Disturbance

RET places a central focus on LSE and considers it to be a primary etiological factor in many forms of psychopathology. In the words of Ellis (1965): "Perhaps the most common self-defeating belief of a highly disturbed patient is his conviction that he is a worthless, inadequate individual who essentially is undeserving of self-respect and happiness" (p. 1).

The authors endorse Ellis's statement and suggest that most clients who seek mental health treatment have self-esteem problems that are either primary or concomitant to other concerns. An explanation of how LSE fits into various emotional-behavioral problems is given later in this chapter, but first it is appropriate to more extensively describe self-rating.

As mentioned earlier, the ideational process by which individuals create LSE and accompanying emotional disturbance is termed "self-rating"—the tendency to rate one's acts, behaviors, and performances as good or bad, and to generalize this evaluation to one's entire worth. It is a habitual tendency that may occur without the individual's awareness, and can exist in episodic bursts or as a chronic and continuous stream of meaning which may monopolize one's mind.

Ellis (1977a) contends that all human beings are predisposed to self-rating, and there is a significant amount of support for his claim. The clinician need not ask *if* the client self-rates, but rather *how much* and *in what manner*. Poorly adjusted individuals chronically engage in self-rating and make it a way of life, and even the most stable people self-rate now and then. For example, we therapists might only rarely put ourselves down for making an everyday goof, but criticize our therapy and look out! We tie our self-worth to our therapeutic expertise, and we angrily defend our perceived competence and/or criticize ourselves for not reaching high standards of success.

Self-rating varies not only in degree but also in form. While each person probably has his or her own personalistic way of self-rating, and it is imperative that the empathic therapist decipher these unique pathologies, it is also possible to identify common forms of self-rating. One fairly standard form for adolescents is a preoccupation with physical appearance. A male college student in therapy with one of the authors is an illustrative case. He walks across campus with his eyes darting from one male to the next, continuously comparing his appearance to theirs. He gives particular attention to couples, asking himself the question: "Would that girl choose me over the guy she's with?" This form of self-rating is not unusual and for most adolescents it passes as they learn to accept their physical appearance.

Another common form of self-rating was demonstrated by a female client who drove herself toward an *ideal self-image*. When her performances and characteristics were not close approximations of the ideal person she *demanded* she be, she would experience acute depression. At other times, when fearing that she would not measure up to her ideal image, she would have anxiety attacks. The seriousness of her striving was directly expressed one day when the therapist asked: "How would you feel if I told you there was a ceiling on your development and you would never reach your ideal self, and that you must live the rest of your life just the way you are?" The client thought for a moment and then said in a very convincing and determined tone: "I wouldn't want to live any longer."

This case is a classic example of what Horney (1950) has termed the "ideal self" in neurotic adjustment. Some people have such a deficit in self-esteem that they create a perfect self to strive toward, a self that is undeniably of high worth. It represents an overcompensation for their perceived low worth, and serves as the criterion for self-rating.

A third form of self-rating which usually leads to LSE, guilt, and depression, is comparing oneself to inflexible and unrealistic moral and religious standards, and then condemning oneself for not being perfectly moral and saintly. The pathology in this form of self-rating does not lie in morality or religion, but in the idea that one is first and foremost worthless, and the only redemption and route to self-worth is attainment of perfect morality and sainthood.

Recently a client sought my (J.B.) help for just such a problem. He was a bright and overly conscientious graduate student who was being strongly influenced by a fundamentalist religious sect. He was laden with guilt and anxiety, and had periodic flights of panic. Every day offered him more evidence that he was a "lost soul": he had not *totally* given his life to the church; he suspected that some of his behavior was motivated by unconscious, immoral motives; and he couldn't read God's "signs" as well as his religious friends. Seeking therapy for his emotional problems was also a sinful act, because he had been told that true Christians "put their lives in the hands of the Lord."

Within the forms and styles of self-rating there are some similar cognitive characteristics. Excessive personalization and introspection are usually present as an overabundance of stimuli are examined for their relationship to one's self and value. Also, Beck (1976) and Berger (1974) advise clinicians to look for thinking disorders such as overgeneralization, dicotomous reasoning, polarized thinking, and adherence to absolutistic rules. These mechanisms create distortions of reality, and compounding this genesis are existing irrational beliefs noted earlier.

To summarize, RET theory says that self-rating is a uniquely human trait that causes defensiveness and LSE, and precipitates a host of other emotional-behavioral disturbances. Self-rating is an irrational cognitive process based on unprovable self-esteem questions, illogical reasoning, and bona fide thinking disorders.

Approval and Performance Anxiety

Two criteria that people frequently use as indicators of self-worth are approval from others and successful performances. The irrational inferences are: "I'm of value if others value me," and "I'm worthwhile because I am good at this performance and because others tell me I'm good when I perform well."

People who use others' approval and excellent performances as self-rating criteria are putting their self-worth on the line at all times. They are constantly under threat, and therefore experience an abundance of anxiety. Unfortunately this anxiety tends to fulfill their worst expectancies because it causes them to be socially inept and clumsy, overly subservient, and to behave in other unattractive ways. As for performances, anxiety can ruin proficiency; and even if individuals can somehow produce a high-level performance their anxiety is hardly worth the price. In RET the stream of meaning behind approval and performance anxiety is brought to awareness, challenged, and worked through. Although each person has unique properties in his or her mediational flow, the four themes of irrationality are usually prominent.

> "I must have their approval; it would be *terrible* to have them dislike me. I *couldn't stand* that; if they don't like me it must mean there's something wrong with me—that I'm *not worthy* of their approval."
>
> "Since this performance is terribly important to me, I've just *got to* do well; I *can't* be satisfied with a mediocre showing; if I don't do well it will prove how ordinary I am, that I'm not really good at anything, just *an incompetent*."

Approval and performance anxiety are LSE symptoms brought on by self-rating. They sometimes indicate a primary self-esteem problem, and frequently they reveal LSE as a concomitant when other problems are first order.

Self-Downing Depression

Most clinicians are trained to treat depression as solely an affective disturbance with secondary symptoms. In contrast to this view, the work of Beck (1972, 1976), Ellis (1962), and Seligman (1975) posits that the distorted views of depressed persons is central to the development and maintenance of their disturbance.

Self-rating is one of the major cognitive dimensions associated with depression. While anticipation of being shown to be worthless leads to anxiety, actually putting yourself down or rating yourself as bad for an act or any other reason will produce guilt and depression. In fact, the anxiety-depression sequence is a typical pattern for people with long-standing emotional problems, for they get anxious before a performance because they may find themselves worthless, and they make themselves depressed afterwards by concluding they are worthless.

Clinicians make a critical mistake when they fail to see self-downing in depression. It is easier to see the client's demandingness and awfulizing, such as in the following monologue: "Life is just overwhelming; I lost my job, my wife left me, what's the use in going on. . . . There's nothing to live for."

In this brief expression the depressed person exhibits the attitude that life should be easier, a catastrophic fate has been unfairly dumped on him, and the future will be just as bad. Also hidden among these depressive ideas is self-downing.

> Life is just overwhelming, *and I'm too weak to handle it.*
> I lost my job, *because I'm so incompetent.*
> My wife left me, *showing that I'm unlovable; she discovered what a louse I am.*
> There's nothing to live for, *I'm so worthless my life doesn't have a value to anyone else, not even to me.*

Sometimes depressed individuals are also guilty, and they advocate more than their own lack of value—they promote their badness. By "self-blaming" they entertain the non sequitur of "I am despicable, totally and forever, because I did a bad act." This attitude leads to acute guilt and depression, and the clinician should watch for suicidal thoughts and plans.

Secondary Gain and Self-Rating

Genuine self-rating and blaming leads to serious levels of anxiety, guilt, and depression—a level of distress which is debilitating. The people doing this self-rating are often not aware of their cognitive habit, and they ignorantly express a true belief in their unworthiness without realizing what they are saying. Their irrational beliefs and self-rating is hidden between the lines, symbolically expressed, and only on occasion does it slip out.

Another type of self-rating has different signs. The level of emotional distress is problematic but not chronic, and the self-raters openly discuss their LSE. These are often signs of self-rating which have become a neurotic way of life, a mode of behavior which is rewarded by secondary gains such as sympathy and attention from others, relief from responsibilities, and an avoidance of other impending problems such as marital difficulties, decisions, or career failures. Masochistic self-blamers have a particularly interesting secondary gain. They admonish themselves, but then follow up this condemnation with the hidden idea that "I'm good for recognizing how bad I am and punishing myself."

Secondary gains are not the only reason for clients to dwell on their LSE during therapy. Their self-flagellating tactic may actually be camouflaging more threatening issues, and the therapist must cut through this defensive maneuver.

In a recent supervision session one of the authors (J.B.) listened to an audio tape of a female client who initiated and engaged the therapist in a discussion of her LSE. The supervisor's sense of "something amiss" grew, and after finally learning that the LSE discussion has extended over two sessions, the pieces fell together. By reevaluating the case a new diagnosis was reached; the client had been *demanding* rather than self-rating. Shoulds, oughts, and musts were responsible for more distress than self-rating, and when the therapist followed this diagnostic path the case quickly improved. Though the client offered some resistance at first, she quickly gained insight into her demandingness, and emotional and behavioral changes followed as the therapist and client entered the "working-through stage" of RET.

Self-Rating and Anger Problems

Another set of problems that often involve self-rating has to do with anger. Grieger (1977) has described an anger reaction which has LSE and self-rating at its core (see the chapter in this text by Grieger). The syndrome begins with one's self-esteem being tied to external critiera (approval, performance, etc.), and the anxiety one feels when these criteria are threatened. Instead of focusing on one's self-worth and feeling anxious or depressed, however, the angry individual takes the protective course of condemning the threatening agent. With defensively aggressive behavior the individual attacks to protect his or her self-esteem.

This kind of defensive anger is difficult to diagnose, because the irrational themes of demandingness, awfulizing, and condemnation of others are all involved. But the reason for these themes— the reason most hidden from the angry person—is a threat to self-esteem. For example, in response to disrespectful treatment the person with "ego or self-worth anger" concludes: "Their actions show disrespect, like I'm not significant and therefore I must not be significant. Those bums shouldn't do such an awful thing to me; I'll show them!"

Self-worth anger illustrates how self-rating interacts with other irrational themes to create a formidable emotional-behavioral problem. It also shows how self-rating and LSE can be hidden at the deepest levels of a neurotic difficulty which seems to belie insecurity. When dealing with anger and aggression clinicians may want to heed Ellis's (1977b) advice: "The first, and perhaps the most important of the emotive methods of overcoming anger, consists of unconditional self-acceptance or self-acknowledgment" (p.8).

Procrastination and Self-Esteem

Procrastination is one of those "little problems" that can mirror larger psychological difficulties. That is, clients at mental health centers and other psychiatric facilities frequently present themselves as "basket cases," completely debilitated by anxiety, depression, or whatever, and as they describe their symptoms and complaints they say in passing: "I can't get anything done; I'm always late; I've put off this appointment for months; somehow I just can't get myself to do the things I want to do," and so forth. Therapists don't give procrastination as the diagnosis in such cases, but procrastination may well be a microcosm of the client's overall difficulties.

At counseling centers and guidance clinics procrastination is more often the sole presenting concern; sometimes it is so commonplace that counselors take it for granted. In academic settings where deadlines abound for tests and term papers, procrastination is indigenous to student life.

There are many ideational antecedents for procrastination, and Ellis and Knaus (1977) have devoted an entire book to the subject. A lack of self-discipline and low frustration tolerance are the most well-known causes of procrastination. But self-rating and LSE also give rise to procrastination, and in a two-step manner. First, individuals are afraid to do a certain act because they unknowingly fear failure or rejection and therewith their self-esteem; so they put off the threatening act, even though its completion would have desirable consequences for them, for fear of proving their worthlessness. Second, they observe the delay they have chosen, find it disgusting, and condemn themselves for it, further fostering LSE.

Miscellaneous Emotional Disturbances and Self-Rating

As mentioned earlier, there are a host of emotional disturb-ances and symptoms which can be precipitated, primarily or in part, by self-rating. In some of these disturbances self-rating is so obvious that laymen can spot it, but in others the client's symptoms may seem to bizarre or serious to be linked with LSE. A couple of case examples will be offered to show how self-rating can be unobtrusively present in psychopathology.

Frank was a young man in his early twenties whose comple-ment of problems justified the label "obsessive-compulsive neuro-sis." Of keenest concern to Frank were sensory obsessions which interfered and sometimes prohibited his work and social life. These obsessions consisted of counting eyeblinks, swallows, breaths, and having obsessive bladder sensations which prompted dry-run bathroom trips. Frank was also susceptible to worrying in general, and an irrational fear about being accosted by homosex-uals caused paranoia-like suspicions.

There were a few situational/learning circumstances in Frank's background which could explain some of the origins for his symptoms. The onset of bladder sensations was traced back to an academic examination which was critical to his professional career; he sat through four hours of testing while fighting off bladder pains, the urge to urinate, and a fear of impairing his performance if he took time to go to the bathroom. Another historical origin was a childhood experience involving an apparent pedophiliac, and a joking comment years later from an adolescent friend who commented that Frank had the physical appearance of a "fag." Frank put these two experiences together and created the fear that he somehow attracted homosexuals, and that he might have latent homosexual strivings.

The mediational core of Frank's obsessional symptoms was two-fold. A symptom would always begin with "awfulizing" thoughts about something which he feared might happen, such as flunking a test, being socially criticized, or becoming a homosexual. As he then became anxious he would then begin to fear that this anxiety would bring on an obsession and, true to his prophesy, it would. The scenario ended as Frank obsessed for hours.

Relaxation training, desensitization, and RET were successful in helping Frank reduce his awfulizing and his approval and performance anxieties. He learned to dispute many of his irrational ideas; through homework assignments he confronted and worked through obsessional tendencies, and after 10 sessions his symptoms were minimal. Even when anxiety and obsessions did crop up he could effectively send them away with concentrated rational thinking. Both Frank and the therapist were pleased with the success of their efforts; presenting problems were overcome, but, there had been a costly omission in therapy. They did not work long enough or hard enough on Frank's LSE and self-rating. Though this aspect of Frank's problems was touched, most of their time in therapy was taken up with other forms of distortion.

Two years later Frank returned to therapy with what seemed like a new set of obsessional tendencies. He was being influenced by a fundamentalist religious sect, experienced excessive guilt and anxiety, and found himself going to extreme lengths to prove his honesty and morality to others. To make a long story short, this time the therapist directly challenged Frank's self-rating practices, and together a successful assault was made on his low opinion of himself. This strategy should have been vigorously employed in Frank's first therapy stint, for self-rating had always been behind his sensory obsessions. It was the irrational foundation which fostered the approval and performance anxiety which eventually escalated into obsessions.

Another set of emotional disturbances which can obfuscate self-rating is relationship and sexual difficulties. Symptoms such as volatile emotions, poor communication, and psychosomatic ailments tend to mask the fact that the self-esteem of both partners is critical to their relationship. When one or both partners have LSE and use the other's behavior for his or her self-rating purposes, a weak and dependent relationship will develop. This point has been beautifully expressed in Gibran's (1976) *The Prophet:*

Give your hearts, but not into each other's keeping.
For only the hand of life can contain your hearts.
And stand together yet not too near together:
For the pillars of the temple stand apart,
And the oak tree and the cypress grow not in each others shadow (p. 16).

Hank and Millie are a tragic story of a couple, each having LSE. They have been married for 18 years, are in their middle 40s, and throughout their marriage have maintained an ongoing series of hostile battles. Each partner feels insecure and demands a constant flow of affection from the other. They expect each other to be completely devoted and to meet their every whim. When their partner fails to meet these demands and expectancies, they feel "hurt" (a loss of esteem), condemn the partner, and retaliate by withholding affection (including sex) and making cruel, derogatory remarks.

Marital therapy for Hank and Millie has been unsuccessful because in each other's presence they refuse to do anything but battle. Individual therapy for each one has been of limited success, but only when the therapist exerts full intervention to self-esteem. Relative calm arrives in their marriage only on rare occasions when each has had a profitable therapy session and has temporarily stopped rating both his or herself and the other party.

RET FOR SELF-ESTEEM PROBLEMS

The bulk of this chapter has explained self-esteem from a RET perspective, and the outline of a diagnostic structure has been sketched. Left untouched, however, has been therapeutic treatment. How can self-esteem problems be effectively resolved through psychotherapy?

In a recent published text (Grieger & Boyd, 1979), the authors have answered the "how" question at length, and to conclude this chapter an overview of RET for self-esteem problems will be offered. As has been presented, the demon which generates LSE is the human predisposition to self-rate, and the ideal solution to the self-rating is a cessation of self-rating and the introduction of self-acceptance. To bring about this, or an approximation thereof, RET progresses through four stages which influence the client to make constructive changes in the cognitive, emotive, and behavioral realms.

The first stage of RET, *psychodiagnosis,* is aimed at helping clients describe their emotional disturbances while simultaneously the therapist is soliciting diagnostically relevant information. A diagnosis is reached when the therapist understands the overall disturbance via the A-B-C paradigm. Diagnosis can be made quickly by experienced RET therapists when client problems are typical, though the therapist remains open and may alter a diagnosis later in therapy. A longer diagnostic stage may be required for unfamiliar or complex disturbances. Regarding self-esteem problems, the diagnostic tasks are to categorize self-rating as a primary or secondary cognitive process, to ferret out the client's personalistic content in self-rating, and to determine if and how other irrational beliefs are contributing to the disturbance.

Following diagnosis is the *insight stage* of RET. Here the objective is to promote clients' understanding of their irrational beliefs and the way they use them to create emotional disturbance. Insights pertaining to LSE revolve around self-rating; clients learn that they do self-rate, how they self-rate, and the emotional and behavioral consequences of self-rating. Attention is given to the antecedents of LSE only if there is an unusual clinical reason to do so. Awareness of past history does not lift present day disturbances or the self-rating habit, but somtimes a client gains motivation to overcome self-rating if he or she can see that it was encouraged and practiced by significant others.

The *working-through stage* of RET overlaps with the insight stage. Working through consists of persistently exerting efforts which are designed to therapeutically rehabilitate the cognitive, emotional, and behavioral aspects of a psychological problem. RET is directed at the tripartite constitution of self-esteem problems: irrational beliefs and cognitive distortions, emotional and imaginal operations, and overt behavior. There are a host of techniques for each modality, such as cognitively disputing irrational beliefs and replacing them with rational attitudes, practicing emotive-imagery exercises, and behavioral homework assignments which force one to confront and give up self-defeating actions. To illustrate, clients having LSE are usually asked within the RET session to challenge and logically argue against their self-rating ideas, or perhaps to switch roles with the therapist and solve a mock LSE problem which parallels their own. Shame-attacking assignments, an emotive method, encourage LSE clients to deliberately do something they neurotically consider shameful, and to thus confront, experience, and defuse a self-rating criterion. A procrastinating self-rater might use the behavioral technique of self-managed reward and penalty in order to get things done.

As the working-through stage progresses there are therapeutic changes in the ideas, emotions, and behavior of LSE clients. A most important change is to slow down the self-rating process, and to wage a battle against it. Clients learn to notice when they are self-rating and to actively dispute these cognitions *in vivo*. Behavior begins to shift toward the confident-assertive realm, through effort rather than magic. New actions may feel foreign and take clients into threatening experiences, such as assertively returning a malfunctioning apparatus to a sharp-tongued store clerk, or entering a competition where your error-laden performance will be seen by a crowd of spectators. From such experiences comes the psychological freedom to be oneself.

As cognition and behavior are changing so also is emotion. Anxiety, guilt, depression, and anger lift in proportion to the decrease in self-rating and the increase in self-acceptance. The tripartite resolution to LSE problems can snowball upward, cognitively-emotively-behaviorally, just as the self-rating process takes one downward.

The last RET stage, *reeducation,* is entered and becomes conjoint with working through when clients' therapeutic changes have begun. The purpose of reeducation is to strengthen and engrain rational ways of thinking and behaving, to help clients acquire additional skills (e.g., assertion, decision making) that will assist them to overcome their disturbances, and to help them synthesize their therapeutic learnings and generalize these to their lives and future.

Elegant RET solutions are developed in the reeducation stage as clients make changes in their life philosophies. The obsessive-compulsive client cited twice in this chapter has made significant shifts in his career aspirations and religious beliefs. He has taken much of the irrationality out of both. No longer a workaholic, he does not feel compelled to be corporate president, and has chosen a life based on personal rather than commercial values. Spiritually, his RET assault on self-condemnation has opened up an inner world of self-acceptance which he now supports through his religion.

EPILOGUE

Self-esteem problems are one of our oldest and deadliest enemies—the price we pay for being the only animal species with self-consciousness. For over 2,000 years we have known the enemy is within us, that certain interpretations of events lead to emotional disturbance; yet, we have done so little about this phenomena. It seems fitting and certainly overdue that the same cognitivie capacity by which we have berated ourselves for so long is turned toward logic and reason for the attainment of self-acceptance, happiness, and contentment. This is an ideal worth that our best efforts, and our emotional health is riding on the outcome.

REFERENCES

Adler, A. *The practice and theory of individual psychology*. New York: Harcourt, 1927.

Adler, A. *Understanding human nature*. New York: Fawcett World, 1974.

Beck, A. *Cognitive therapy and the emotional disorders*. New York: International-al Universities Press, 1976.

Beck, A. T. *Depression: Causes and treatment*. Philadelphia: University of Pennsylvania Press, 1972.

Berger, E. Irrational self-censure: The problem and its correction. *Personnel and Guidance Journal*, 1974, *53*(3), 193–198.

Berne, E. *Games people play*. New York: Grove Press, 1964.

Branden, N. *Psychology of self-esteem*. New York: Bantam, 1971.

Coopersmith, S. *The antecedents of self-esteem*. San Francisco: W. H. Freeman and Company, 1967.

Ellis, A. *Reason and emotion in psychotherapy*. New York: Lyle Stuart, 1962.

Ellis, A. *Sex without guilt*. New York: Lyle Stuart, 1965.

Ellis, A. *Growth through reason*. Hollywood, Calif.: Wilshire Books, 1973.

Ellis, A. *Humanistic psychotherapy: The rational-emotive approch*. New York: McGraw-Hill, 1974.

Ellis, A. *How to live with a "neurotic."* New York: Crown, 1975.

Ellis, A. RET abolishes most of the human ego. *Psychotherapy: Theory, Research and Practice*, 1976, *13*(4), 343–348.

Ellis, A. Rational-emotive therapy: Research data that supports the clinical and personality hypotheses of RET and other modes of cognitive-behavior therapy. *The Counseling Psychologist*, 1977, *7*, (1), 2–42. (a)

Ellis, A. *How to live with and without anger*. New York: Thomas Y. Crowell, 1977. (b)

Ellis, A., & Grieger, R. *Handbook of rational-emotive therapy*. New York: Springer, 1977.

Ellis, A., & Harper, R. A. *A new guide to rational living*. Hollywood, Calif.: Wilshire Book Co., 1975.

Ellis, A., & Knaus, W. *Overcoming procrastination*, New York: Institute for Rational Living, 1977.

Epstein, S. The self concept revisited. *American Psychologist*, 1973, *28*(5), 404–416.

Freud, S. *Collected papers*. New York: Collier, 1963.

Fromm, E. *Man for himself*. New York: Rinehart, 1947.

Gibran, Kahlil. *The prophet*. New York: Knopf, 1976.

Grieger, R. Self-concept, self-esteem and rational-emotive theory. *Rational Living*, 1975, *10*, 13–17.

Grieger, R. M. An existential component of anger. *Rational Living*, 1977, *12*(2), 3–8.

Grieger, R., & Boyd, J. *Rational-emotive therapy: A skills-based approach*. New York: Van Nostrand Reinhold, 1979.

Horney, K. *Neurosis and human growth*. New York: W. W. Norton, 1950.

James, W. *Principles of psychology*. New York: Holt, 1890.

Jung, C. *The practice of psychotherapy*. New York: Pantheon Press; 1954.

Mead, G. H. *Mind, self and society*. Chicago: University of Chicago Press, 1934.

Perls, F. *Gestalt therapy verbatim*. Lafayette, California: Real People Press, 1969.

Rogers, C. R. *On becoming a person*. Boston: Houghton Mifflin, 1961.

Schneider, D. J., & Turkat, D. Self-presentation following success or failure: Defensive self-esteem. *Journal of Personality*, 1975, *43*, 127–135.

Seligman, M. *Helplessness: On depression, development and death*. San Francisco: W. H. Freeman, 1975.

Sullivan, H. S. *The interpersonal theory of psychiatry*. New York: W. W. Norton, 1953.

Chapter 5

COGNITION AND MAJOR MENTAL DISORDERS

Eliot Abrahms

In an area which is obviously highly complex and does not easily lend itself to naive oversimplification, it is useful to think of the components of any given major mental disorder as genetic, environmental, and cognitive. These components do not seem in any sense pure; rather, they appear inseparable. Individuals bring their biological make-up to their life experiences, and view these experiences in light of their genetic limitations. In this sense, cognitions can never be divorced from their biological underpinnings. In the major mental disorders, the appearance and maintenance of symptoms seems to be determined by an individual's genetic potential, the kind and degree of his environmental stresses, and the individual's view of these stresses.

To some psychoanalysts and others, the distraught person's associations provide the key to uncovering the role of cognitions for these severe states of emotional disturbance. It is true that any particular experience can evoke widely different meanings and associations, but people symptomatic for a given major mental disorder tend to hold quite similar cognitions relevant to their particular condition. For instance, the depressed person reveals impaired reasoning when he or she thinks his or her worth is at stake, the anxious individual when he or she thinks he or she is in danger (Beck, 1976). Such impaired reasoning can take a number of forms, and vary in degree and intensity. But their variety seems relatively limited and reduceable to a few self-defeating thought patterns, such as, "I *must* have my way, otherwise it is catastrophic and I am a worthless individual!" And, "If others frustrate me in any way, it is horrible!" Given the genetic predisposition toward a particular major mental disorder and faced with stressful life experiences, the individual's irrational cognitions seem to play a principle role in the appearance and continuation of signs and symptoms of severe psychopathology.

Given all this, it seems that the distorted and irrational cognitions of those with major mental disorders are by and large the same as those with other forms of emotional disorders. Because of this, instead of going through much of the same material that is contained in other chapters in this book, I will mention mental disorders and will indicate how cognitions play a role in these.

SCHIZOPHRENIA

Schizophrenia appears to be an excellent example of how genetic, environmental, and cognitive components combine in the manifestation and continuation of major mental disorders. In understanding the etiology of schizophrenia, it has been suggested that genetic factors seem to account for about 80% of the variability and environmental factors account for perhaps 20% (Gottesman, 1979). In this model the so-called "environmental factors" can be seen as comprising both the life experiences and the individual's cognitions about those experiences.

It is believed that this relationship among the biology, environment, and cognitions contributing to a major mental disorder is a dynamic process. In the course of this mechanism, afflicted individuals may vary from being symptomatic to being asymptomatic depending on his or her stress threshold. Given a particular genetic make-up, a particular mental disorder may or may not develop depending on the degree to which environmental stresses are *considered* traumatic. These stressful events are only truly "traumatic" if they are perceived as such.

Stress

Studies examining the association between life events and the signs and symptoms of major mental disorders reveal striking correlations. The onset of psychiatric disorders has been shown to be preceded by an increase in stressful life events (Birley & Brown, 1970; Paykel, Myers, Dienelt, Klerman, Lindenthal, & Pepper, 1969). The accumulation of stresses is more likely to influence psychiatric disorder than the presence of any single stress (Langner & Michael, 1963). Further studies indicate that the greater the stress, the greater the risk of the manifestations of a major mental disorder, regardless of socioeconomic status (Berkman, 1971). But it has been noted that this research has not settled the issue of whether life events can actually cause mental disorders or only cause transient symptoms, thereby increasing the chance that preexisting illness will come to treatment (Robins, 1978).

In the vein of this text, one study concludes that the distressing quality of life events, not merely the life change that they cause, is associated with later onset of a major mental disorder (Tennant & Andrews, 1978). Such a finding seems to imply the importance of cognitive factors in the development of a major mental disorder. Cognitive theory focuses on the attitude that people take toward changes in their life events, rather than on those events themselves. From this point of view, is it not suprising that upsetting cognitions appear to be associated with the development of major mental disorders.

Stressful life events have consistently been found to be related to psychological problems. Relevant studies have concentrated on past stressful changes or events, many fortuitous, most time-limited (Cooper & Sylph, 1978). But it is current social stressors which seem to have an even stronger association with depressive symptoms. Research indicates that current marital stressors appear to have the highest and most significant relationship with depression. Parental stressors (for mothers) and job stressors (for married men) have a statistically significant correlation with depression (Ilfeld, 1977). Making a comparison with past sources of stress, Ilfeld states, "My view is that current social stressors that are patterned into our everyday roles as marital partners, breadwinners, and parents are equally as important in affecting mental status" (Ilfeld, 1977).

Current stressors, then, may be far more important in affecting mental status than past stressors. Traditional theory holds that adverse early life experiences sensitize an individual to future psychological trouble. It appears more likely, however, that a person's vulnerability to stress, in combination with his or her cognitions about this stress, more accurately pinpoint the sources of emotional disturbances.

A disturbed individual who appears to have been made upset by certain early experiences was in all probability vulnerable to disturbance by such experiences to begin with. A negative cognitive set, which continues to the present day, may have been brought to those early "upsetting" life events. In this sense, the stresses that primarily affect mental status have always been and continue to be "current" stressors.

Conscious and Unconscious Factors

Theories emphasizing "the unconscious" place most cognitions out of awareness. Opinions differ on the role of the unconscious in regard to individuals afflicted by major mental disorders. Traditional neuropsychiatry, psychoanalysis, and classical behavior therapy all share the same basic assumption: that the emotionally disturbed individual is victimized by concealed forces over which he or she has no control. The psychoanalytic view has long been that most emotional disturbance rests within the unconscious. Beck (1976) disagrees.

"Freud assumed that peculiar behavior has its roots in the Unconscious, and that any irrationalities observed on the conscious level are only manifestations of the underlying Unconscious drive. The presence of self-deception and distortions, however, does not require the postulation of the Unconscious, as conceived by Freud. Irrationality can be understood in terms of inadequacies in organizing and interpreting reality."

Beck stresses that the theory and practice of cognitively oriented therapy rests on the assumption that "the root to the emotions" lays completely within the realm of consciousness. Contrasting his orientation to that of the psychoanalysts and the behaviorists, he states: "The cognitive approach, however, brings the whole matter of arousal of emotion back within the range of common-sense observation."

Taking an opposing view, Silvano Arieti notes, "Beck believes a person's depression is caused by unpleasant thoughts that are fully conscious . . . But Beck analyzes only the superficial layers . . . The conscious negative ideas that Beck takes into consideration are used by the patient to justify his depression, which has much deeper sources" (Arieti, 1979).

Indeed, Beck may be only partially correct. While some sources of emotional disturbance seem conscious, it also appears that much emotionally and behaviorally associated cognition is out of awareness. Many self-defeating cognitions seem to be within the realm of what is typically considered the preconscious—out of awareness, yet readily acknowledged if inquired about (Ellis & Abrahms, 1978). For instance, many distraught people, first unable to recognize or express thoughts that may be associated with emotional turmoil, will readily admit that they believe their situation is "awful" when asked.

Even in cases in which people consciously verbalize irrational thoughts, they are frequently unaware of any connection between these thoughts and their inappropriate feelings and behaviors. For example, a 42-year-old high school teacher who complained bitterly about feelings of shame and worthlessness was fully aware of his beliefs: "I must impress my students that I am extremely competent during each class, otherwise it is terrible." He was quite unaware, however, of any possible connection between these thoughts and his feeling ashamed and worthless.

SEVERE DEPRESSION

The typical losses precipitating a depressive episode may be apparent, as in the case of a sudden unexpected professional failure. It may also develop from a cumulation of events which the individual may feel relatively deprived for failing to strike an acceptable level in the emotional "give-get balance" (Saul, 1947).

Regardless of the precise nature of adverse experiences inciting depression, cognitive theorists believe that it is one's self-defeating evaluation of these experiences that is more directly responsible for the depression than the experiences themselves (Ellis & Abrahms, 1978). If an individual thinks that he or she is deprived in the emotional "give-get balance," he or she may well believe he or she *should* not be so deprived, and that it is *terrible* that he or she has suffered this deprivation. Therefore, in the individual vulnerable to depression, it appears that precipitating experiences, while contributing to depression, cannot accurately be separated from the individual's view of these experiences.

With this in mind, a number of cognitively oriented theorists take a pluralistic view to the etiology and classification of depression, as they do with all major mental disorders. No single factor is considered "the cause." Biological components, environmental stresses, and cognitions are all considered interactionally in the creation and maintenance of depression. Consistent with this viewpoint, depression is perceived, not as a single discrete condition, but as a variety of associated syndromes.

Personality Factors

Evidence indicates that personality factors influence the development, maintenance, and recurrence of depressive episodes.

Individuals with long-standing neurotic malfunctioning tend to have recurring problems of depression and unfavorable long-term outcomes. This research indicates that personality, not the initial severity of symptoms or past history of depression, is the single most important factor in the prediction of ultimate outcome (Weissman, Prusoff, & Klerman, 1978).

This data is consistent with cognitive theory, for "personality" is closely associated with an individual's characteristic thoughts, attitudes, and evaluations about life experiences. These aspects of personality, which comprise one's cognitive style, appear more closely correlated with ultimate outcome than with any single depressive episode (see Rush & Weissenburger's chapter on depression). Yet, any particular depressive episode suffered by a vulnerable individual may more closely reflect an unusually stressful set of precipitating events than a characteristic manner of evaluating life experiences.

Primary and Secondary Depression

The differences between primary and secondary depression also have implications for cognitive theorists. An individual is said to have a primary affective disturbance when (1) he or she has a manic or a depressive episode and was previously well, or (2) he or she had no other prior major mental disorder except mania or depression. By contrast, an individual is said to have a secondary depression if: (1) he or she has depressive illness after a diagnosis of another major mental disorder; or if (2) a physical illness preceded the symptoms of depression.

One discussion of major interest to cognitive theorists states, "It is possible to conceptualize certain psychiatric illnesses . . . as consisting of a core phasic disorder complicated by secondary defenses, adaptations, and maladaptations. For instance, endogenous-like depression may be secondarily complicated by demoralization" (Zitrin, Klein & Woerner, 1978). It seems that, when disturbed, people often tend to think about their disturbances, whatever that initial disturbance might be, and thereby create additional anxiety, depression, guilt, and hostility (Ellis & Abrahms, 1978). More specifically, some afflicted individuals tend to define their major mental disorders as *awful,* and thereby disturb themselves about their disorders.

Until recently, it has been said that there are no treatment implications in the differentation between primary and secondary depression. A more recent view, however, is that the primary-secondary categorization is perhaps the most useful classification scheme of depression. Under "standard" psychiatric treatment for depressive disorders—pharmacotherapy, electroconvulsive therapy, support, and family counseling—primary depression has a relatively good outcome. On the other hand, evidence indicates that the prognosis for the depressed individual with a physical illness may depend largely on the prognosis of this nonaffective disorder (Akiskal, Briton, Puzantian, Rosenthal, & Walker, 1978).

This suggests that cognitions play a major part in the outcome of affective disorders, including both primary and secondary depression. Many people apparently define a nonremitting disease as catastrophic; in disproportionate numbers some even become hopeless. That cognitive state—hopelessness—has been found to be the best single indicator of an individual's suicidal intent (Beck, 1976).

Unipolar and Bipolar Depression

By definition, those who experience either a single episode or recurrent episodes of depression are said to have major unipolar affective disorder, while those having a history of euphoria, either with or without episodes of depression, are considered to have bipolar major affective disorder.

Unipolar depressives and bipolar individuals in the depressed phase can be distinguished symptomatically in certain ways that indicate broad differences in their cognitions. Compared to bipolar depressed people, those in a unipolar depression seem characterized more by agitated psychomotor activity, hyposomnia, somatic complaints and hypochondriasis, anger directed at self and others (see the Grieger chapter), and possibly increased feelings of anxiety (see chapter by Ellis). On the other hand, bipolar individuals in the depressed phase more often show psychomotor retardation, hypersomnia, fewer somatic complaints, mild or no anger, and possibly less anxiety (Depue & Monroe, 1978).

In terms of cognitive theory and rational-emotive theory in particular, unipolar depressives appear to "awfulize" and "catastrophize" more than those in the depressed phase of bipolar affective disorder. In both unipolar and bipolar major affective disorder, however, self-defeating cognitions, often about stressful life conditions, contribute to the vulnerable individual's major mental disorder.

The nature of the cognitions and associated behaviors of manic-depressives has long intrigued students of human behavior. Psychoanalysts believe that denial is a prominent defense mechanism of the elated stage, and cognitive therapists add that self-defeating thoughts underlie such defenses (Ellis & Abrahms, 1978; Lewin, 1950). According to this reasoning, an individual uses the mechanism of denial to keep out of awareness that which he thinks is "horrible."

The view that particular sets of cognitions may be the foundation for the behavior of persons with bipolar disorder is shared by Beck. He notes that the manic or hypomanic individual sees a substantial improvement in life, and believes that it is these optimistic evaluations which lead to euphoric feelings (Beck, 1976). As Shakespeare said in *Hamlet*, "There's nothing either good or bad, but thinking makes it so." Looking at another aspect of the state of euphoria, the Roman slave Epictitus said, "Men are disturbed, not by things, but by the view which they take of them." The disturbances in this instance are unrealistic and inappropriate feelings and behaviors of overoptimism, and they appear to stem largely from distorted, though pleasure-oriented, perceptions.

Psychoanalysis holds that an abnormal dependent character formation is present in the manic-depressive during remission (Freud, 1936). The manic-depressive, says Arieti, tends "to be a

conformist, willing to accept what he is given by his surroundings
. . . and to rely less than the average person on his own interpretations and evaluations of the external world" (Arieti, 1957).

Research now indicates that remitted manic-depressives do
not differ in terms of positive mental health from those without a
history of emotional disorder. There was no significant difference
in desire to win social approval or in the extent to which they
viewed events in their lives as being under their control (MacVane,
Long, Brown, & Zayat, 1978). "The findings cast serious doubts
on the view pervasive among both the professional and lay
popoulations that holds that remitted individuals with this disorder
are consistently less healthy than the general population," say the
authors of this controlled study, "and casts doubt as well on the
psychodynamic view that these individuals tend to be dependent
on others and the environment to the point of being extremely
externally oriented and other-directed in behavior, attitudes, and
values" (MacVane et al., 1978). By implication of this study,
manic-depressives in remission do not hold irrational ideas to any
greater extent than those in the general population.

PHOBIA

The individual afflicted with a phobic disorder characteristically experiences "irrational, overwhelming, and at times crip-
pling anxiety in the face of a variety of objects or situations that
present, realistically speaking, little or no actual danger" (Nemiah,
1978). But some degree of realistic fear is appropriate for many
objects of phobic anxiety. Lightning does strike people, and planes
do crash—but these outcomes are statistically quite low.

Phobic individuals typically show both logical and empirical
cognitive distortions. The logical misperceptions of a flight phobic
might commonly include such self-statements as: "If I have to take
a plane flight it will be awful, and I couldn't stand the experience!"
The same person, when thinking about the feared flight, may make
the empirical error: "The chance of a plane crash must certainly be
at least fifty-fifty!"

One formulation holds that "antiempirical" evaluations actually stem from "logical" defects in thinking. For instance, the reason our flight phobic may believe he or she has about an even chance of suffering a plane crash is that he or she believes that such a crash would be "awful" (Ellis & Abrahms, 1978).

Looking at another aspect of phobia, Beck notes that one woman with a fear of heights, who experienced intense anxiety while on the 20th floor, visually imagined the floors tilting and disintegrating. "The patient's cognitive response to the stimulus situation," he concluded "may be expressed in purely verbal form or in the form of imagery" (Beck, 1976). Cognitions, then, can be expressed other than verbally.

Borderline and Narcissistic Conditions

Otto F. Kernberg uses the term "borderline personality organization," which includes the narcissistic personality disorder, to describe a psychopathological constellation having a specific ego structure and a variety of other characteristics (Kernberg, 1975). According to Kernberg, the borderline individual may complain of a wide variety of symptoms, and will demonstrate specific and nonspecific indications of ego weakness.

Psychiatrist John Gunderson of the Harvard Medical School believes that the "core conflicts" of borderline patients are an inability to acknowledge wants and to discriminate them from needs (Gunderson, 1977). From the vantage point of cognitive theory, this observation speaks to the heart of the philosophical source of the emotional and behavioral disorders of the borderline individual. For that matter, it appears that any disturbed person's "core conflict" is an escalation of wants into needs.

One system of classification holds that anger is frequently experienced by borderline individuals in many aspects of their lives. This hostility can be expressed both covertly or overtly toward varying targets. Such a classification scheme views borderline patients as vascillating in their relationships, and sees their inability to commit themselves to others as one reason for feelings of depression (Grinker, Werble, & Drye, 1968).

Implicit in this description of the affectual and behavioral characteristics of borderlines is the self-defeating cognitive set through which they view themselves, others, and the world. Those who vacillate in their relationships tend to believe that they *must* make the correct choice, and that the consequences of the wrong decision would be *catastrophic*. Along similar lines, the anger which is so pervasive in borderlines seems likely to stem from the notion that others *should* act well toward them and that conditions of the world *must* be easy or it is *awful* (Ellis & Abrahms, 1978).

The central problem of the narcissistic individual, a variant of the borderline personality organization, is continuous effort to protect self-esteem. Some individuals afflicted by a narcissistic disorder persistently assume an air of moral superiority, but with depression and lack of pleasure resulting (Kernberg, 1975). An air of moral superiority seems to imply that the individual believes: "I must think and act respectively and therefore be a superior person." Lack of pleasure, too, appears closely bound to self-defeating cognitions. For if an individual continually reasons, as those who think of themselves as morally superior to others do, that he or she has to *prove* himself or herself, as opposed to *enjoy* him or herself, he or she is clearly denying pleasure.

It has been noted that those who are limited to primarily narcissistic relations are vulnerable to separation and loss "with its threat of catastrophy" (Stanton, 1978). From a cognitively oriented theoretical view, such people are vulnerable to separation and loss because they define such a separation or loss as catastrophic. Those who view the same loss from a more self-enhancing cognitive set simply are not subject to this "threat of catastrophy."

Presumed Etiology and Appropriate Treatment

Oftentimes, when genetic influences are shown to operate in the genesis of a major mental disorder, misunderstanding arises concerning the immutability of these disorders and of their unresponsiveness to psychological treatment. This is unfortunate. Just as drug therapy can be very helpful for conditions apparently related largely to environmental stress, psychological treatment often proves appropriate for conditions which seem based largely on organic pathology (Cancro, 1979).

What remains sadly unrecognized is that in emotional disturbance, regardless of its specific nature, we are witnessing the apparently inseparable interactions of genetic, environmental, and cognitive components.

REFERENCES

Akiskal, H., Briton, A., Puzantian, V., Rosenthal, T., & Walker, P. The nosological status of neurotic depression. *Archives of General Psychiatry*, 1979, *35*, 756–766.

Arieti, S. Manic-depressive psychosis. In S. Arieti (Ed.): *American handbook of psychiatry*. New York: Basic Books Inc., 1957.

Arieti, S. The power of the dominant other. *Psychology Today*, April, 1979.

Beck, A.T. *Cognitive therapy and the emotional disorders*. New York: International Universities Press, 1976.

Berkman, P. Life stress and psychological well being: an evaluation of Langner's analysis in the midtown Manhattan area. *Health and Social Behavior*, 1971, *12*, 35–45.

Birley, F.L.T., & Brown, G. W. Crises and life changes preceding the onset or relapse of acute schizophrenia: clinical aspects. *British Journal of Psychiatry*, 1970, *116*, 327–333.

Cancro, R. The clinical relevance of genetic studies in schizophrenia. *Psychiatric Annals*, 1979, *9*, 103–111.

Cooper, B., & Sylph, J. Life events in the onset of neurosis in an investigation in general practice. *Psychological Medical Bulletin*, 1978, *11*, 13–18.

Depue, R., & Monroe, S. The unipolar-bipolar distinction in the depressive disorders. *Psychological Bulletin*, 1978, *85*, 1001–10029.

Ellis, A. The biological basis of human irrationality. *Journal of Individual Psychology*, 1976, *32*, 145–168.

Ellis, A., & Abrahms, E. *Brief psychotherapy in medical and health practice*. New York: Springer Publishing Co., 1978.

Ellis, A., & Grieger, R. *Handbook of rational-emotive therapy*. New York: Springer Publishing Co., 1977.

Freud, A. *The ego and the mechanisms of defense.* London: Hogarth Press, 1936.

Gottesman, I. Schizophrenia and genetics: Toward understanding uncertainty. *Psychiatric Annals,* 1979, *9,* 54–78.

Grinker, R.R., Werble, B., & Drye, R. *The borderline syndrome: A behavior study of ego functions.* New York: Basic Books, Inc., 1968.

Gunderson, J.G. Discriminating characteristics of borderlines and their families. Unpublished paper, 1977.

Ilfeld, F. Current social stressors and symptoms of depression. *American Journal of Psychiatry,* 1977, *134,* 2.

Kernberg, O.F. *Borderline conditions and pathological narcissism.* New York: Jason Aronson, 1975.

Kety, S.S., Rosenthal, D., Wendor, P., Schulsinger, S., & Jacoben, B. Mental illness in the biological and adoptive individuals who have become schizophrenic: A preliminary report based upon a psychiatric interview. In J. Fifver, D. Rosenthal, & H. Brill (Eds.), *Genetic research in psychiatry.* Baltimore: Johns Hopkins University Press, 1975, pp. 147–165.

Kidd, K.K., & Matthyse, E. Research designs for the study of gene-environment interactions in psychiatric disorders. *Archives of General Psychiatry,* 1978, *34,* 925–922.

Langner, T., & Michael, S. *Life stress and mental health.* Toronto: Glencoe Free Press, 1963.

Lewin, B.D. *The psychoanalysis of elation.* New York: W.W. Norton & Co., 1950.

MacVane, J., Lange, L.J., Brown, W., & Zayat, N. Psychological functioning of bipolar manic-depressives in remission. *Archives of General Psychiatry,* 1978, *35,* 1351–1354.

Nemiah, J. Psychoneurotic disorders. In A. Nicholi (Ed.), *The Harvard guide to modern psychiatry.* Cambridge, Mass.: Belknap Press, 1978.

Paykel, E., Myers, J., Dienelt, M., Klerman, G., Lindenthal, J., & Pepper, M. *Archives of General Psychiatry,* 1969, *21,* 753–760.

Robins, L.M. Psychiatric epidemiology. *Archives of General Psychiatry,* 1978, *35,* 697–702.

Saul, L.J. *Emotional maturity: The development and dynamics of personality.* Philadelphia: Lippincott Press, 1947.

Stanton, A.H. Personality disorders. In A. Nicholi (Ed.), *The Harvard guide to modern psychiatry.* Cambridge, Mass.: Belknap Press, 1978.

Tennant, C., & Andrews, G. The pathogenic quality of life event stress in neurotic impairment. *Archives of General Psychiatry,* 1978, *35,* 859–863.

Weissman, M., Prusoff, B., & Klerman, G. Personality and the prediction of long-term outcome of depression. *American Journal of Psychiatry*, 1978, *135*, 7.

Zitrin, C., Klein, D., & Woerner, M. Behavior therapy, supportive psychotherapy, imipramine, and phobias. *Archives of General Psychiatry*, 1978, *35*, 307–315.

Chapter 6

COGNITIVE FACTORS
IN SEXUAL BEHAVIOR

Janet Wolfe
Susan Walen

It has been said that while sex is perfectly natural, it is rarely naturally perfect. This statement implies that a great deal of our sexual behavior entails utilizing new learning. Learning can be broadly conceptualized into two major forms: that in which stimuli acquire new meaning for the individual (classical conditioning), and that in which new responses are added to the individual's repertoire (operant conditioning). It is likely that many of the changes we observe in our overt sexual behaviors are mediated by the principles of operant conditioning (reinforcement and punishment). Overt sexual behavior, however is usually elicited by external events (e.g., a sexual approach by a partner) or by internal events (e.g., sexual thoughts or feelings of arousal). These eliciting stimuli for sexual behavior probably acquire their erotic meaning for the individual through the principles of classical conditioning. Thus, it seems that people not only learn (a) "how to do sex," but also (b) to give certain external stimuli sexual meaning, and (c) to identify and label certain internal stimuli (physiologic arousal) as erotic.

It is common knowledge by now that our greatest sex organ is not located below the belt, but between our ears. The cognitive activity of our brain can either augment or inhibit the sexual response cycle. The two major forms of cognitive behavior which we will examine in this chapter are perceptions and evaluation.

PERCEPTIONS

Perception entails three processes: detection, labeling, and attribution. Let us briefly review each in turn. *Detection* simply refers to the individual's ability to note the presence of a stimulus or to discriminate it from other stimuli. For example, an individual may note a change in heart rate. Obviously, unless this step is accomplished the stimulus is functionally "not there" for the individual. *Labeling* refers to the descriptors that the individual uses to categorize the stimulus event; it is a classifying operation. The person who notes the sensations in heart activity may label it, "my heart just skipped a beat." The third step is *attribution,* finding an explanation for the perception. The attribution selected by the individual may depend most heavily on contextual cues (Schachter & Singer, 1962). Using the example above, the skipped heart beat may be attributed to "true love" or fear, depending, at least in part, on the situational cues of the moment.

Perception, therefore, is a process of gathering data correctly and drawing accurate conclusions from the data. In a sense, the perceiver is functioning as a data collector, and had better scientifically check out the accuracy of his or her reality testing. Inability to detect sexual stimuli, incorrect labeling, or misattribution of them may significantly impede sexual performance.

Aaron Beck (1976, 1978) has done a great deal of work on cognitive errors of perception in problems of depression. Let us now take Beck's work out of the mood clinic and usefully apply it in the sex clinic. The major cognitive errors described by Beck are the following:

Selective abstraction—focusing only on certain details from a complex situation and using the detail to describe the entire experience

Arbitrary inference—drawing a conclusion without evidence or in the face of evidence to the contrary

Overgeneralization—drawing a conclusion on the basis of a single incident

Personalization—relating events to oneself without clear evidence

Dichotomous thinking—classifying events into either/or or all/none categories instead of as existing on a continuum

We will return to these cognitive errors later, and illustrate their role in perception as part of the sexual response cycle.

EVALUATIONS

The second major cognitive behavior that can affect sexual functioning is evaluation, which in essence entails rating events on a continuum from good to bad. The cognitive theory of RET, as evolved by Albert Ellis (Ellis & Harper, 1975), has focused primarily on evaluative beliefs.

Obviously, when an individual evaluates a sexual stimulus as good or positive, sexual functioning will be enhanced. Equally obvious, when a stimulus is evaluated negatively, sexuality will be diminished. Still more destructive are exaggerated negative evaluations which Ellis refers to as "awfulizing" or "catastrophizing." If a man fails to get an erection during sex play, he can rationally evaluate this event as bad. Such an evaluation would be sensible if he had held expectations of intercourse in the sexual encounter, but may not inhibit other sexual behaviors which do not require an erection. Irrationally, however, he may go on to evaluate his flaccid state as "terrible, awful, and horrible." Such an overly negative evaluation will typically set up an intense cycle of anxiety or guilt which, in turn, will probably block further attempts at sexual arousal of the individual or his partner.

A New Conception of the Sexual Arousal Cycle

While arousal need not preceed the initiation of overt sexual behaviors, it certainly will affect the individual's enjoyment of a sexual encounter and thus will affect how he or she behaves. Arousal, we suggest, is a product of both *perception* and *evaluation* of events, and, in turn, leads to further cognitive appraisal. Thus, we propose the arousal cycle (see Figure 6–1).

Note that this system suggests a feedback model, in which each of the eight links in the chain functions as both a cue for the next link and a reinforcer for the preceding event. Let us take each succeeding link and discuss its contribution to a positive sexual experience.

Link I: Perception of a Sexual Stimulus

The perception or identification of a stimulus as erotic in large part is learned, a conclusion which seems clear from an examination of cross-cultural studies of sexual behavior. Ford and Beach (1951), for example, state:

> "Human sexuality is affected by experience in two ways: First, the kinds of stimulation and the types of situations that become capable of evoking sexual excitement are determined in large measure by learning. Second, the overt behavior through which this excitement is expressed depends largely upon the individual's previous experience" (p. 263).

How does this happen? How do we learn to identify certain people or body parts or inanimate objects as erotic? A number of processes may come into play, one of which involves modeling and social reinforcement. The culture in which we live sets the stage for detection and labeling of a stimulus as erotic. For example, Americans for many years seemed to focus erotic energy on

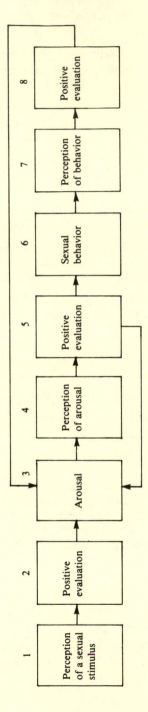

Figure 6–1. Proposed Feedback Loop of a Positive Sexual Experience

women's breasts, much to the amazement of many Europeans and certainly to many African tribes in which breasts are usually bared, and despite the fact that for a large percentage of women the breasts are not erotically sensitive.

Not only cultural expectations, but the existence of an adequate vocabulary are important to the perception process. For instance, the dearth of words (synonyms or descriptors) in our language for the female sex organ, the clitoris, may contribute in large part to the relatively high percentage of women who are sexually dysfunctional in our society.

Finally, through a process of stimulus pairing, an event which has been repeatedly experienced with arousal or orgasm, will acquire erotic potential. The study by Rachman and Hodgson (1968) provided a laboratory model which suggests how this process may work. An analogue of a fetish was created through classical conditioning by repeatedly pairing slides of high black boots with slides of attractive naked women. Using normal male subjects and measuring changes in penile volume, conditioning, stimulus generalization, extinction, and spontaneous recovery were all demonstrated.

Link 2: Evaluation of the Sexual Stimulus

Once the stimulus is identified as erotic, it will be evaluated by the individual. If the evaluation is positive, arousal will proceed. If, however, the individual evaluates the stimulus negatively, arousal may be blocked. Thus, an individual who evaluates a sexual picture or sexual approach as "disgusting," "not nice," or "unseemly" will probably fail to be aroused by it. When the range of sexual stimuli that are considered acceptable to the individual is very restricted, the probability of arousal will be low and the sexual repertoire will be perforce limited.

Link 3: Arousal

Physiologic arousal is a generalized phenomenon, and much the same kind of responses will be noted after a variety of human experiences, both negative and positive. The early stages of sexual arousal (e.g., increased heart rate, blood pressure, muscle tension) show the same responses as do those that occur under a number of conditions ranging from simple physical exertion to painful stimulation to anxiety-arousing events.

According to Schachter's (1964) model of emotion, two elements are required for the experience of emotion: (a) a physiological state of arousal, and (b) situational cues that enable the individual to label the arousal as a specific emotion. In the classic study of this model by Schachter and Singer (1962), physiologic arousal was induced in subjects by injections of epinepherine. Subjects were then exposed to highly emotional displays of behavior (euphoria or anger) by a confederate of the experimenters. Those subjects who were correctly informed of the expected phenomenologic effects of the drug were less affected by the confederate's behavior than were subjects who were misinformed or uninformed. The latter subjects displayed more emotional responses, modeling those of the confederate, presumably because the context allowed them to provide an emotional label for their aroused state.

By derivation, we presume that appropriate environmental cues can help an individual to label physiologic arousal as the sensations of love or sexual excitation. Because the arousal is nonspecific, however, inaccurate labeling may easily result. For example, a young woman may be dating a man whose approach behaviors are extremely unpredictable. He might court her avidly for a few days and then not phone again for weeks, following which the cycle is repeated. The young woman's hopes and expectations would be very confused, and her partner's inconsistent and inconsiderate behavior might result in a strong state of arousal. If she labels her arousal as feelings of intense love rather than those of anxiety or anger, she may remain in what may be an unfulfilling relationship. The accurate perception of arousal, therefore, will be an extremely important aspect of good erotic functioning. Once correctly perceived, arousal may lead to further focusing on erotic sensations and to increased sexual behavior, which will further increase arousal.

Link 4: Perception of Arousal

Research by Julia Heiman (1977) has indicated a significant sex difference in the ability to detect and report erotic arousal. Male and female college students were presented with erotic and nonerotic auditory stimuli. Their reactions were measured by objective recordings of genital vasocongestion and by subjective reports of arousal. A significant discrepancy between these two measures was found for the female subjects, indicating either that they are less able to discriminate their own arousal and/or are less likely to report it. What factors could be responsible for this difference between the sexes?

Cultural taboos and rigid sex norms for females may certainly play a role. Women are known to engage less frequently in masturbation; in fact, commonly a first step in the treatment of sexually dysfunctional women is permission-giving and instruction in masturbation, thus providing a training ground for recognizing and labeling genital sensations.

Young women frequently do not attend to their own arousal, concentrating instead on making sure that their partner doesn't "go too far." While she is busy policing his behavior, she is distracted from monitoring her own sensations. When women are fully sexually active, they may still be inattentive to their arousal because they may be more attuned to pleasing their partners, thus following the cultural model of women as passive caretakers of others.

Also, quite simply, a woman's vasocongestive arousal is often not as obvious as is a man's. One can hardly miss detecting an erection, but many of a woman's early arousal signals are internal, subtle, and ambiguous. A slight dampening of the vulva, if detected, could be interpreted as perspiration or urine, and nipples certainly erect to the cold. Many women, in fact, are not even certain if they have had an orgasm. Since women tend to do less verbal or physical sharing of early masturbatory experiences or other sexual behaviors than do men, their ability to detect and correctly label their arousal may be hindered.

Another important aspect of the identification of arousal in both men and women relates to the criteria used in the inspection process. The earliest physiological changes in sexual arousal consist of increases in heart rate, muscular tension, skin temperature, and respiration. All of these, however, are fairly nonspecific, and research indicates that we are not particularly adept at discriminating them (Heiman, 1977). With the addition or more intense and localized vasocongestive changes (copious lubrication or erection) the signals become clearer.

Trouble can still arise, however, if the individual sets the criteria for signs of physiological arousal too stringently. How full must an erection be before the male identifies it as a "sure" sign of arousal? How much lubrication must be noticed in the woman? What, in fact, happens if he or she *only* uses the magnitude of erection or lubrication as the signal? One possibility is that the individual may engage in further sexual behavior before arousal is maximal, thus often leading to nonattainment of orgasm or a relatively anhedonic orgasm. Or, if the specific signal is delayed or doesn't match rigid criteria, the individual may conclude that he or she is not aroused at all, and may abandon further attempts at the sexual pursuit.

Attending to multiple cues and not setting rigid criteria for these cues would seem to be the most helpful. If the individual is focusing on only one cue, particularly a genital cue, he or she may not augment the arousal cycle by self-reinforcing and arousal-facilitating cognitions, but instead may further reduce arousal with inhibitory cognitions.

The attribution for a perceived state of arousal will also be important, since arousal is so nonspecific. Two studies of misattribution cited by Rook and Hammen (1977) are relevant to this point. Cantor, Zillman, and Bryant (1975) found that male subjects' subjective reports of sexual arousal and liking of an erotic film were enhanced by residual physiologic arousal produced by physical exercise. Dutton and Aron (1974) arranged to have male subjects approached by an attractive female experimenter while on a fear-arousing suspension bridge. These men gave more sexual responses to Thematic Apperception Test (TAT) cards and made more attempts to contact the experimenter after the study than did male subjects tested on a less threatening bridge or those approached by a male experimenter.

It may be suggested, therefore, that situational cues are an important determinant in the interpretation or attribution that an individual makes to a perception of arousal. Possibly such a phenomenon is involved in the establishment of problematic or unusual sexual behaviors. Misattribution of an arousal sequence as sexual may come to elicit sexual arousal or ultimately restrict the individual to the unusual eliciting stimuli.

Link 5: Evaluation of Arousal

If an individual has learned to label arousal as bad, the negative emotional consequences to this evaluation may block the sexual arousal cycle. Thus, the woman who thinks of her vulva as dirty or smelly, and evaluates her own lubrication as merely "sticky" or, worse, as "disgusting" may end up feeling embarrassed by her arousal, an emotion hardly compatible with a positive sexual experience. Similarly, the man who decides that he "shouldn't" have erections in certain situations may find himself consumed with guilt rather than further arousal. It is for these reasons that much of the work of the sex counselor consists of instilling a new set of sex-positive attitudes vis-à-vis arousal.

Link 6: Overt Sexual Behavior

If arousal is present, and it is accurately labeled and evaluated, typically the individual moves on to initiate or to further engage in sexual behavior, and thereby augments arousal. Here again, however, differences between the sexes may emerge. Many women inhibit themselves at this stage, blocking their pursuit of sexual arousal with cognitions such as:

—I can't take over the control.
—I couldn't do that (or ask for that).

—He won't like it if I do that.

—As long as he's happy, I'm happy.

—It's not nice (or ladylike) to do that.

—What will he think of me if I do?

Thus, while the partner is liable to time his behaviors and movements to his state of arousal, she may not. She may even be repeatedly engaging in sexual behavior when she is at a low or even zero level of arousal. If so, it is easy to imagine how this pairing could result in further sexual difficulties.

Link 7: Perception of Sexual Behavior

Individuals react to their own spontaneous expressions as indicators of their arousal. They may monitor cries, laughter, tears, or movements. If accurately perceived and labeled and evaluated positively, they may further augment the perception of arousal. In addition, since movement and other expressive behaviors may increase cardiac output, they may directly contribute to the general arousal level.

At this link, however, an important distinction needs to be made between *observation* of sexual or expressive behaviors and *spectatoring* them. The latter implies not merely detection and labeling, but a *self-rating* process which has a goal-oriented focus. When the individual is spectatoring his or her performance, the here-and-now experience of pleasure will be lost, and sex becomes work rather than play. When the self-rating of the individual is critical, the results can certainly be a troublesome distraction from the arousal cycle.

Link 8: Evaluation of Sexual Behavior

Evaluation of one's sexual behavior is the core problem in the majority of the common sexual dysfunctions brought to the sex counselor. In fact, rational-emotive therapists make a distinction between sexual *dysfunction* and sexual *disturbance*. The individual may have a dysfunction (e.g., erectile difficulty) and yet choose to be relatively undisturbed about it emotionally. If disturbed, of course, the emotional turmoil will further inhibit good sexual functioning. The disturbance, according to RET, stems from the individual's *evaluation* of the sexual difficulty.

The erectile failure will be problematic to the man and his partner only if they evaluate it as "awful." If they go on to attribute the failure to some enduring characteristic of themselves, and evaluate this characteristic as horrid, they will not only impede their performance at the moment, but will be making dire and probably self-fulfilling propheses of the future. On the other hand, if they are able to conclude that the erectile failure is not catastrophic, that they can still function as good sex partners using other techniques, that their "self" is still intact even if the erection is not, the erection may very well be recovered, or at least the couple may go on to their next sexual encounter unencumbered by fear, anxiety, or self-downing.

Synthesis

Positive sexual experiences are a smooth amalgam of stimuli and responses, the flow between them guided by correct perceptions and positive evaluations. When this process occurs, the emotional climate of the individual will be untroubled, and sex play will be pleasant or even joyful.

Negative sexual experiences occur when the linkages between stimuli and responses are blocked by incorrect or negative cognitions. The following are some examples of these kinds of cognitive errors:

PERCEPTUAL ERRORS.

selective abstraction: "I don't see a sex flush on my chest . . . I guess I'm not aroused."

arbitrary inference: "I haven't come yet . . . I'm probably not going to."

overgeneralization: "My erection is smaller . . . I knew I was becoming impotent."

personalization: "I've taken off my clothes and he doesn't
    have an erection. He doesn't find me attractive any
    more."

dichotomous thinking: "I'm not orgasmic." "I'm not a real
    man."

EVALUATIVE ERRORS.   None of the statements above need to impede
the process of the arousal cycle, unless the individual ascribes an
exaggerated negative evaluation to the cognition. For instance,
from the first example above, the woman could conclude that she
is not aroused, and evaluate this finding nonhurtfully: e.g., "Well,
so I'm not aroused. There's always next time. I'll just make this a
super loving session for my partner." On the other hand, consider
what would occur if perceptions such as the above were followed
by an evaluation such as:

"How awful!"
"It shouldn't be this way!"
"I can't stand it!"
"I've got to do better!"
"What a sad sack I am!"
"It's all my (or his or her) fault!"

The flooding of anxiety, misery, guilt, or anger will certainly get
in the way of happy, playful sex.

    With regard to sexual dysfunctions, it is interesting to note
that sex therapists have developed various classificatory systems
for the common sexual dysfunctions, typically delimiting premature ejaculation, retarded ejaculation, and impotency among men,
and preorgasmia, dyspareunia, and vaginismus among women.
These categories are often broken down still further into primary
dysfunctions (occurring under all conditions) and situational dysfunctions (occurring only under specific conditions).

    Closer examination of these categories, however, suggests
that the same dysfunctional processes are operative in virtually all

cases. For example, most premature ejaculators *assume* that they orgasm rapidly because they are too highly aroused, and the typically ineffective self-help procedures they evolve consist of distracting themselves from the sexual encounter (e.g., by reciting multiplication tables) or minimizing stimulation (e.g., not allowing their partner to touch their genitals). Counselors who have worked with premature ejaculators find, however, that rather than being overaroused, they are usually underaroused. In fact, when such clients acquire the ability to exert some control over the reflex, they typically report that the orgasm, when it occurs, is significantly more pleasurable.

It appears, then, that the core ingredients in all of the diagnostic categories are a high level of emotional distress induced by *cognitive errors of evaluation,* often coupled with *cognitive errors of perception.* The end product is an individual who approaches the job of sex (rather than the joy of sex) as a way to prove him or herself (rather than to enjoy him or herself)—certainly a very unsexy attitude.

SEX THERAPY

For roughly the first half of the 20th century the treatment of sex disorders consisted largely of psychoanalytic or psychodynamically oriented therapy. Treatment was posited on the notion that healthy sexual functioning could be achieved by gaining insight into early psychosexual problems and resolving the oedipal conflicts, and the penis envy or castration anxiety resulting from them, which normally would require years of individual probing. While essentially cognitive in nature, psychoanalytically oriented therapies rarely focus directly (or even indirectly) on inaccurate perceptions and dysfunctional evaluations of sexual stimuli, arousal, or behavior. To the extent that any of these links are discussed, they are typically not followed by instruction for remediation. For example, if an oedipal conflict is identified as a "reason" for premature ejaculation, the patient is rarely instructed in techniques that could effectively influence the perception and evaluation of the stages of arousal leading to ejaculation, or reduce the emotional distress following a rapid ejaculation. To date there has been little evidence of the success of this type of treatment in significantly altering dysfunctional sexual behavior, and in innumerable instances, especially in cases of women in classical psychoanalysis, there may actually be a further increase in sexual disturbance during and following treatment.

More practical forms of sex therapy have also existed since at least the early part of the 20th century, largely practiced by nonanalytic physicians and often described in detail in manuals for the general public. Sexologists, including August Forel (1922), Havelock Ellis (1935), Magnus Hirschfeld (1935), William J. Robinson (1929), W. F. Robie (1925), Theodore Van de Velde (1926), G. Lombard Kelly (1948), and Hannah and Abraham Stone (1935), contributed works read by millions who wanted to learn what to do to feel more sexually adequate. Although their approaches were largely ignored by psychoanalytic practitioners, there is some evidence that their writings dealt more directly with the various links in our model and had positive effects in terms of attitudinal and behavioral changes.

Still more recently, the focus in sex research and sex therapy has followed a more or less explicit behavioral model. One of the first modern psychologists to break completely from the Freudian model and emphasize an active cognitive and behavioral approach to sex therapy was Albert Ellis (1953, 1960). Subsequently, the experimental and clinical work of Masters and Johnson (1970) established the efficacy of directed behavioral change and *in vivo* practice as important ingredients in improved sexual functioning. The carefully documented procedures and effectiveness of the work of Masters and Johnson received wide publicity, and significantly influenced even the work of psychoanalytically oriented practitioners such as Kaplan (1974). From the work of Masters and Johnson, Ellis, and other pioneers, behavior therapy procedures began to be systematically applied to problems of sexual inadequacy and disturbance (Annon, 1974; Barbach, 1975; Feldman &

MacCulloch, 1971; Hartman & Fithian, 1972; Heiman, LoPiccolo, & LoPiccolo, 1976; Lazarus, 1971; Semans, 1956; Wolpe & Lazarus, 1966).

In addition to the often highly creative behavioral methods used in contemporary sex therapy, a significant component of behavior change used by most of these theorists and practitioners is a focus on altering cognitions. Directly or indirectly, cognitions about sexual stimulation and sexual behavior are addressed. Clients' attitudes based on myth and misinformation about themselves, their bodies, and their sexual functioning are replaced with more accurate beliefs about sex and sexuality. Ellis (1960, 1976, 1979), in particular, has elaborated cognitive restructuring techniques that focus on changing attitudes toward sexual performance in general and toward oneself when a sexual dysfunction is present. The goal of such procedures is to reduce anxiety and self-downing, thus providing a better psychological set for approaching the more technical behavioral aspects of a sex therapy program.

Let us now examine some of the current and most widely practiced sex therapy approaches in terms of our 8-stage model, focusing on two of the more common sexual disorders.

Female Orgasmic Dysfunction

The main treatment modality for both primary and secondary orgasmic dysfunction is a series of graduated masturbation homework assignments (Barbach, 1975; Heiman, LoPiccolo, & LoPiccolo, 1976; Kaplan, 1974). Adjunctive techniques for secondary orgasmic dysfunction may include sensate focus (Masters & Johnson, 1970), systematic desensitization (Wolpe, 1969), and assertiveness training (Wolfe, 1976).

In a variety of ways, treatment focuses on getting the woman to develop an expanded set of situations and stimuli capable of evoking sexual excitement (Link 1). This is done in a number of ways. Through giving corrective information about the female pelvic anatomy and physiology, women are urged to think of their clitoris, and not the vaginal walls, as being the site of erotic stimulation most likely to lead to orgasm. The use of fantasy (and not just romantic thoughts of one's husband of 30 years) is encouraged. Fantasies, often previously used with anxiety (or perhaps not used at all) are relabeled by the therapist as good, fun, healthy sexual stimuli. And fingers, vibrators, pillows, and other physical stimuli are given "status" as valid sexual stimuli. While expanding their set of stimuli that can potentiate sexual arousal and enjoyment, clients are also learning a new vocabulary with which to describe these stimuli both to themselves and to their partners. Through repeated pairing of the new sexual stimuli with higher arousal, the new erotic potential of these stimuli gets better established. In addition, clients are helped to identify those stimuli that "turn them off," rather than turn them on (e.g., body odor, unresolved hurts and anger), and to bring about changes in these stimuli and /or in their evaluations of them in order to reduce or eliminate their off-turning potential.

Corrective information is also given regarding Link 4, perception of arousal, by information-giving coupled with masturbatory practice. Thus, the client may be looking for exploding skyrockets, copious lubrication, or shockwaves through her body as signals of arousal. Failing to experience these, by selective abstraction she may fail to label and acknowledge her body's far more subtle indications of arousal (e.g., a tickling or tingling sensation in her vulva, tensing of her thigh muscles, contractions of her abdominal and perineal muscles, or increased breath rate). By providing the client with a variety of indicants of arousal, with accompanying labels for them, and by encouraging her to look for her own changes in sensations during her masturbatory practice sessions, she becomes trained to more accurately perceive a wide variety of sexual sensations. At Link 5, positive evaluation of arousal is facilitated through various kinds of verbal coaching, aimed at reeducating and reassuring the client about her sexual arousal, and the things that aid or interfere with it. In addition, the client is helped to identify and label those physical and mental signals that distract her from tuning in to her arousal (e.g., discomfort from too-hard clitoral stimulation, anxiety about rejection, overfocus on pleasing her partner, or more general mind-wandering), and is provided with ways of reducing her interfering thoughts and feelings.

Kaplan (1974), Barbach (1975), and Heiman, LoPiccolo, and LoPiccolo (1976) aid this process of positive evaluation of arousal by telling the client that it's all right to take as long as she needs, by showing her that her feelings and fears are normal, and that she's not such a bad person since lots of other women have this problem. However, perhaps no therapy as effectively and directly attacks the negative evaluations and attendant anxiety, guilt, or depression that block arousal and interfere with orgasm as well as Ellis' (1960, 1975, 1979) RET, in which the client is taught to vigorously and actively debate her ideas that "It's awful not to feel excited"; "I should be coming more quickly"; or "What a hopeless sexual failure I am."

One of the staples in the armamentarium of the sex therapist, especially useful in the treatment of secondary anorgasmia, is sensate focus. This procedure consists of a two-phased sequence of mutual partner stimulation exercises designed to take the focus off intercourse and to redirect it to sensual pleasure from many parts of the body. It also provides a means for the sexual partners to communicate their likes and dislikes and feelings to each other. In the first phase, first one partner, then the other caresses the partner's body from head to toes, experimenting with different touches, and giving feedback to each other on what feels good, and what produces discomfort. Breasts and genitals are excluded. In the second part, breasts and genitals are added with additional instruction to experiment not with producing orgasm, but with finding ways of touching that produce higher states of arousal. Again, both participants learn to reduce their rigid fixation on the usual erogenous zones, and to extend their sources of erotic stimulation and arousal to a variety of areas often not previously perceived as stimulating. They learn to talk about these places in a

new way, to touch them in new way, and to evaluate the arousal
and sexual behavior positively (e.g., sensations in the scalp, feet,
ears, etc.). The overall cognitive/emotive effect is generally a
reduction in tension in sexual interactions, a freeing of the pressure
to have an orgasm (or an erection) or intercourse. Because it
becomes almost impossible to fail when the sexual goals of
orgasm, erection, and intercourse are eliminated, all the kinds of
stimulation and arousal that occur tend to become more positively
evaluated with a concomitant reduction of interfering negative
thoughts and feelings.

If the woman is to transmit to her partner some of the new
information about what sexual behaviors feel arousing to her so
that they may be incorporated into their sexual encounters, she
may profit from assertivenss training, to help her become more
skilled and comfortable in communicating sexual preferences and
feelings. Assertiveness training consists of helping the individual—via the techniques of behavior rehearsal, modeling, and
coaching—to communicate feelings and preferences in a direct,
clear fashion (for example, that she would like her partner to
perform oral-genital contact, or that she'd like to rub her clitoris
during intercourse to facilitate orgasm). A usual part of this process involves the uncovering of feelings that block communication
(e.g., anxiety about sounding foolish, or about being rejected),
and helping the client to develop a new set of beliefs that support
assertive expression ("I have a right to express my preferences"; "I
have a right to sexual satisfaction"; "If the other person feels put
upon by my request, it's disappointing and frustrating, but not
awful."). The process of expanding the repertoire of stimuli and
arousal cues and overt sexual behaviors, and of evaluating them
positively, is thus extended to the woman's partner.

Experimentation in a wide variety of sexual behaviors (Link
6) is encouraged between the partners, with the therapist giving
permission to talk about what's liked and what's uncomfortable as
a further means of helping the clients to develop more comfortable
and positive feelings and evaluations of their newly extended set of
sexual behaviors. The woman may also be encouraged to practice

new behavioral expression on her own (e.g., stimulating herself to a noisy orgasm, or role-playing orgasm), to help her strengthen both the behavior and the positive experience of it.

Premature Ejaculation

Let us now apply our model to a common male problem, that of premature ejaculation. A core condition in cases of premature ejaculation is an inability to recognize (and consequently control) the sensations premonitory to ejaculation (Link 4). An important step in treatment may involve *in vivo* training, in which the client learns to "get in touch" with his preorgastic sensations toward the goal of increasing his threshold of excitability. As Walen, Hauserman, and Lavin (1977, p. 301) state: "It appears that the active ingredient of the successful therapy methods consists of overcoming the immediate obstacle to ejaculatory continence by inducing the man to experience the previously avoided perception of high levels of erotic arousal while he is with his sexual partner." The therapist also helps the client to focus on the thoughts and feelings (e.g., fear of failure, anger or insensitivity toward his spouse) which interfere with this sensual focus, and replace them with more positive evaluations. The client is also helped to identify and positively evaluate other stimuli and behaviors (e.g., fantasies, ways of stimulating himself) which will aid in becoming aroused and better controlling the pacing of the arousal (Links 1 and 6).

When, as is frequently the case, there is an additional problem of negative evaluation of the problem behavior (Link 8), the client may be greatly helped by the addition of a RET approach (Ellis, 1976) in which he is counseled to challenge his anxiety-creating thoughts ("It's awful if I come too fast") or self-attacking thoughts ("What an inadequate sexual partner I am for coming so fast"). This work on countering possible negative evaluations of sexual behavior is also done by most of the leading sex therapists by reassuring the client that it is not necessary for him to be able to have prolonged intercourse or an erect penis in order to be able to enjoy sex or to satisfy his partner.

A Case Example

What is evident from the examples above is that the links in the proposed feedback-loop model do not necessarily follow each other in a step-by-step, sequenced fashion, but rather reverberate to each other in different ways. What the model can hopefully facilitate is the identification of which links may be especially problematic in an individual case so that therapeutic strategies may thereby be more clearly selected.

The following case illustrates a session in which various links in the model are dealt with, within a rational therapy framework, as the therapist helps the client clarify her misperceptions and exaggeratedly negative evaluations and dispute these irrationalities to produce cognitive, emotive, and behavioral changes. The client is a 32-year-old woman with secondary orgasmic dysfunction. The woman has been divorced for 4 years, during which she has had several sexual partners but has become increasingly "turned off" by sex. In the session, she is discussing a man she has dated three times with whom she enjoys talking and going out, but at whom she is beginning to feel angry as he has orgasms easily and she does not. Though a major goal is helping her to identify the kinds of stimulation she likes and to become more assertive in going after her preferences, the larger goal is to help the client to develop a belief system that supports her right to have pleasure, and one that helps her antiawfulize about the possibility of being rejected (the underlying issue that is probably the root of a large percentage of sexual disturbances).

C: I don't know what's wrong with me. I really liked Bob—but after we had sex the other night, I just felt angry and crummy and couldn't wait for him to get out the door. Maybe I'm just too fussy or messed up and won't ever find anyone I can relate to.

T: You seemed to feel so positively about him. What happened, do you think, that led up to your feeling angry?

C: Hmmmm. I think it was when we had sex. We did a lot of

necking . . . I really like that a lot and was getting very turned on. Then we started having intercourse. He came in about 3 minutes, then we sort of lay in bed and talked for awhile and I just wished he'd disappear. I think that's the thing that really made me mad.

T: *It* made you mad? Remember . . . How is it that we cause our feelings in reaction to certain things according to RET?

C: Oh, yeah . . . by my thoughts about what happened . . . Let me see. I guess I told myself he should have been more interested in my pleasure. And that he was a pretty selfish person . . . he doesn't really give a damn about me at all.

T: Gee, that doesn't sound like the way you were describing him a couple of weeks ago. Let's assume he may be acting selfishly or insensitively with you sexually; that is, not taking the time to check with you and see if you are satisfied. Can you see how this selfish behavior doesn't mean he's a totally selfish person?

C: I guess he's not really a selfish person. He's actually been very nice and generous to me, and from what I've seen, to his family and friends. But he *shouldn't* just have his orgasm and roll over, should he? I mean, I don't like that!

T: And where is it written that he *must* behave the way you'd like him to?

C: I guess he doesn't *have* to . . . but I want him to.

T: Great! Now, I'd like to check things out and see if you have some handle on how to dispute your "should," your demands that he must give you an orgasm. Because if you want at least to explore the possibility of a relationship with him, and improve your sexual enjoyment, I think it's important that you really learn how to stop this kind of "should-ing," else you probably are going to get so angry you're just going to want to run . . . a pattern you've said you'd like to break.

C: I guess I can tell myself, I don't like his neglecting my orgasm, but I can stand it (I already have—three times!).

(Laughs) And I can try to remember he's not a rotten selfish person . . . just somewhat fallible.

T: Good. Now, let's see if we can brainstorm some ways of going about trying to see if you can wind up with more orgasms. Any thoughts on this? What are some of the things that turn you on, some of the ways you think you're most likely to orgasm?

C: Uh . . . (awkwardly) uh . . . well, I can just about always have an orgasm with my vibrator. And almost always . . . uh . . . if a guy does oral sex on me. And I love when he touches my body, rubs my back.

T: Good, so you've got some pretty good ideas to give him.

C: Yeah . . . but I could *never* ask him to do . . . like, go down on me. He'd probably think I was a weirdo, to need these kinds of things, and to just come out and ask for them. Just the thought makes me really anxious.

T: Let's assume that he might . . . though lots and lots of men I've talked to have said just the opposite . . . that they'd welcome some feedback from their partners, 'cause half the time they don't know if she's really turned on, or if she's come. And they say that if she'd open her mouth, he wouldn't have to go through so much mind-reading or spend half an hour screwing her when she'd really like her back massaged and her nipples licked! But anyway . . . Let's assume Stan does think you're a weirdo. What do you suppose you're telling yourself about this to create anxiety?

C: That's easy, That it would be awful if he thought that, and that he'd never want to see me again.

T: And if he didn't want to see you again?

C: I guess, when I think about it, it wouldn't be so awful. Pretty disappointing, 'cause I guess I do think he's one of the nicest guys I've met in a long time . . . but I guess if I've survived without him all this time, I could still get by if he split.

T: Good. Now if you can keep those rational thoughts firmly planted in your mind . . . and especially at the times you're anxious about letting him know where you're at sexually . . . you'll be in a better place to take the risk of speaking up.

Because of the client's religious background, and awkwardness in discussing her sexual preferences, behavior rehearsal was done to help reduce her anxiety and increase her facility in expressing herself. Next session, she reported great success; Stan had expressed surprise at learning that she hadn't been satisfied since her noises had led him to assume she had come, and was eager to do the things she indicated she liked.

CONCLUSION

Positive sexual experiences are a result of more than good sex technique. They result from accurate and realistic perceptions and positive evaluations. Without these mediating links, no amount of "sexpertise" can overcome inhibitions, guilt, anxiety, depression, or anger. Sexual dysfunctions of the male or the female client can therefore be regarded as stemming from blockages in these final common pathways.

It will seem obvious that good diagnosis will maximize the selection of an appropriate treatment procedure, which in turn may enhance the probability of successful treatment. It is suggested that a diagnosis based on the proposed feedback-loop model of a positive sexual experience may enable the therapist to (a) select the most relevant cognitive-behavioral procedures for the client, and (b) emphasize the most relevant aspects of these procedures for an individual case.

REFERENCES

Annon, J. S. *The behavioral treatment of sexual problems. Vol. 1, Brief therapy.* Honolulu: Enabling Systems, Inc., 1974.

Barbach, L. G. *For yourself: The fulfillment of female sexuality.* New York: Doubleday, 1975.

Beck, A. T. *Cognitive therapy and the emotional disorders*. New York: International Universities Press, 1976.

Beck, A. T., Rush, A. J., Shaw, B. F., & Emery, G. *Cognitive therapy of depression: A treatment manual*. Copyright by A. T. Beck, 1978.

Cantor, J., Zillman, D., & Bryant, J. Enhancement of experienced sexual arousal in response to erotic stimuli through misattribution of unrelated residual excitation. *Journal of Personality and Social Psychology*, 1975, *32*, 69–75.

Dutton, D., & Aron, A. Some evidence for heightened sexual attraction under conditions of high anxiety. *Journal of Personality and Social Psychology*, 1974, *30*, 510–517.

Ellis, A. Is the vaginal orgasm a myth? In A. P. Pillay & A. Ellis (Eds.), *Sex, society and the individual*. Bombay: International Journal of Sexology Press, 1953.

Ellis, A. *The art and science of love*. New York: Lyle Stuart, 1960.

Ellis, A. *Sex and the liberated man*. New York: Lyle Stuart, 1976.

Ellis, A. *Intelligent woman's guide to dating and mating*. Secaucus, New Jersey: Lyle Stuart, 1979.

Ellis, A., & Harper, R. A. *A new guide to rational living*. Hollywood, Calif.: Wilshire Books, 1975.

Ellis, H. *Studies in the psychology of sex*. New York: Random House, 1936.

Feldman, M. P., & MacCulloch, M. J. *Homosexual behavior: Therapy and assessment*. New York: Pergamon, 1971.

Ford, C., & Beach, F. *Patterns of sexual behavior*. New York: Paul Hoeber, 1951.

Forel, A. *The sexual question*. New York: Physician's and Surgeon's Book Co., 1922.

Hartman, W., & Fithian, M. *The treatment of the sexual dysfunctions*. Long Beach, Calif: Center for Marital and Sexual Studies, 1972.

Heiman, J. R. A psychophysiological exploration of sexual arousal patterns in males and females. *Psychophysiology*, 1977, *14*, 266–274.

Heiman, J. R., LoPiccolo, L., & LoPiccolo, J. *Becoming orgasmic: A sexual growth program for women*. Englewood Cliffs, N. J.: Prentice-Hall, 1976.

Hirschfeld, M. *Sex in human relationships*. London: Lane, 1935.

Kaplan, H. S. *The new sex therapy: Active treatment of sexual dysfunctions*. New York: Brunner/Mazel, 1974.

Kelly, G. L. *Sexual manual for those married or about to be*. Augusta, Ga.: S. Medical Supply Co., 1948.

Lazarus, A. *Behavior therapy and beyond*. New York: McGraw-Hill, 1971.

Masters, W. H., & Johnson, V. E. *Human sexual inadequacy*. Boston: Little, Brown, 1970.

Rachman, S., & Hodgson, R. J. Experimentally-induced "sexual fetishism": replication and development. *Psychological Record*, 1968, *18*, 25–27.

Robie, W. F. *The art of love*. Ithaca, N.Y.: Rational Life Press, 1925.

Robinson, W. *Woman: Her sex and love life*. New York: Eugenics Publishing Co., 1929.

Rook, K. S., & Hammen, C. L. A cognitive perspective on the experience of sexual arousal. *Journal of Social Issues*, 1977, *33*, 7–29.

Schachter, S. The interaction of cognitive and physiological determinants of emotional state. In L. Berkowitz (Ed.), *Advances in Experimental Social Psychology*. New York: Academic Press, 1964.

Schachter, S., & Singer, J. Cognitive, social, and physiological determinants of emotional state. *Psychological Review*, 1962, *69*, 379–399.

Semans, J. H. Premature ejaculation: a new approach. *Southern Medical Journal*, *49*, 353–357.

Stone, H., & Stone, A. *A marriage manual*. New York: Simon & Schuster, 1935.

Van de Velde, T. H. *Ideal marriage*. New York: Covici-Friede, 1926.

Walen, S. R., Hauserman, N., & Lavin, P. *A clinical guide to behavior therapy*. New York: Oxford University Press, 1977.

Wolfe, J. *How to be sexually assertive*. New York: Institute for Rational Living, 1976.

Wolpe, J. *The practice of behavior therapy*. New York: Pergamon Press, 1969.

Wolpe, J., & Lazarus, A. *Behavior therapy techniques*. New York: Pergamon Press, 1966.

Chapter 7

THE PARAMETERS OF PROCRASTINATION[1]

William Knaus

Procrastination refers to a behavior pattern of delaying what one construes as unpleasant or uncomfortable. Generally, it has come to be known not only as a harmless but annoying failure of so-called "normals" to utilize time wisely, but also a recognizable symptom of a myriad of psychopathological states.

Despite the almost universal occurrence of procrastination, the issues it poses are underrepresented in the literature. Although mentioned by writers and investigators, such as Bolles (1972), Back and Goldberg (1974), Lakin (1973), Dyer (1976), Dell (1973), Sieveking, Campbell, Raleigh, and Savitsky (1971), Krumboltz and Thoresen (1976), Wessman (1973), and Dewey (1904), little has been done to outline the parameters of and

[1]In this paper I am using procrastination and avoidance somewhat interchangeably. Procrastination reflects putting off the uncomfortable task until later; avoidance involves movement away from threatening circumstances. Avoidance is generally considered a response to fear. Procrastination sometimes includes the major factor of fear avoidance but also reflects other motives such as rebelliousness, inadequacy feelings, and so forth.

treatment of procrastination with the exceptions of the work of Knaus (1973), Ellis and Knaus (1977), and Knaus (1979). This chapter, therefore, represents an attempt at refining the definition of procrastination, delineating parameters in terms of its critical features, and describing general procrastination reduction strategies.

DEFINING PROCRASTINATION

Most of us will periodically and purposely delay doing something *relevant* we perceive as unpleasant and uncomfortable, and rationalize this delay by promising ourselves to begin later. Typically this discomfort dodging tactic is short-lived and is within the parameters of normal or adaptive functioning. But, when acts of procrastinating become recognizable patterns and are highly resistive to change, the pattern is indicative of mild to severe forms of psychological disturbance. Indeed, multiple procrastination problems that are durable and intense are symptomatic of almost all psychopathology, particularly the neurotic disorders where some relevant acts are put off indefinitely.

In contrast to a pattern of needlessly delaying relevant activities, there are, of course, numerous downright unnecessary activities rightly unattended. Not routinely sanding and polishing the rafters of my unfinished basement crawl space hardly justifies my behavior as procrastinating. Also, if my delay is legitimately strategic, or due to illness or other like factors, it may not be considered procrastination. So, part of the concept of the procrastinating pattern centers on the assumption that relevant activities are needlessly delayed and this pattern of delay tends to be more or less habitual.

Procrastination is obviously not the central issue in all forms of psychological disturbance. The least of our therapeutic concerns about a floridly psychotic person centers on whether he or she is prompt in sending out his or her résumé to a prospective employer. The hyperactive, enuretic 5-year-old probably would not be viewed as procrastinating on learning to stay in focus or in overcoming bedwetting. So, another feature of procrastination is that it is a behavior largely under the control of conscious processes; and the person makes a *choice* to delay or to act.

Procrastination can be relative, variable, situational, multifaceted, or multidimensional. What Maher (1966) and Lang (1969) have reported about anxiety, that it is not the consequence of each threatening circumstance or always expressed in the same degree, also describes procrastination. For example, a person prone to procrastinating under one set of stressful conditions sometimes becomes quite efficient under different forms of stress, and indeed may take the initiative and work to complete work ahead of schedule.

The implications of the variations in procrastinating behaviors may render its detection and measurement more difficult. However, procrastination can be tied to observable criteria, thus giving the behavior clinical and scientific value.

Needless Delays of Relevant Activities

Chiefly, we are interested in the *extent* to which a person engages in procrastination behaviors, and to make that determination we would be advised to clarify what is meant by needless delays of relevant activities. Describing relevant activities and needless delays can be a complex undertaking. This is because much of the activities in life that a person avoids and the reasons for avoiding them are not open to public inspection.

Even under highly structured work conditions, a person's procrastinating may not be readily apparent because this individual is actively involved in a relevant, but *not a priority* work activity. For example, a purchase department agent has multiple responsibilities. Let's assume that the company has a clear job description outlining the legitimate activities and performance standards which reflect a reasonable rate of productivity. One of these functions is assuring that invoices are routinely filed. As it so happens, the day we observe this person, he or she must make an unpleasant but necessary phone call to a supplier. He or she normally enjoys dealing with this person, but today has been directed to immediately inform the person that his or her company has contracted with a new supplier; so when his or her contract expires, it won't be renewed. We observe on this day that he or she is actively filing invoices (this is normally a low priority, routinely delegated to one of his or her subordinates). Then, nearing the end of the work day, he or she places the phone call. Assuming there was no objective advantage in placing the phone call near the end of the day, we might conclude that our purchase department agent had substituted a relevant but lower-priority activity for a higher priority but more unpleasant activity. We conclude that he or she needlessly delayed making the phone call, define the delay as procrastinating, and make this decision because we are aware of the objective priorities.

Subjectively, our purchase agent had another agenda. He or she wanted to delay tension by avoiding transmitting disappointing news. Like many others in similar circumstances, our purchase agent put off the inevitable until the last possible moment, thus engaging in procrastination.

While it is sometimes difficult to detect procrastination under *formal-structured* conditions where performance guidelines are specified, *self-structured* situations present even greater detection problems. These self-structured situations are conditions where a person has full responsibility for developing his or her own structure, as, for example, the time structuring of self-employed persons and most people outside of a formal work structure. Self-structured compares with formally structured situations in that low-priority tasks may be stretched out and high-priority activities relegated to the future.

At least part of the complications occur because an individual operating under less formal work conditions has varied options and choices about how the options can be prioritized. Under more open-ended conditions, priorities are likely to be more variable, personal interests may fluctuate, and deadlines and scheduling needs can be more flexible.

However, even under self-structured conditions, there are *definable objectives*. For example, if a professional artist strongly wishes to profit financially from his efforts, but makes only marginal efforts to market his or her creations, one can raise the question as to why. If the artist's objectives are to create and sell those creations, then we have a criteria against which to evaluate this individual's efforts. If the prioritizing of the artist's work activities is based upon subjective factors, such as what is comfortable, but not on the basis of what is objectively important, we might rightly infer he or she is procrastinating.

Once we have identified procrastination behaviors, it is important to distinguish between isolated procrastination acts and *procrastination patterns*. Isolated acts, in all probability, will not require psychotherapeutic intervention, while patterns, depending upon their severity and persistence, may. For example, the purchasing agent may rarely exhibit procrastination behaviors on the job and when he or she does may successfully counter the problem. Psychotherapeutic intervention therefore would be contraindicated. On the other hand, the artist whose failure to follow through on his planning may need help to examine his or her objectives and plan, to sort out the reasons for the persistence of his or her procrastination problem, and to develop a counter-procrastination action plan. The basis for recommending psychotherapeutic intervention, however, would depend upon the persistence of the procrastination symptom and the degree to which he or she is, or perceived him or herself to be, debilitated.

Procrastination Inventory

If a therapist wanted to identify a client's procrastination patterns and did not wish to rely on verbal self-reports or time-consuming direct observation, a procrastination inventory I constructed (Knaus, 1979) may prove helpful to identify procrastination problem areas. Because this inventory uniquely requires the respondent to cite data supporting each listed category prior to rating him or herself along a frequency dimension, the respondent is more likely to have a substantive basis for the ratings. Thus, the general dimensions of this performance disability become more readily identified along with specific procrastination behaviors. Figure 7–1 is a sample of the procrastination inventory.

General Procrastination Categories

Typically, acts and patterns of procrastination, whether normal or neurotic, fall into two broad, often overlapping categories: maintenance functions and self-development (Knaus, 1973). Maintenance function procrastination occurs when people put off daily routines they view as onerous, unpleasant, or mundane, such as house cleaning, auto inspections, filing merchandise guaran-

Figure 7–1. Procrastination Inventory

Complete this inventory by citing examples from your life that support or refute each item. Then, based upon your own written testimony, place a check in the column (R = rarely; O = occasionally, SO = somewhat often; VF = very frequently) that you believe best summarizes your written description.

Problem	Evidence	Summary			
		R	O	SO	VF
1. I delay until the eleventh hour before beginning important projects.					
2. I live my life in a state of disorganization.					
3. I show up late for appointments.					
4. I repeatedly replay arguments in my head.					
5. I feel I lack drive or energy.					

tees, paying bills, or disgarding unwanted materials (old clothing, newspapers, furniture). When this pattern is deeply entrenched, people will often report feeling depressed, partially because their living environment appears disheveled and they tend to perceive themselves as hopelessly disorganized.

Self-development procrastination is observed when a person routinely: (1) delays dealing with a troublesome personal problem (agoraphobic fear of going outside the home by oneself, excessive cigarette smoking, overeating, remaining in a destructive relationship, suppression of self-expression); (2) delays taking advantage of leisure-time activities (planning a vacation, joining a pottery class, going on a picnic, building a stamp collection, and so forth); or (3) delays improving career opportunities (seeking to improve work skills, seeking challenging opportunities).

When this pattern is pronounced, the person will often report feeling depressed, immobilized, or in a "rut." Raiport (1976) presents another interesting typology that provides a framework for identifying procrastination dynamics. He classifies people into two categories based upon whether they are dominated by time or space considerations. Time people he sees as dominated by memory, intellect, and abstract thought. They are inclined toward depression and physical passivity. Thus, they are likely to be imprisoned in a world of thought where action is deemphasized. People who are space-oriented tend toward impulsivity, spontaneity, expediency; they live in the present. Space-oriented people generally focus on immediate gratification and thus put off long-term gain if it takes much effort to get what they want. Both time- and space-dominated individuals procrastinate for different reasons, and both thus fail to act in the interest of their future. Ideally, according to Raiport, when space and time dimensions are harmonized, creativity, productivity, and spontaneity result.

The Roots of Procrastination

Procrastination, as I defined it, is an umbrella concept associated with a wide spectrum of relevant but needlessly delayed activities. It is a concept whose broadness can have practical value if the many different procrastination acts and patterns are factored down to a few clinically sound formulations. At the very least, this simplifies our understanding of the dynamics of procrastination and enables us to accurately target on and help clients directly deal with its foundations. I will now describe two major dynamic factors in this section, and will point to five other dimensions further on in this chapter.

Self-Doubt Downing Procrastination

In an earlier publication I advanced that self-doubt downing and low-tension tolerance are pivotal to the procrastination pattern (Knaus, 1979).[2] These are primarily idiosyncratic, change-resistive conceptual formulations attached to situations or events associated with somatically unpleasant affective states. Some people will have a greater natural affinity for acquiring and maintaining them. Further, both formulations generally coexist and are mutually adulterating.

Self-doubt downing reflects a self-destructive, procrastination-generating process. It occurs in instances such as when people judge their abilities as inadequate and then define their adequacy as people on the basis of these questioned qualities. Often, the end product of this process is self-denigration and tension, as well as procrastination. And this negative introspective process is characteristic of Raiport's time-bound personality type.

As indicated in Boyd and Grieger's chapter, self-doubt downing develops in the context of daily living. Through daily experiences people learn faulty concepts from others or creatively invent them (after all, creativity is a bipolar process wherein both constructive insights as well as destructive insights arise). Thus, self-doubt downing often begins as a consequence of a misconception of misattribution which leads to irrational conclusions. For

---

[2]See Knaus (1979) for a description of how these two conceptual dynamics lend to feelings of helplessness, hostility, and guilt and to acts of resistance and rebelliousness

example, one of the more common of the many possible self-defeating erroneous ideas which sets the stage for self-doubt downing procrastination is the belief that almost anything one does ought to be done both easily and of excellent quality. At least part of the problem with this premise is due to the sufferer sematically confusing *easy* with *quickly,* and then expecting his or her performance to reflect the standard. So, if a naturally talented writer comes to believe that he or she *ought* to be able to easily (quickly) write an excellent novel, he or she will probably be disappointed with his or her pace. Contrasting this actual performance against the standard could lead him or her to conclude that he or she is a poor writer and that he or she is wasting time writing. And failing to try or giving only half-hearted efforts reinforces the original opinion that he or she is not talented. Thus, the writer continues to avoid the work (procrastinates) and develops further doubts about his or her capabilities. Doubting one's capabilities, the person is likely (particularly if depressed) to show significantly lower levels of self-expectation and self-reward (Lobitz & DeePost, 1979; Shrauger & Terbovic, 1976). Not uncommonly the next link in this sad chain is self-downing anxiety (ego anxiety) and further procrastination.

Before describing low tension tolerance procrastination, I want to make the point that self-doubt downing is a more basic term than ones like self-concept or self-image. Self-doubt downing implies a *process* of doing or acting; it refers to a chain of cognitive-affective-behavioral associations that develop and change over time. And it seems descriptive of the sort of maladaptive mental processes underlying low self-esteem, poor self-concept, and poor self-image, terms usually employed in the literature.

Indeed, the use of such global terms to describe various states of psychological disturbance by clinicians and researchers of different theoretic orientations, such as Horney (1939), Syngg and Combs (1949), and Rogers (1960), Bandura (1974, 1978), and Lazarus (1971), testifies to the importance these practitioners place upon the impact self-view has on performance. Thus, it is not an unreasonable hypothesis that procrastination, in part, is a reflection of a disparaging self-view, which in turn is a reflection of the self-doubt downing chain.

Low Tension Tolerance Procrastination

Compared to concepts like self-worth, tension tolerance is less frequently highlighted in the literature. But, it has been identified and described in different terms by therapists and researchers as a salient factor in psychological distress. For example, Low (1950) refers to chronic comfort-seeking/discomfort-avoiding tendencies as reflective of psychological disturbance. Freud (1933) has spoken of the pleasure principle wherein individuals will seek pleasure and avoid pain. Thorndike's (1932, 1935) reinforcement theories also refer to the satisfaction-seeking, pain-avoiding tendencies of humans. Horney (1950) insightfully describes neurotic measures to relieve tension in terms of "auxillary approaches to artificial harmony." These are self-alienating defenses which are credible sounding and compensatory, but utterly self-defeating, compulsive strivings. And, as Horney implies, striving to avoid tension without tending to the "impairment of the inner condition" only exacerbates neurotic conflict. Further, the RET system, developed by Ellis, has emphasized low frustration tolerance as a major factor in human psychological disturbance and has made this concept central in treatment programs (Ellis & Knaus, 1979). And this tension-avoiding/comfort-seeking passion is characteristic of Raiport's (1976) time-space orientation.

Persons who have low tolerance for tension overrespond to circumstances where their goals are hindered or blocked. They tend to be emotionally and somatically oversensitized to almost any strain or tension, including mildly unpleasant but normal variations in their biological condition, as well as the normal and inevitable irritations of life. These sensitized individuals unfortunately preoccupy themselves by focusing on their tensions, and they self-generate psychological stress by magnifying the negative importance of these feelings while simultaneously striving to neutralize them by various means. As has been noted by Wine (1971), Duval and Wickland (1972), and Weeks (1976), this sensitization tendency is a major component in anxiety as it serves to make them in part very afraid of their own bad feelings. This general process may be termed "discomfort anxiety." At least part of the procrastination syndrome rests on a foundation of tension avoidance where the procrastinating person's covert goal is avoidance or termination of tension brought on by the demands of a relevant activity or task.

Diversionary Ploys

Although pivotal in a procrastination syndrome, self-doubt downing and low tension tolerance are often shaded by the defenses people muster to divert themselves from experiencing these unpleasant states. Such distortions frequently lead to much unnecessary pain and suffering in the long run, even though their short-term effect may be tension reduction (Freud, 1936; Coleman, 1964). And, in goal-seeking behavior where immediate tension reduction is the implicit objective, people tend to skip over effective long-term solutions (Doob, 1969; Ainslie, 1974) by seeking paliative but specious short-term rewards. Specious solutions in a procrastination pattern often take the form of diversionary tactics which fall into three overlapping categories: mental, action, and emotional.

The best known of the *mental diversions* is the *mañana attitude* where procrastination is cloaked by a decision that a timely activity would be better done later, tomorrow perhaps, when one is in a better mood or better prepared. It is the decision to put off until tomorrow that conveys a false sense of security that the project will eventually be completed. This same decision is evident in a more elaborate mental diversion, the *contingency mañana*, where the uncomfortable activity is put off pending the completion of an invented preliminary step which is also put off. A destructive version of the contingency mañana is the analytic game where procrastination is perpetuated pending a complete analysis of oneself and one's motives, an analysis which tends to remain incomplete.

An important contingency mañana is the happiness contingency. People who are malcontented often strive to obtain perfection, control, approval, and comfort as a means of obtaining inner peace. These individuals believe that attainment of one or more of these four happiness contingencies will make their life wonderful and will make it possible for them to do what they have been putting off. Unfortunately, mental efforts are absorbed in this impossible dream while action awaits the date when the contingencies arrive.

A more extreme form of a mental diversion is the *Catch 22 system* often manifested by more disturbed and rigid persons in which they trap themselves in no-win conceptualizations. For example, a client expressed: "I really want to date attractive women, but they only want to go out with men who are more intelligent than I am; so, I can't see trying to meet one." Since this person was demeaning toward women he viewed as unattractive, and since there was no middle ground in his conceptual network, there was no way he could establish a workable relationship with a woman. Thus the Catch 22 falsely excused his procrastination.

A most debilitating "mental prison trap" is observed in instances where a person introspects into inaction by self-critical ruminations *(the analytic diversion)*. He or she then comes to identify with his or her cruddy self-evaluation, believes he or she cannot change, and simultaneously fears change because he or she fears losing identity and losing self. The obvious outcome of this often deeply rooted trap is a strong avoidance of engaging in personal growth and a strong striving to keep "everything" the same.

Action diversions, like mental diversions, exist along a continuum from mild to severe psychological disturbance. At the mild end of the continuum we find the person putting off trying to solve a relevant high-priority problem by substituting a lower one. At this point in the continuum, substitution behavior is short-lived and occasionally serves an adaptive function. At more disturbed levels, the substitute activity often involves compulsions, addictions, and manias. And like mental diversions, both mild and severe action diversions become stabilized because they are routinely reinforced since they temporarily reduce stress.

Some persons are particularly fearful of conditions in which they might feel tension, and are especially afraid of feeling negative affects such as anxiety. Situations which are associated with tension tend to be avoided, and tense feelings are suppressed. People who try to *emotionally divert* from feeling tense by dodging the stress situation and squelching the tenseness usually find their efforts backfire, for they typically experience considerably more anguished feelings than they would if they directly coped with the feared situation. They manufacture they very feelings they want to avoid.

It is interesting to note that the three diversionary systems often operate in profusion. While one may clearly dominate, the other two are almost always part of the procrastination pattern. As self-doubt downing and low tension tolerance play off each other, the other three diversionary systems also tend to interact. Indeed, where procrastination is chronic a person may spend much time analyzing his or her procrastination symptoms until he or she knows everything about the symptom and makes the symptom into everything. In so doing he or she is trapped into a labyrinth of interlocking emotional, mental, and action complications.

Procrastination Complications

The pathways of the labyrinth can be quite tangled, particularly if the procrastinating individual falsely externalizes blame onto others for the plight. Then, the solutions to the problems involve changing other persons held responsible for one's own unnecessary delays, a most formidable task in many instances.

At times the pathways lead to more time wasting, as when the procrastinating individual shelves his or her own problem, takes the offense, and impatiently lectures and chastizes others (particularly intimates) for real or imagined procrastinating. The expressed expectation is that the criticizing lectures will prove expedient. But, these are projections and tend to incite anger in others. And, despite poor results, critical lecturing is resistant to extinction because it serves the covert purpose of creating (1) a sense of superiority, (2) a sense of mission, and (3) the avoidance of select maintenance and growth functions which might be threatening or frustrating.

Sometimes the labyrinth has conflicting cognitions blocking exit pathways. For example, the boy who originally took pleasure in listening to the sound of the trumpet began to take lessons and enjoyed them, but began to hate the trumpet when his parents began to yell at him to practice more. He came to associate pleasurable experiences with anger and rebellion. These countervailing concepts play off each other, and if anger becomes compelling, it dominates and generalizes and the person avoids pleasure.

Obviously, there are breakdowns in the diversionary systems. During these breakdown periods the person may feel immobilized, incompetent, and self-disgusted. Sometimes frenzied activity to complete the overhanging projects occurs, and immobilization is successfully countered. But, such magificent efforts are only part of an overall pattern of procrastination-action-procrastination-action. And, often this habit-prone person lives in eternal hope that one frenzied action will forever end the problem. But that hope is as likely to materialize as would the hope that one thorough garden weeding would forever end weed growth.

An Interactive-Reciprocity Model

Generally the relationship between self-doubt downing, low tension tolerance, procrastination, somatic sensitization, and diversionary ploys is interactive, reciprocal, and intertwined with social-personal norms and situational contexts (see Figure 7–2).

The seven dimensions in Figure 7–2 fluctuate in salience. For example, procrastination originally may have been the symptom of severe self-doubts experienced under unusually provocative

Figure 7–2.   Procrastination Reciprocal-Interaction Model

Procrastination Reciprocal-Interaction Model

Diversions

Self-Doubt Downing   Procrastination   Low Tension
                             Tolerance

Somatic Sensitization

CONTEXT

circumstances (context) when the person expected more than he or she could deliver (personal norms). The procrastination habit established during this period generalizes to other mild-to-moderately stress-stimulating conditions. Now the symptom, procrastination, becomes the source of stressful contemplations, and escalating self-doubts and fears of feeling tense become reciprocal responses. Somatic sensitization becomes prepotent in the sequence and serves as a powerful avoidance-procrastination signal.

Normally, constructive changes in one of these interlocking factors thins the flow of this reciprocal-interactive process and makes the other dimensions more alterable. Thus, the model may be helpful as a general guideline to the professional interested in examining and therapeutically altering a general procrastination pattern, or as a guideline to the counselor concerned with dealing with a specific procrastination pattern. Thus, if the symptomatic complaints represented a major problem like agoraphobia, shyness, obesity, lateness, or failure to complete assignments on schedule, that particular procrastination complaint would be the treatment focus, and a conceptual-behavioral diagnosis made of that symptom pattern.

Working with clients to overcome specific procrastination problems, like shyness, would involve a careful conceptual-behavioral analysis of self-descriptions and images (self-doubts and so forth), diversionary activities, intensity of somatic sensitivity reactions, perception of and response to tension, performance standards, and variances within specific interpersonal contexts. With a solid conceptual-behavioral diagnosis, *action* planning and therapeutic interventions to disrupt the malfunctional shyness-procrastination pattern are likely to be more realistic and effective.

PROCRASTINATION REDUCTION

Kluver (1933) has noted that human behavior reflects attitudes, sets, complexes, determining tendencies, needs, or quasineeds. In developing strategies for helping a client reduce procrastinating activities, the more we know about that client's attitudes, determining tendencies, and so forth, the closer we can come to understanding the client and the more likely we will be to help him or her.

Obviously, to maximize our therapeutic effectiveness, a solid conceptual-behavioral diagnosis is important so that we can proceed in our therapeutic efforts with greater confidence and with a greater likelihood of being effective. With this diagnosis we see more clearly how a person thinks, what determines that thinking, and what he or she is likely to feel and do as a result.

The diagnosis involves identifying and clarifying procrastination problem dimensions from what we observe, what a person tells us, and what we can infer and then validate. Sometimes our diagnosis makes it possible for us to proceed to use a high-structured action program. At other times, we will not be able to develop a clear conceptual picture so the therapy process becomes one of ongoing diagnosis and intervention.

Regardless of whether a person's procrastination difficulties can be therapeutically approached through a highly structured or through an ongoing diagnostic-interventionist process, two major dimensions are kept in focus. These dimensions are *awareness* and *action*.

When a person changes from malfunctional to adaptive modes of thinking and behaving, he or she does so because of constructive self-awareness and/or constructive efforts. Thus, it is important to organize therapy along the lines of an awareness-action format to maximize therapeutic effectiveness.

An awareness and action format for organizing therapy is inclusive of scientifically valid psychotherapeutic methods. Many of these methods have been developed and refined through secular action therapy systems such as behavior therapy (Wolpe, 1969), RET (Ellis, 1973), and multimodal therapy (Lazarus, 1973). This format also embraces clinically valid concepts formulated by neoanalysts like Horney (1937) and ego-analysts like Hartman (1968).

An awareness-action therapy organization can be effectively tied to the procrastination reciprocity-interaction model (PRIM). Most procrastination acts and patterns can be treated at the conceptual-behavioral level suggested by PRIM. And cognitive (awareness) and/or behavior (action) systems such as rational-emotive, multimodal, and behavior therapy can be combined and employed to treat procrastination. These three psychotherapy delivery systems are empirically testable, support client actions to do better to get better, and therefore seem most adaptable among contemporary therapy systems for alleviating human procrastination patterns.

The three psychotherapy delivery systems can be integrated into a high-structured treatment program. This high-structured program includes: effective methods targeted toward procrastination problem clusters with clearly specified objectives for the therapeutic process. Figure 7–3 illustrates a high-structured procrastination reduction treatment plan.

Such a highly structured procrastination reduction program limits client evasiveness by reducing side-tracking. With minimizing opportunities for side-tracking, client's efforts can be more effectively targeted to deal with his or her troublesome procrastination pattern(s). Indeed, therapy systems like behavioral and rational-emotive, which have a clearly structured treatment proce-

Figure 7–3 High-Structure Procrastination Reduction Treatment Plan

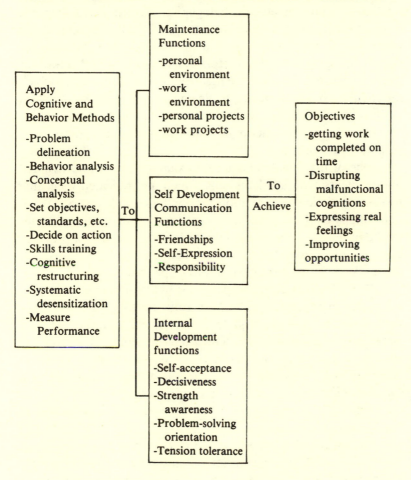

dure, tend to be the most effective. Perhaps high structure is an important variable for behavior change.

High-structured formal treatment programs are sometimes counterindicated at the beginning phases of therapy. Substantive conceptual diagnoses often take time, particularly if the client's problems are abstract, diffuse, or multiple. Thus, it is not always possible to establish and implement a quality, high-structured, counterprocrastination program. Instead, a more loosely structured but forceful therapeutic dialogue between client and therapist is required (1) to gain a solid conceptual understanding of the person's problems and (2) to identify and clarify difficult-to-detect, but centrally important associative-conceptual links. Indeed, sometimes the effective therapeutic process is one in which the client becomes aware of the dynamic interrelationship between various life experiences, conceptual associations to those experiences, and current functioning, and uses this awareness as a springboard to change.

One of my female clients, for example, repeatedly avoided involvements with available single men and repeatedly became involved with dead-end relationships with married men. She came into therapy convinced she had an irreversible commitment "hang-up." She had worked on her commitment problem in a previous therapy and felt marginally better about herself, but was still exasperated by the continuation of her pattern.

When I first began to help her stop procrastinating in meeting available single men, I did a brief retrospective analysis of her pattern. Significantly, the pattern analysis led to a discussion of her family relationships. It seemed that considerable rivalry existed between her and her mother. Indeed, the mother stood between her and her father, to the extent that to communicate with each other she and her father would pass notes. So, at least part of her problem reflected a continuing repetition of a pathological family pattern.

Once aware that she was still carrying on the family battle that now had generalized the conflict to married men and their wives, she began to avoid married men and started to date single men. Unfortunately she began to see singles who seemed tied to their mothers' apron strings. When this pattern became obvious, it too was intercepted and the client began to date less disturbed but available men. At the time of this writing she is successfully living with one.

As best as I could determine, her pattern began when she was about 8 years of age, when her mother seemed to be experiencing a "nervous breakdown." The relationship between her and her father did not seem sexually oriented. Her father would periodically abandon the home when he and his wife fought. Part of her relationship difficulties involved abandonment fears. The rapidity with which she changed with each new awareness was partially a function of orienting herself toward thinking how she could work toward improving her relationship, reducing self-doubts, and tolerating her fears and thereby avoiding self-restriction.

Clearly the complex interplay between critical experiences, critical cognitions concerning these experiences, and, in many instances, conflicting cognitions, abstractions, generalizations, and semantic confusions, point to the importance of a solid conceptual analysis of a person's procrastination pattern. And, this conceptual analysis may take time as the client and therapist may initially be unaware of important problem areas.

SUMMARY

I have delineated the parameters of procrastination in this chapter. I do not expect this delineation to be the final one. Indeed, I have developed this chapter as a catalyst for thought, discussion, and research with the view that there are many loose ends to be tied, issues to be fleshed out, and contradictions to be resolved.

The parameters of procrastination involve the assumptions that:

- procrastination is an umbrella concept that describes a wide spectrum of maladaptive behaviors.
- procrastination represents a needless delay of a relevant activity.
- each act of procrastination represents a choice.
- procrastination is variable, relative, multidimensional, situational, and multifaceted.
- the concept is clinically observable and empirically testable.

- procrastination primarily reflects self-doubts and intolerance for tension.
- mental, emotional, and action diversions are recognizable symptoms of a procrastination pattern.
- procrastination may reflect somatic sensitization and personal-social norms.
- procrastination is part of a reciprocal-interactive process that includes self-doubt, low tension tolerance, somatic sensitization, diversions, personal-social norms, and context.
- constructive alteration in one or more of the seven reciprocal-interacting dimensions weakens the flow of the reciprocal-interactive process.
- time-bound persons are likely to procrastinate as a result of a process of thinking excessively.
- space-bound persons will procrastinate because they will emphasize specious rather than long-term rewards.

I have also provided an awareness-action structure for organizing empirically valid systems of psychotherapy. The structure is obviously in its germinal stage. It does, however, have the potential for being an inclusive system that ties methods together that can be useful to help clients optimize their performance by getting on with the relevant high-priority aspects of their lives. And since all good therapists tend to help their clients obtain realistic awarenesses and become involved in problem-solving and growth-developing actions, awareness-action is a logical way of organizing such efforts.

Finally, there are two therapy assumptions:

- Most procrastination patterns are best treated through a high-structured therapy format.
- Some procrastination patterns yield most readily to a focused, informally structured, awareness-action centered therapy structure.

REFERENCES

Ainslie, G. Specious reward: A behavioral theory of impulsiveness and impulse control. *Psychological Bulletin,* 1975, *82,* 463–496.

Bach, G. R., & Goldberg, H. *Creative aggression.* New York: Doubleday and Co., 1974.

Bandura, A. Behavior theory and the models of man. *American Psychologist,* 1974, *29,* 859–869.

Bandura, A. The self-system in reciprocal determinism. *American Psychologist,* 1978, *33,* 344–358.

Bolles, R.N. *What color is your parachute?* Berkeley, Calif.: Ten Speed Press, 1977.

Coleman, J.C. *Abnormal psychology and modern life* (3rd ed.). Glenville, Ill.: Scott Foresman, 1964.

Dell, D.M. Counselor power base, influence attempt, and behavior change in counseling. *Journal of Counseling Psychology,* 1973, *20,* 399–405.

Dewey, J. *Moral principle in education.* New York: Houghton Mifflin Co., 1909.

Doob, L. *Patterning of time.* New Haven: Yale University Press, 1971.

Duval, S., & Wickland, R. *A theory of objective self-awareness.* New York: Academic Press, 1972.

Dyer, W.W. *Your erroneous zones.* New York: Funk and Wagnalls, 1976.

Ellis, A. *Reason and emotion in psychotherapy.* New York: Lyle Stuart, 1962.

Ellis, A. *Humanistic psychotherapy: The rational-emotive approach.* New York: Julian Press, 1973.

Ellis, A., & Knaus, W.J. *Overcoming procrastination.* New York: New American Library, 1979.

Freud, A. *The ego and the mechanisms of defense.* New York: International Universities Press, 1956.

Freud, S. *New introductory lectures on psychoanalysis.* New York: Norton, 1933.

Hartman, H. *Ego psychology and the problem of adaptation.* New York: International Universities Press, 1968.

Horney, K. *The neurotic personality of our times.* New York: W. W. Norton, 1937.

Horney, K. *Neurosis and human growth.* New York: W. W. Norton, 1950.

Kluver, H. *Behavior mechanisms in monkeys.* Chicago: University of Chicago Press, 1933.

Knaus, W.J. Overcoming procrastination. *Rational Living.* 1973, *8,* 2–7.

Knaus, W.J. *Do it now: How to stop procrastinating.* Englewood Cliffs, N. J.: Prentice-Hall, 1979.

Krumboltz, J., & Thoresen, C. *Counseling methods.* New York: Holt, Rinehart, and Winston, 1976.

Lakin, A.L. *How to get control of your time and your life*. New York: Peter Wyden, 1973.

Lang, P.J. The mechanisms of desensitization and the laboratory study of fear. In C.M. Franks (Ed.), *Behavior therapy: Appraisal and status*, New York: McGraw-Hill, 1969.

Lazarus, A. *Behavior therapy and beyond*. New York: McGraw-Hill, 1971.

Lazarus, A. *Multi-modal psychotherapy*. New York: Springer, 1976.

Lobitz, W. C. & DeePost, R. Parameters of self-reinforcement and depression. *Journal of Abnormal Psychology*, 1979, *88*, 33–41.

Low, A. *Mental health through will training*. Boston: Christopher Publishing House, 1950.

Maher, B.A. *Principles of psychopathology: An experimental approach*. New York: McGraw-Hill, 1966.

Raiport, G. Personality typology based upon space-time involvement, Unpublished paper, 1979. (Available from G. Raiport, 250 E. 87th St., N.Y., N.Y. 10028.)

Raiport, G. The personality through time-space involvement. *Journal of Academy of Science*, Tbilisi, U.S.S.R., 1976, *2*, 115–125.

Rogers, C.L. *On becoming a person*. Boston: Houghton Mifflin, 1961.

Shrauger, J.S., & Terbovic, M.L. Self-evaluation and assessments of performance by self and others. *Journal of Consulting and Clinical Psychology*, 1976, *44*, 564–572.

Sieveking, N.A., Campbell, M.C., Raleigh, W.J., & Savitsky, S. Mass intervention by mail for academic impediment, *Journal of Consulting and Clinical Psychology*, 1971, *18*, 601–602.

Syngg, D., & Combs, A.W. *Individual behavior*. New York: Harper, 1949.

Thorndike, E.L. *The fundamentals of learning*. New York: Teachers College, 1932.

Thorndike, E.L. *The psychology of wants, interests, and attitudes*. New York: Appleton-Century, 1935.

Weeks, C. *Simple, effective treatment of agoraphobia*. New York: Hawthorn Books, 1976.

Wessman, A. Personality and the subjective experience of time. *Journal of Personality Assessment*. 1933, *37*, 103–114.

Wine, J. Test anxiety and direction of attention. *Psychological Bulletin*, 1971, *76*, 92–104.

Wolpe, J. *The practice of behavior therapy*. New York: Pergamon Press, 1969.

Chapter 8

THE COGNITIVE BASIS OF WOMEN'S PROBLEMS

Ingrid Zachary Grieger

The question of how and why women become emotionally disturbed constitutes one of the most controversial, heated, and vociferous debates in psychology. The views of the various camps involved in the controversy are remarkably divergent, both in terms of etiology and treatment. Positions range from the universal inevitability of feminine craziness inherent in the Freudian view all the way to a basic questioning by feminists of whether women are mad at all, as opposed to being profoundly oppressed. This chapter will present both of those positions as a prelude to examining the internal cognitive variables which by themselves or in interaction with the environment form what I believe to be the most heuristic and tenable construct for understanding emotional disturbance in women.

THE PSYCHOANALYTIC VIEW

In the Freudian scheme of things, a female is virtually doomed to experience some form of emotional disturbance from the moment she realizes that she doesn't have a penis. As a child, she immediately recognizes the superiority of the male organ and develops a sense of inferiority and contempt for herself and other females; her inevitable penis envy generalizes into the feminine trait of jealousy, and she becomes narcissistic and vain as a reaction to her basic sense of shame. Should she refuse to accept "the fact of being castrated," a woman will develop a masculinity complex which is clearly neurotic and may, in fact, form the beginnings of a psychosis (Freud, 1925).

The only "normal" path a woman can follow in developing her femininity is to exchange her mother for her father as primary love object and to relinquish her clitoris for her vagina as her leading genital zone (Freud, 1931). The goal of this process is marriage and the birth of a male child, in order that a woman experience fulfillment and mental adjustment; to do otherwise would be neurotic. However, Freud stated that marriage, too, is extremely neurosis-inducing; furthermore, once a woman becomes aware that her marriage is driving her crazy and considers eluding it, perhaps via unfaithfulness, she will seek refuge in yet another neurosis (Freud, 1947). Thus, no matter which course of action a woman follows, the traditional route of marriage or the nontraditional path of a profession, she is inexorably bound to be neurotic.

Another factor in the genesis of emotional disturbance in women for Freud is the differential sequence of the castration complex and the Oedipal conflict in males and females. In males the castration complex follows the Oedipal conflict, thus providing the impetus for the formation of a strong super-ego and the resolution of the Oedipal conflict. In females, however, the castration complex precedes the Oedipal complex; thus there is no strong impetus for the resolution of the Oedipal complex or the formation of a strong super-ego. Thus, Freud concluded that,

> For women the level of what is ethically normal is different from what it is in men . . . character-traits which critics of every epoch have brought up against women—that they show less sense of jus-

tice than men, that they are less ready to submit to the great exigencies of life, that they are more often influenced in their judgements by feelings of affection or hostility—all of these would be amply accounted for by the modification in the formation of their super-ego (Freud, 1925).

Deutsch (1944), like Freud, stressed that passivity, narcissism, and masochism form the core of the feminine personality. According to Deutsch, the healthy woman renounces her achievements, does not insist upon her rights, is easily influenced, and is intuitive rather than objective and intellectual. In fact, it is unhealthy for a woman to turn her attention to objective intellectual endeavors; contemporary education thus overburdens females by destroying their emotionality and intuition. For Deutsch, these women are disturbed when they engage in "masculine" pursuits like working and thinking objectively, which diverts them from their true emotional nature and from their ultimate destiny, which is to be "the servant of reproduction."

The notion that passivity and especially masochism are not only normal, but quintessential feminine characteristics was strongly reiterated by Marie Bonaparte (1953). Somewhat more benignly, Erikson (1968) has reframed the concept of female masochism from the traditional definition of taking pleasure in pain to the understanding of pain "as a meaningful aspect of human experience, in general, and of the feminine role in particular." Erikson explains this contention by postulating a sense of "inner space" in females which permits them to experience an emptiness, despair, and hurt that is quite beyond that of males. This sense of "inner space" in females also suggests that a woman can fulfill herself only via marriage and reproduction. In fact, Erikson contends that a woman cannot fully have an identity before marriage because she must keep a part of her identity "open for the peculiarities of the man to be joined and of the children to be brought up."

In summary, it appears that for the Freudians a woman's sole desire in life being to marry and have (preferably male) children is normal. Deviations from this goal are viewed as neurotic because they represent a woman's refusal to be happy in the feminine role, which is resultant of unresolved penis envy and an unresolved Oedipal complex. On the other hand, masochism, narcissism, jealousy, passivity, shame, and inferiority are viewed as perfectly normal feminine characteristics. In males, of course, these traits would be seen as neurotic "symptoms."

Lest we be too quick to relegate this antiquated double standard of mental health to the psychiatric archives, the reader is reminded that in the now classic Broverman study, conducted in 1970, it was found that clinicians had one standard of mental health for healthy males and healthy adults, sex unspecified, and a different standard of mental health for adult women. Broverman, Broverman, Rosenkrantz, & Vogel (1970), concluded that,

> Clinicians are more likely to suggest that healthy women differ from healthy men by being more submissive, less independent, less adventurous, more easily influenced, less aggressive, less competitive, more excitable in minor crises, having their feelings more easily hurt, being more emotional, more conceited about their appearance, less objective and disliking math and science.

This finding is a contemporary recapitulation of the Freudian double bind: a woman can be a psychologically healthy female, but then she is an unhealthy adult and conversely, if she demonstrates the characteristics of a healthy adult, she is an emotionally disturbed woman. In the traditional view, thus, there are sex-role stereotypical criteria of adjustment for both males and females and deviations from these norms were seen as "disturbed." The link between sex role and psychopathology is expounded more fully by some contemporary writers, particularly Phyllis Chesler, (1972) and will be discussed in the next section.

SOCIOLOGICAL VIEWS

In a clear contradistinction to the anatomically based etiology of emotional disturbance in women delineated above, Clara Thompson offers a cultural and, indeed, a political reinterpretation of the Freudian position. Thompson (1942) maintained that Freud's theory is clearly based only upon observations of Victorian women and remains relevant only to the extent that vestiges of Victorianism are present in our own culture today. Thompson (1942) maintains that Freud's notions about penis envy, narcissism, and lack of strong conviction in women can be adequately explained by the extremely restrictive and repressive nature of Victorian society.

Thompson (1950) questions whether envy for the penis, as a physical organ, exists at all or whether the penis is merely a symbol for the power and autonomy which men, potentially, enjoy. Thus, it is not the lack of a penis that may engender feelings of envy, or even of hostility, in women; rather, it is the lack of independence and freedom to take control over one's life. Thompson concludes that so-called "penis envy" is *not* a neurotic symptom; rather it is a symbol of real and legitimate grievances against the limitations of a patriarchal and phallocentric society.

Similarly, a woman's alleged narcissism may arise out of a need to maintain physical attractiveness in order to survive economically (Thompson, 1942). Likewise a woman's apparent lack of strong convictions are not resultant of a weak superego; rather a woman needed to remain flexible in order to adopt the ideology which would put her in good stead with the man who would be her protector (Thompson, 1942). Thompson has also hypothesized that in today's patriarchal culture a woman is more likely to experience emotional difficulties than previously, as her jobs of raising children and maintaining a home have become less time and energy consuming and, hence, less valued. Thus, many of today's women become emotionally upset, at least in part, because they find themselves without a meaningful and respected occupation.

Friedan (1963) has offered a contemporary reiteration of Thompson's thesis. Many of today's women, Friedan contends, are plagued by "the problem that has no name," which encompasses feelings of isolation, helplessness, depression, and utter futility, resultant of the uncomfortable and persistent suspicion that there has to be more to life than childrearing and housework. For

Friedan, the housewife is "neurotic" because she has no viable means to come to full, healthy adulthood. As a woman becomes older, in fact, the problem is intensified as her children and husband slip farther and farther away from her, often leaving her with no reason to go on. For Friedan, the solution to feminine neurosis lies in massive social and political change in which marriage and motherhood may become a part, but certainly not the sum total, of a woman's life. Friedan believes that only when women commit themselves to life-spanning pursuits of their own can they take control of their lives and experience competence and fulfillment via their own accomplishments, rather than living through husbands and children for feelings of self-worth. By fulfilling competent adult roles and defining their own lives, women can overcome the "neurotic housewife" syndrome.

Like Thompson (1941, 1942, 1943, 1950) and Friedan (1963), Chesler (1972) contends that "psychopathology" in women can be aptly explained by oppressive conditions in society and sex-role sterotyping rather than by intrapsychic factors resultant of penis envy. Chesler asserts that women often seek psychiatric help for symptoms which are, in fact, conditioned and socially approved of self-destructive feminine behaviors, such as depression, excessive worries, feelings of inferiority, and lack of self-confidence. In discussing depression, in particular, Chesler alludes to the traditional Freudian explanation of depression as a response to loss and suggests that perhaps women are in a perpetual state of mourning for the loss of the love of their mothers, their husbands, and for their own ideal selves which were never fully realized. Chesler stresses that depression, rather than aggression, is the socially approved of vehicle for a woman to react to disappointment. A woman who acts out aggressively achieves no secondary gains and is usually abandoned rather than protected. The woman who acts out against her sex role, who does become violent, angry, and insensitive to her appearance is, according to Chesler, often labeled as "schizophrenic." These women do, however, retain some "feminine" symptoms such as helplessness, dependence, and feelings of inferiority.

Observations of the symptomology of emotional disturbance in women have led Chesler to the theoretical proposition that what we label as "madness" is either the acting out of the devalued female role or the total or partial rejection of one's sex-role stereotype (Chesler, 1972, p.56). Thus, women tend to be hospitilized for such feminine disturbances as depression, anxiety neurosis, and paranoia, or for such unfeminine behaviors as schizophrenia or lesbianism.

As one would imagine, Chesler (1972) rejects traditional psychotherapy as the panacea for women's ills. Chesler views psychotherapy as a patriarchal institution which mirrors the position of the woman in the family and in society at large. Chesler contends that a relationship in which the man is viewed as the superior, the expert, the helper, and the woman is viewed as the dependent, help-seeking subordinate is distructive and debilitating to women. Traditional psychotherapists tend to reinforce stereotypical female roles by assuring female clients that they will find fulfillment via marriage, children, and vaginal orgasms, while they ignore the objective fact of women's oppression in a sexist society. Unhappiness, discontent, and depression, then, are viewed as intrapsychic illnesses rather than as natural concomitants of being "trained to be passive and dependent in a world that values activity and strength" (Chesler, 1971).

The views presented thus far have attributed emotional disturbance in women to either intrapsychic conflicts resultant of anatomical inferiority or to reactions to oppressive conditions of a patriarchal and sexist society. In the remainder of this chapter I shall turn my attention to cognitive factors in the etiology of emotional disturbance in women and suggestions for remediation.

COGNITIVE VIEWS

Martin Seligman (1973) stumbled across the phenomenon of learned helplessness rather serendipitously when he discovered that dogs who were exposed to inescapable, uncontrollable shock simply lay down passively and accepted the aversive stimulus. In subsequent phases of the experiment, when the dogs could escape the shock, they made no attempt to do so. In short, they had learned that they were helpless. Experiments by Donald Hiroto (1974) revealed that human subjects reacted similarly to the aversive stimulus of uncontrollable noise. Seligman (1973) suggests that there are striking parallels between subjects who had developed experimentally induced learned helplessness and individuals who are depressed. Both experience cognitive, emotional, and motivational disturbances.

Seligman's (1975) original model of learned helplessness is based on the premise that when an individual expects an aversive outcome and believes that his or her response to a given situation and the contingency of outcome upon that response are independent of one another, he or she is rendered helpless; i.e., when a person believes that his or her response is irrelevant, he or she will become depressed. It is Seligman's (1975) assertion that learned helplessness and unipolar depressions are remarkably similar in terms of symptomology, etiology, cure, and prevention. In terms of symptomology, Seligman notes that both learned helplessness and depression are characterized by lowered initiation of voluntary responses, a negative cognitive set, lowered aggression, lowered self-esteem, physiological and neurophysiological changes, and passivity.

Beck and Greenberg (1974) suggest that the learned helplessness model of depression is particularly relevant to understanding depression in women. Beck and Greenberg note that women in our society have had a variety of experiences that would tend to facilitate their belief that they are helpless. For example, female children are often taught that their survival depends upon their physical attractiveness, rather than upon their competence in responding to and controlling life situations. Furthermore, throughout adolescence, they are subjected to parental, societal, and institutional constraints which further restrict their exerting control over their own lives. According to Seligman (1975), the best inoculation against learned helplessness depression is early experience with competence and mastery. What Beck and Greenberg

(1974) are suggesting, then, is that since females have had such few opportunities to experience their own sense of competence and mastery early in life, they are particularly vulnerable to depression as adults. In short, they have learned that their own skilled response to a situation is irrelevant.

More recently (1979) Seligman has developed a refinement of his original learned helplessness model of depression. Seligman now contends that when people experience failure, they look for explanations or attributions. Seligman has found that the attributions that people make regarding their own success or failure have three dimensions: (1) internal/external; (2) stable/unstable; and (3) global/specific. Depressed persons make attributions that are internal, stable, and global with regard to failure. Thus, when a depressed individual experiences failure he or she believes that it is all his or her fault (internal) because he or she is a failure in everything (global) and will always be (stable). For example, a depressed student who fails a test will tell her or himself that he or she failed because he or she is stupid, which is an attribution which is internal, stable, and global. A nondepressed person will tell him or herself that this particular test was just too hard, an attribution which is external, unstable, and specific.

Seligman (1979) notes that the ratio between male and female depression may be as high as 1:10. He attributes this to women's belief in the noncontingency of their responses and to their attributional style. Seligman has found that as early as 4th grade females tend to make internal, stable, and global attributions ("I am stupid"). One reason for this, contends Seligman, is that teachers tend to make more unstable, specific, and external statements to boys regarding failure, and more internal, stable, and global statements to girls. Why this is the case is not clear, nor is this by any means the total explanation for the attributional style of females. The exploration of how females develop their self-defeating attributional style is certainly fertile ground for future research. It appears, thus, that Seligman has certainly presented a heuristic model for understanding the role of cognition in depression in women.

To summarize, then, an individual is likely to become depressed when he or she expects a negative occurrence, believes that there is nothing that he or she can do to prevent that occurrence, and attributes this failure to factors that are internal, stable, and global. Seligman (1979) suggests that four modes of therapeutic interventions are implied by his reformulated theory of depression. They are as follows.

ENRICHING THE ENVIRONMENT.   Since a depressed individual expects aversive outcomes, one way of altering this expectation is to help him or her change the environment in positive ways. The therapist becomes a change agent, a manipulator of the client's external environment, and a liaison with other social agencies and resources within the community. Environmental enrichment may include assistance in the areas of vocational training and job placement, housing, financial aid, medical care, and rehabilitation, finding day care centers and social outlets.

TRAIN IN PERSONAL CONTROL.   The depressed individual believes that aversive events are uncontrollable, i.e., there is nothing he or she can do about it. Training an individual in personal control skills should aid in changing the cognition of uncontrollability to one of controllability. Examples include training in social skills, assertiveness, time management, money management, decision making, problem solving, and graded task assignments.

RESIGNATION TRAINING.   In this strategy, the goal of the therapist is to help the client to reduce the aversiveness of an expected negative outcome and reduce the attractiveness of a desired, but probably unattainable, positive outcome. An effective way to help the client achieve this goal is via RET (Ellis, 1962). The RET therapist directly and vigorously challenges the client's basic assumptions about the desirability or aversiveness of a particular outcome. For example, a client may decide that to be in a relationship with a particular man is a highly desirable outcome and to lose him would be most aversive. When this relationship ends, she becomes depressed by telling herself that this is so aversive that it is awful, that she cannot go on living, and that she is unlovable because she lost this particular man. The RET therapist would challenge each of these assumptions in an effort to help this client to stop awfulizing about the aversiveness of this outcome and to put it in a more rational perspective, i.e., that it is unfortunate and regretful, but not awful.

REATTRIBUTION TRAINING.   Since the depressed client makes attributions that are internal, global, and stable for failure and external, specific, and unstable for success, the goal of the therapist is to reverse this process, of course, within the limits of reality. Thus, for example, a woman who fails to get a promotion to executive rank in her company may conclude that it was because she is an incompetent individual (internal), and that she always will be (stable), and that she will never advance in any job (global). The therapist will aid her in substituting these cognitions for ones like: The system often discriminates against women (external), but things are changing (unstable), and perhaps your company is particularly discriminatory (specific).

RET can be helpful, as well, in disputing the entire notion of any character trait being global, internal, and stable. RET specifically changes the belief that we can ever evaluate ourselves totally and for all time. Rather, it suggests that we are a composite of many performances which are constantly changing over time. Thus, although an individual may not succeed at a given performance, he or she can never be "a failure," as that suggests that in each and every endeavor in that person's life, he or she only and always fails. It should be noted, however, that within Seligman's model RET would be extremely powerful with regard to reattribution for failure but not for success.

In summary, Seligman's learned helplessness model of depression is a prime example of the role of cognition in the etiology of depression. The individual disturbs herself by setting up a set of beliefs that are self-defeating and self-downing. The use of behavioral, environmental, and cognitive interventions, however, can ameliorate and even reverse the effects of learned helplessness. When dealing with female clients, this is a particularly relevant and powerful schema for conceptualizing the dynamics and antecedents of depression.

IRRATIONAL PHILOSOPHIES

Like Seligman (1979), Aaron Beck (1972) suggests that depressed individuals have a unique mode of viewing their experiences. Beck contends that depressed persons hold a systematic bias against themselves, the world, and the future. (This "cognitive triad" is quite similar to what Seligman is saying about attributional style; as a negative set about one's self, the world and the future is, in fact, internal, global, and stable.) Beck and Greenberg (1974) suggest that with regard to a negative view of self, a woman's depression may be exacerbated by the fact that our culture tends to reinforce her negative self-evaluations. Thus, messages in the society that woman are ineffectual, dependent, and passive and that a depressed woman is either a "manipulative bitch" or "a dishrag" can only feed into a woman's depression. In short then, when a depressed woman tells herself "I am worthless," society answers "Yes, you are," thus reinforcing her self-defeating systematic bias against herself. I would suggest also that once depressed, a man has more effective coping strategies than does a woman, as a proactive, aggressive posture is certainly more effective than a passive, helpless one in breaking up depression.

The cognitive process, then, is the same for both women and men regarding depression; however, society tends to reinforce the negative messages that women tell themselves. Ellis (1974) presents a similar view in discussing sex and love problems in women. Ellis (1974) suggests that women tend to be "love slobs" because society reinforces women telling themselves that they *must* be a part of a couple in order to be fulfilled and worthwhile. Thus, when a woman is not in a relationship with a man or has been rejected by her lover, she disturbs herself emotionally by holding "mustubatory," awfulizing, and self-downing beliefs and philosophies and society reinforces these beliefs.

In addition, Beck and Greenberg (1974) suggest that women and men tend to get depressed around sex-typed events. Thus, a man may become depressed around crises in his career, whereas a woman may be more likely to become depressed around relationship crises, children leaving home, or some issues such as rape, the career/housewife conflict, or abortion, which are unique to women.

This view is entirely consistent with my own which I have discussed elsewhere (Zachary, 1979). It is my contention that cognition plays a pivotal role in the emotional disturbance of both men and women. All human beings become angry, depressed, guilty or anxious when they hold self-defeating irrational beliefs (Ellis & Harper, 1975). Thus, in the A (activating event)-B (beliefs, cognitions, philosophies)-C (emotional consequences) theory of RET, the B's and C's tend to be the same for both males and females; however, the A's may be very different. Thus women tend to upset themselves around different concerns and there may, in fact, be more issues and events in a woman's life that are facilitative of emotional disturbance.

CONCLUSION

The cognitive view of emotional disturbance in women is clearly a radical departure from the biology-equals-psychology stance posited by the Freudians. Rather than adhering to such constructs as penis envy, narcissism, and masculine protest, cognitive theory posits intervening cognitive variables which mediate between the environment and the individual. In this regard, the cognitive view breaks with purely sociological theories, as well. This is not to say that sex-role stereotyping, discrimination, and derogatory attitudes towards women do not exist in the environment; indeed they do. However, for the cognitive therapist, the critical variable is not that these conditions exist, but how the client filters this state of affairs through her own cognitive processes. Thus, society may send a woman messages about her helplessness and incompetence, but they become potent only when she incorporates these messages and begins to tell them to herself. Similarly, society may proscribe traditional and limiting roles and expectations for women, but this becomes emotionally disturbing only when a woman tells herself, "I must be feminine. I shouldn't compete. I need a husband and children in order to be fulfilled. . . . " A woman, then, creates her own emotional disturbance, her own depression, guilt, anger, anxiety, or frustration, by propagandizing herself with self-defeating and self-deprecating self-talk.

The role of the cognitive therapist in working with an emotionally disturbed woman is to focus rigorously and actively on the "B's," the cognitions. The cognitive therapist does not deny the derogatory messages sent to women by our society; rather he or she helps the client to dispute these messages in a logical, empirical, and powerful manner. By helping a woman to correct her irrational beliefs, her systematic bias against herself, the cognitive therapist can aid her in defining her own roles, expectations, goals, and potentials well beyond the limits proscribed by society, if this is her choice. Giving a woman this freedom to choose, to find her own way, to create her destiny (regardless of anatomy) is perhaps the most powerful and humanistic aspect of cognitive therapy in helping women to overcome their emotional disturbances.

REFERENCES

Beck, A.T. *Depression: Causes and treatment*. Philadelphia: University of Pennsylvania Press, 1972.

Beck, A. T. & Greenberg, R. L. Cognitive therapy with depressed women. In V. Franks & V. Burtle (Eds.), *Women in therapy*. New York: Brunner/Mazel Publishers, 1974.

Bonaparte, M. *Female sexuality*. New York: Grove Press, 1965. First published by International Universities Press, 1953.

Broverman, I. K., Broverman, D. M., Rosenkrantz, P. S, & Vogel S. R. Sex-role stereotypes and clinical judgments of mental health. *Journal of Consulting and Clinical Psychology*, 1970 *34*, 1–7.

Chesler, P. Women as psychiatric and psychotherapeutic patients. *Journal of Marriage and the Family,* November, 1971.

Chesler, P. *Women and madness.* New York: Doubleday, 1972.

Deutsch, H. *The psychology of women* (1944). New York: Bantam, 1973.

Ellis, A. The treatment of love and sex problems in women. In V. Franks & V. Burtle (Eds.), *Women in therapy.* New York: Brunner/Mazel Publishers, 1974.

Ellis, A. *Reason and emotion in psychotherapy.* New York: Lyle Stuart, 1962.

Ellis, A., & Harper, R. *The new guide to rational living* Hollywood, Calif.: Wilshire Publishing Company, 1975.

Erikson, E. *Womanhood and the innerspace. Identity, youth and crisis.* New York: W. W. Norton and Company, Inc., 1968.

Freud, S. Some psychical consequences of the anatomical distinction between the sexes (1925). In J. Strousse (Ed.), *Women and analysis.* New York: Grossman Publishers, 1974.

Freud, S. Female sexuality (1931). In J. Strousse (Ed.), *Women and analysis.* New York: Grossman Publishers, 1974.

Freud, S. *On war, sex, and neurosis,* S. Katz (Ed.). New York: Arts and Science Press, 1947.

Friedan, B. *The feminine mystique.* New York: Dell, 1963.

Hiroto, D. S. Laws of control and learned helplessness. *Journal of Experimantal Psychology,* 1974, *102,* 187–193.

Seligman, M. E. P. Fall into helplessness. *Psychology Today, 7,* June, 1973.

Seligman, M. E. P. *Helplessness.* San Francisco: W. H. Freeman and Company, 1975.

Seligman, M. E. P. Conference on Learned Helplessness. Charlottesville, Virginia, 1979.

Thompson, C. M. The role of women in the culture. *Psychiatry,* 1941, *4,* 1–8.

Thompson, C. M. Cultural pressures in the psychology of women. *Psychiatry,* 1942, *5,* 331–39.

Thompson, C. M. Penis envy in women. *Psychiatry,* 1943, *6,* 123–125.

Thompson, C. M. Some effects of the derogatory attitude toward female sexuality. *Psychiatry,* 1950, *13,* 349–54.

Zachary, I. RET with women, some special issues. In R. Grieger & J. Boyd (Eds.), Rational emotive therapy: a skills-based approach. New York: Van Nostrand Reinhold, 1979.

Chapter 9

PROBLEMS OF CHILDREN AND THEIR PARENTS

Raymond DiGiuseppe

In recent years clinical child psychology has been dominated by advances in behavioral and family therapies. While different in origins and content, these approaches share a strong environmental, deterministic view. They believe the etiology of childhood behavior problems lies outside the child, caused either by the presence of positive or negative reinforcers or by one's family-system dynamics. Such views fail to explicate the role of internal mechanisms which mediate environmental events in children. While behavioral and family theories hold much that is valuable, a more complete understanding of childhood psychopathology would result from considering the balance of both environmental as well as cognitive variables.

The failure to conceptualize the internal mechanisms which play an active role in children's behavior disorders arises from several sources, one of which is the general zietgeist in child development and socialization research. Psychologists study the effects of divorce, siblings, schools, food additives, teacher expectancies, etc. on children; in all this children are perceived as passive. More recent research, however, suggests that from early infancy on children are active participants in the socialization process and tend to control or influence their caretakers as much as, or possibly more than, their caretakers influence them (Bell & Harper, 1977). Such an active view of childhood development allows the idea that children's thoughts mediate their behavior. The paucity of theory and research on the role of cognition in childhood psychopathology seems puzzling given the voluminous literature in child cognitive development. It appears that psychologists believe that children think about everything but personal problems. Children's thinking on social and personal matters remains an uncharted region.

Several methodological difficulties also seem to have discouraged researchers from assessing the role of cognition in childhood psychopathology. Children, since less articulate, have difficulty verbalizing their cognitive processes. Psychological researchers appear to believe that because they cannot measure children's cognitions, the cognitions do not occur. It is erroneous to assume that the inability to assess children's cognitions implies that cognitions have no role in maladaptive behaviors. Since cognitive variables have been known to affect most other learned behaviors in childhood, such as modeling (Bandura, 1979), it would appear likely that cognitive factors affect disturbed behavior as well.

The referral of children for mental health services may also make it difficult to assess the role of cognition in childhood psychopathology. Children are rarely, if ever, self-referred. Rather, clinicians usually see children because their behavior is disturbing to someone else. Nevertheless, the child's behavior need not be disturbed to be disturbing; the parents or teachers may be upsetting themselves about normal behavior. For example, Lobitz and Johnson (1975) studied referred and nonreferred impulsive children. On most dependent measures, the mean differences between the two groups were in the predicted direction, but with considerable overlap. The variable that most distinguished the two groups, however, was parental attitudes about the children's impulsivity. The referred children's parents were more intolerant of their children's behavior than the parents of the nonreferred children. Research focusing on referred and nonreferred populations might very well, then, fail to note cognitive differences between the groups because of the high degree of overlap in children's actual behavior and falsely conclude that cognitions play no role in pathological behavior.

In addition, cognition is *un*likely to play a major role in childhood disorders when the child's behavior is labeled disturbed, yet adults continue to reinforce it. In such situations the behavior may be adaptive given the child's environment. Thus a behavior problem could exist with no cognitive distortions at all. For example, Gary, a 9-year-old male, who preferred sports to all other activities held no joy for academic pursuits. He played soccer, basketball, and football seasonally and rarely studied or completed homework. His parents applied no penalties for his poor academic track record. When the report card came they were deeply concerned about Gary's academic underachievement and sought professional counseling. Despite their concern, they refused to change their contingencies and still praised the athletic and tolerated the sloppy academic work. Gary was perfectly happy with things. Do we consider his behavior disturbed? Is his thinking distorted and irrational? Gary's behavior seemed to make good sense given his values and the reinforcement contingencies in his life. Children's cognitive mechanisms will not account for "disturbed" behavior when the disturbance is more a result of reinforcement contingencies in the environment than in the child's behavior.

Another reason for the lack of theory and research in the role of cognition in childhood psychopathology is the general lack of agreement of the nature of childhood psychopathology itself. For example, Achenbach and Edelbrock (1978) have noted: "The study of psychopathology in children has long lacked coherent taxonomic framework in which training, treatment, epidemiology and research could be integrated." Researchers have identified several "narrow band syndromes" in children surrounding behaviors which are more disturbing to other people rather than those that cause psychic pain to the child (Abikoff, 1979). As a result we see cognitive-behavioral researchers focusing more on the aggressive, hyperactive, and delinquent behaviors than we do on the anxious, depressed, somatic, and withdrawn behaviors. One reason for this research emphasis may be the manner of referral mentioned above.

The present chapter will attempt to review and outline some of the major theories and research on cognitive factors effecting childhood behavior problems. Cognitive views of childhood disturbance appear to fall into two main categories: (1) positions that see psychopathology as resulting from the absence of appropriate cognitions; (2) positions that believe that psychopathology results from the presence of maladaptive distorted cognitions.

ABSENCE OF APPROPRIATE COGNITIONS

The Soviet psychologists Vygotsky (1962) and Luria (1961) have had a large influence on cognitive behavior theory. Their model concerns the systematic development of linguisitic control over behavior. Initially toddlers learn to direct their behavior by the language of others. With maturity children learn to use their own overt language to direct behavior. Finally, behavioral control is transferred to internal self-talk. This model has been used to explain behavioral excesses such as aggressivesness, impulsivity, hyperactivity and acting out. These behaviors are thought to occur because a child has failed to develop the necessary cognitive and linguistic mechanisms to inhibit behavioral excesses or because no self-instruction exists for incompatible appropriate behavior. Accordingly, maladjusted behavior could develop because the child has failed to reach the final developmental stage in this sequence.

This view gains support from Camp's (1977) study of hyper-aggressive boys. Her clinical population showed no deficits in verbal ability; but they did not mediate their behavior or guide it with verbal rules which they could later recite upon questioning. Similarly, Meichenbaum (1978) reported that some but not all hyperactive/impulsive children could advise others on effective strategies to avoid making errors in academic tasks. However, these same children failed to employ their own advice when performing the same tasks. Thus, some children appear to have a reproduction deficit. That is, they appear to know what to do and what to say but do not generate such cognitions at the appropriate time.

A second reason why children may fail to emit the appropriate behavior according to the self-instructional model is the lack of the appropriate cognitions, that is, a deficit in their cognitive or linguistic repertoire. They would naturally, then, be unable to reproduce guiding self-instruction at the appropriate time.

The Vygotsky and Luria model does not specify the reasons why children do not possess sufficient repetoires of self-instructions to guide effective behavior. The deficit could develop because of limited exposure to a coping model, failure to receive positive feedback for use of self-instruction, organismatic variables such as low intelligence, or brain dysfuntion which inhibits generation of self-instruction. The self-instructional deficit hypothesis has spawned considerable research focusing on impulsivity, and impulsive, hyperactive children. Most studies, however, have attempted to devise self-instructional treatment packages to remediate the deficit rather than to devise ways of uncovering the missing exact cognitive elements. Little research has been done on investigating exactly how normal populations develop appropriate self-instruction. It appears that this strategy may be most helpful in devising preventative techniques and could also be helpful in devising clinical strategies as well.

Interpersonal Cognitive Problem-Solving Skill Deficits

Another major area of theory and research focuses on interpersonal cognitive problem-solving skills (ICPS) (Spivak &

Shure, 1975). From clinical observations Spivak hypothesized that disturbed populations appear to lack specific thinking processes that would enable them to adequately solve social problems, the result being anxiety or inappropriate behavioral excesses. He then proceeded to identify specific ICPS skills and develop measures for each of these. In further research he measured the presence or absence of ICPS skills in normal and abnormal populations. ICPS skills have been shown to differentiate the behavior of impulsive from normal boys, delinquent from nondelinquent adolescents, and adult inpatient psychotics and outpatient neurotics from normals. The first ICPS skill is the ability to notice that a social conflict or problem exists. The second is what Spivak labeled "alternative solution thinking," which is the ability to generate several possible solutions to a single social problem. The third is consequential thinking which represents the ability to predict the social consequences of one's behavior. The way in which a child employs alternative solution thinking and consequential thinking also become important in predicting adjustment.

It appears that adjusted populations are more likely to first think of all the possible solutions and then to evaluate the consequences of each solution. After evaluating all consequences a choice is made. Maladaptive samples are more likely to end their search as soon as they find a consequence that is acceptable, thereby limiting their chances of finding the best possible choice.

Two other important ICPS skills are means-ends thinking and causal thinking. Means-ends thinking refers to the child's ability to plan a specific course of action to achieve a goal, understand or predict the obstacles that may arise in carrying out the plan, and devise strategies to deal with the obstacles. Causal thinking reflects an understanding of human motivation, i.e., the events which significant people in the child's life may get upset about. This skill actually refers to a lack of egocentrism whereby the child notices that people can get upset about issues that are their own rather than child-oriented ones.

Research on ICPS skills (cited by Spivak, Platt, & Shure, 1976) indicates some surprising facts. First, measures of ICPS skills have shown no relations to a child's language usage; neither the degree of verbal production, the rate of speech, fluency, correct syntax, or vocabulary development are related to ICPS. Second, measures of ICPS do not correlate well with intelligence. While there is a low correlation, low-IQ children appear to show the whole range of scores on IPCS skills. Finally, measures of ICPS skills show no relationship to measures of nonsocial problem-solving tasks. In short these skills represent an independant area of cognitive functioning with no immediate transfer to the interpersonal sphere.

Several other studies (Egan & DiGiuseppe, 1981; Merrigan & DiGiuseppe, 1981) noted that even within a specific ICPS skill there may not be generalization. Both studies cited above discovered that a training program in ICPS would significantly increase the number of alternative solutions that a child would make to peer problems but not necessarily increase the number of solutions the child could generate to parent problems. This research, as well as that by Spivak et al. appears to indicate that social problem-solving ability may not automatically generalize and that any psychological treatment or educational programs may require specific steps built in to foster genralization of these cognitive skills.

Many questions remain unanswered concerning the role of ICPS skills in adjustment and pathology. More research is needed with behavioral measures to corroborate the notions of Spivak and Shure (1975). Also, we need to know how children learn ICPS. Some initial research by Shure and Spivak (1978) suggests that mothers can be taught to use ICPS skills to increase their children's use of these skills. An interesting finding emerged from their study. Girl's scores on measures of ICPS were more closely related to and more positively effected by their mother's ICPS skills than were boys. We do not know how socialization or cultural variables account for this sex difference or how males learn ICPS skills since their cognitions are not that easily influenced by their mothers. Also of interest is the degree to which ICPS skills influence psychopathology. By this I mean: do all disturbed children have poor ICPS skills? It would appear that while the absence of those skills could theoretically limit the ability of the child to cope effectively, it remains possible for a child to be disturbed even if he or she possesses good ICPS skills. For instance, other types of cognitions may block the child from using the skills already in their repertoire or may override instructions to carry out the best possible solutions. It would appear valuable to focus on the exceptions to the rule by comparing those disturbed children who have good problem-solving skills with those who have poor problem-solving skills to see if other cognitions mediate the adapted behavior as well. Despite the many unanswered questions, social problem solving provides rich information for both clinicians and researchers to understand childhood psychopathology and will continue to be a strong area of research interest in the future.

The areas of self-instructional training and interpersonal cognitive problem-solving skills have been presented as two separate systems. In actuality many researchers have attempted to combine these systems in a single treatment package. A word of caution appears to be in order. While there has been a great deal of enthusiasm about the new cognitive movement in behavior therapy, the enthusiasm is not totally warranted by the outcome studies. Abikoff's 1979 review of the literature suggested again that cognitive training may not always generalize across situations. That is, cognitive training focusing on cognition effecting academic performance will encourage academic behavior but might not transfer to classroom behavior and other social situations, and vice versa. Such failures may be due to the inefficiency of cognitive training procedures or, as Michenbaum (1978) has suggested, to an inappropriate task analysis. Regardless, the clinician is encouraged to complete a functional analysis on the client's presenting problem and encourage specific training on the cognitions necessary for the remediation of that specific target behavior. In light of the evidence, it would be wrong to assume cognitive training, such as an alternative solution for fighting with one's peers in the classroom, would generalize to problems outside the classroom, such as fighting with your mother or paying attention to your reading material. All these behaviors require separate interventions.

The Presence of Maladaptive Cognitions

Beck (1976) and Ellis (1962, 1972) view the role of cognitions in maladaptive behaviors somewhat similarly. They stress the existence of maladaptive thoughts which bring about disturbed emotional states such as anxiety, depression, or anger. Maladaptive thoughts are illogical and/or exaggerated ideas which falsely represent reality. Beck refers to these cognitions as automatic thoughts and points out how logical errors such as arbitrary inference, overgeneralization, selective abstraction, and minimization/maximization lead to emotional disturbance. Ellis emphasizes the role of irrational beliefs in psychopathology. These are ideas which reflect absolutistic thinking and/or catastrophizing statements.

Both Beck's and Ellis's theories recognize that the client can make logical errors of two kinds. First, they can draw false inferences about what has occurred or will occur, and second, they can make evaluative errors concerning what they believe has occurred or will occur. For example, 7-year-old Ralph was referred for psychotherapy because of persistant crying whenever his parents argued. Ralph's thinking went something like this: "If my parents fight, that means they don't love each other. If they don't love each other they will divorce. If they get divorced I will have to live with one of them and miss the other. I can't stand to be without either one of them and I need both of them together." Ralph's thoughts contain both faulty inferential statements about his parent's behavior (they don't love each other; they will get divorced; I will have to live with only one of them), and irrational evaluations about these inferences (I couldn't stand to be without one of them. I need both of them.). The presence of both thoughts would be necessary for Ralph to feel anxious. If he did not believe there was a chance of divorce, he would feel safe regardless of how negatively he evaluated that event. On the other hand, if he believed that the divorce was imminent, he would not feel anxious if he only evaluated this situation as only moderately or mildly aversive or even pleasant.

In treatment one could ameliorate Ralph's anxiety by changing either his inferential statements or his evaluations. Beck and Ellis would teach Ralph to challenge both through a logical, scientific process. However, they would differ in the importance they would place on each of these arenas and on the types of logical errors causing Ralph's anxiety. Beck focuses primarily but not exclusively on the client's inferences about events, while Ellis focuses primarily, albeit not exclusively, on evaluations.

Despite the growing popularity of cognitive therapy and RET, and the increased evidence for the efficacy of both these therapies (DiGiuseppe, Miller, & Trexler, 1977; Rush, Beck, Kovacs, & Hollon, 1977), there have been few attempts to extend these approaches to explaining and treating childhood behavioral disorders. Only one of Ellis's 30-odd books is devoted to children (Ellis, Wolfe, & Moseley, 1966), and Beck has only produced one article concerning children (Kovacs & Beck, 1977). However, the presence of maladaptive cognitions in the form of both false inferences and irrational evaluations appears to be a valid conceptualization for explaining the etiology of childhood psychopathology. Since both irrational beliefs and automatic thoughts result from illogical thinking, and since children are less cognitively sophisticated than adults (Piaget, 1952), one would expect children to commit more logical errors than adults and thus have more irrational beliefs and faulty automatic thoughts than adults. If this were true, such a cognitive theory may explain more of the variance in childhood psychopathology than it does in adult psychopathology; and children would then predictably have greater incidences of depression and anxiety than adults.

This second hypothesis is exactly the case that has been found with depression. After reviewing the research literature on childhood depression, Lobitz and Johnson (1975) concluded that the emotional and behavioral characteristics of depression occur so frequently among children that it would be wrong to call it a disorder. In addition Kovacs and Beck (1977) administered a children's version of the Beck Depression Inventory to normal children. The majority of their sample received scores which placed them in the moderate or severe range of depression using the adult cut-off scores. Similarly, texts on child development point out how frequently occur fears among childhood populations.

Despite the seeming association between children's thinking and their emotional state, there has been little research directly related to the presence of irrational beliefs and automatic thought and their emotional state. In one of the only studies Kassinove, Crisci, and Tiegerman (1977) showed that rational thinking, as measured on a self-report inventory, was related to self-report measures of emotional adjustment in a normal cross-section of children in grades 4 through 12. Their study also showed that children's irrational beliefs changed with age in the direction of becoming more rational.

In a similar vein, Knaus (1975) postulated that RET could be adopted as a primary prevention intervention with children. He devised an elementary school rational-emotive education program for classroom use to train youngsters to think rationally. To date, long-term follow-up studies assessing the effect of Rational-Emotive Education (REE) on the incidence of psychopathology has yet to appear. However, studies exist indicating that children who receive REE show improvement on self-report measures of adjustment (DiGiuseppe & Kassinove, 1976; Miller, 1977). While these studies have many methodological limitations and a general lack of solid behavioral measures, they are encouraging. The study by DiGiuseppe and Kassinove suggested that the earlier the intervention the more positive the outcome. They compared REE and a control treatment with 4th and 8th graders. Despite the fact that there were no differences in rational thinking between the grades at pretest, the younger children improved much more in both rational thinking and emotional adjustment than the 8th graders. DiGiuseppe and Kassinove hypothesized that these results are due to differences in commitment to the irrational philosophies. The older group had more social and personal indoctrination to the irrational belief and thus may have been more resistant to change. While younger children may be more likely to generate irrational thoughts because of their cognitive immaturity, they also may be more amenable to intervention because of their shorter learning histories.

There has as yet been no research or clinical report for the most common types of logical errors or specific irrational beliefs associated with specific childhood disorders. My clinical experience with children suggests that, while they are in many ways different from adults, they appear to develop the same kinds of irrational beliefs as their adult counterparts, and there appear to be no differences in type or kind of irrational thinking among children of different ages. It may be reassuring that they catastrophize and demand just as well as their parents. What children demand or catastrophize about may be different, but the process appears to be the same.

There is only one area worth noting, however, where children's thinking may be different from adults that has significant implications for part of RET. Many children who arrive for therapy appear not to have learned that thoughts or ideas are open to scrutiny. They appear to believe that an idea is true because it is believed rather than the reverse. It is the idea of challenging beliefs that children have difficulty understanding. Thus, a therapist needs to assess a child's critical thinking skills and his or her notions about believing things on faith; and if they are amiss or remiss, which they usually are, the therapist starts by teaching the child the rules of logic and the need for empirical validation in assessing the validity of ideas. It is uncertain at this point whether this difference in private epistomology is the cause of childhood pathology or whether its incidence is the same in both disturbed and normal populations. It is possible that those children who do come for treatment are those who have not yet learned to challenge their own thinking, while those who have come to understand the validation process avoid emotional distress. This would appear to be a fertile research area and one which would clarify many of the assumptions of cognitive theory with children.

Final Note

I have focused in this chapter on cognitive factors in children
that seem to account for emotional disturbances and maladaptive
behaviors. In so doing I have ignored the role that parents play in
their children's problems. By so doing I neither mean to suggest
that parent behavior is unimportant in child development nor that
parental pathology is irrelevant to child disturbance. Emotional
disturbance in parents in general, as well as cognitive distortions of
parents vis-á-vis their children and their own role as parents,
clearly play a significant role in children's adjustment, and the
wise clinician will never ignore the parents when working with
disturbed children. To round out the cognitive understanding of
children's problems, therefore, I strongly urge the reader to con-
sult Hauck (1967, 1977).

References

Abikoff, H. Cognitive training interventions with children: A review of a new
approach. *Journal of Learning Disabilities,* 1979, *12,* 123–135.

Achenback, T. M., & Edelbrock, C. S. The classification of child psychopathology: A review of empirical efforts. *Psychological Bulletin,* 1978, *85,*
1275–1301.

Bandura, A. *Social learning theory.* New York: Prentice-Hall, 1979.

Beck, A. T. *Cognitive therapy and the emotional disorders.* New York: International Universities Press, 1976.

Beck, A. T., Rush, A. J., Shaw, B. F., & Emery, G. *Cognitive therapy of
depression.* New York: Guilford Press, 1980.

Bell, R. Q., & Harper, L. V. *Child effects on adults.* Hillsdale, New Jersey:
Ellbaum, 1977.

Camp, B. Verbal mediation in young aggressive boys. *Journal of Abnormal
Psychology,* 1977, *86,* 145–153.

DiGiuseppe, R. A., & Kassinove, R. Effects of a rational-emotive school mental
health program on children's adjustment. *Journal of Community Psychology,* 1976, *4,* 382–387.

DiGiuseppe, R. A., Miller, N. J., & Trexler, L. A review of rational-emotive
psychotherapy: Outcome studies. *The Counseling Psychologist,* 1977, *7,*
64–72.

Egan, F., & DiGiuseppe, R. A. Interpersonal cognitive problem solving skills: A components analysis. Unpublished manuscript, Hofstra University, 1981.

Ellis, A. *Reason and emotion in psychotherapy.* New York: Lyle Stuart, 1962.

Ellis, A. *Humanistic psychotherapy.* New York: Crown Publishers and McGraw-Hill Paperbacks, 1972.

Ellis, A. Rejoiner: Elegant and inelegant RET. *The Counseling Psychologist,* 1977, *7,* 73–82.

Ellis, A., Wolfe, J. L., & Moseley, S. How to prevent your child from becoming a neurotic adult. New York: Crown Publishers, 1966.

Hauck, P. A. In A. Ellis & R. Grieger (Eds.), *Handbook of rational-emotive therapy.* New York: Springer Publishing Co., 1977.

Hauck, P. A. *The rational management of children.* New York: Libra Publishers, Inc., 1967.

Kassinove, H., Crisci, R., & Tiegerman, S. Developmental trends in rational thinking: implications for rational-emotive school mental health programs. *Journal of Community Psychology,* 1977, *5,* 216–224.

Knaus, W. *Rational-Emotive Education.* New York: Institute for Rational Living, 1970.

Kovacs, M., & Beck, A. T. An empirical clinical approach towards a definition of childhood depression. In. G. J. Schulterbranet & A. Raskin (Eds.), *Depression in children: Diagnosis, treatment and conceptual models.* New York: Ruben Press, 1977.

Lobitz, C. W., & Johnson, S. M. Parental manipulation of the behavior of normal and abnormal children. *Child Development,* 1975, *46,* 719–726.

Luria, A. *The role of speech in the regulation of normal and abnormal behaviors.* New York: Liveright, 1961.

Meichenbaum, D. *Cognitive behavior modification and the treatment of impulse disorders.* New York: BMA Audio Cassettes, 1978.

Merrigan, E., & DiGiuseppe, R. The effects of role play and modeling in the acquisition of interpersonal problem solving skills. Unpublished manuscript, Hofstra University, 1981.

Piaget, J. *The origins of intelligence in children.* New York: Harper and Row, 1952.

Rush, A. J., Beck, A. T., Kovacs, M., & Hollon, S. Comparative efficacy of cognitive therapy and pharmacotherapy in the treatment of depressed outpatients. *Cognitive Therapy and Research,* 1977, *1,* 17–37.

Shure, M., & Spivak, G. *Problem solving techniques in child rearing.* San Francisco: Jossey-Bass, 1978.

Spivak, G., Platt, J. & Shure, M. *The problem solving approach to adjustment.* San Francisco: Jossey-Bass, 1976.

Spivak, G., & Shure, M. *The social adjustment of young children.* San Francisco: Jossey-Bass, 1975.

Vygotsky, L. *Thought and language.* New York: Wiley, 1962.

INDEX